Helping Families with
Special Problems

HELPING FAMILIES WITH SPECIAL PROBLEMS

Edited by
Martin R. Textor, Dipl.-Paed.

New York • JASON ARONSON • London

Sourcenotes

"Treating Schizophrenia in a Family Context" is reprinted with permission from the *Canadian Psychiatric Association Journal* 23(1978):51–58 and the *Psychiatric Journal of the University of Ottawa* 6(1981):229–233.

"Behavioral Therapy for Families with Child Management Problems" appeared in *Theorie und Praxis der Familientherapie* and is reprinted with the permission of the authors, editor, and publisher.

"Therapy with the Remarried Family System" is reprinted with permission from the *Journal of Marital and Family Therapy* 7(1981):3–13.

Copyright © 1983 by **Jason Aronson, Inc.**

10 9 8 7 6 5 4 3 2 1

Library of Congress Cataloging in Publication Data
Main entry under title:

Helping families with special problems.

   Bibliography.
   Includes index.
   1. Family psychotherapy—Addresses, essays, lectures.
2. Mentally ill—Family relationships—Addresses,
essays, lectures. I. Textor, Martin R.
[DNLM: 1. Family therapy. WM 430.5.F2 F198]
RC488.5.F328 1983   616.89′156   82-24471
ISBN 0-87668-635-8

Manufactured in the United States of America.

To
Marion and Gerda,
Haflidi and Reiner

Contents

Preface

The first family therapy approaches were developed some 30 years ago. Most pioneers worked with families having schizophrenic children. Five or ten years later this focus was broadened to include families with neurotic, alcoholic, and acting-out members. And since the beginning of the last decade, families with members exhibiting symptoms of drug abuse, psychosomatic illness, sexual dysfunctions, and learning disorders also have been treated. In addition, family therapy is used to alleviate the problems of families with disabled, sick, or dying members and with divorcing, divorced, or remarried spouses. There are only a few reports, however, on the treatment of families with members exhibiting symptoms of sexual disorder, depression, hysteria, phobia, personality disorder, and the like. Family therapists focus on the pathogenic processes in these families that cause symptoms in one of the members and treat the whole family according to various theoretical approaches.

In this book we discuss more than 11 pathological family types and their treatment. We also differentiate among these types according to the medical, psychiatric, or psychological "diagnosis" (e.g., anorexia nervosa, schizophrenia, drug abuse, learning disorder) of one or more of the family members. This approach will certainly lead to some criticism. First, many family therapists might say that the same pathogenic mechanisms work in different pathological family types and that, therefore, such a differentiation is unnecessary. We accept this criticism as one coming from well-known theoretical approaches that are considered in this book. But these differentiations are useful for family therapists because they show that different symptoms are caused by similar pathogenic mechanisms working more or less intensely, in various combinations, in different situations, and so on.

Second, some family therapists may object that this differentiation focuses on the individual, thus blaming him or her for the family problems. This makes it difficult to de-emphasize the role of the "identified patient" and to stress the contribution of other family members to the pathology or to point out pathogenic characteristics of the family system. We also accept this criticism but see no other possibility. We could use one of the few classifications of pathological families, but none is as widely used and as well understood as the above-mentioned distinctions. Moreover, these distinctions usually differentiate among only a small number of pathological families, do not use a sufficiently large number of categories, are founded on only one theoretical approach, and are supported by too little research. To develop our own classification, however, is certainly beyond the scope and intent of this book. Thus we have used a classification based on labeling the identified patient, but we stress the interpersonal character of all pathologies mentioned in this book.

Each contributor considers the relevant knowledge, theories, and assumptions concerning pathogenic mechanisms and pathological characteristics of one or more family types. Most of the contributors also describe the different family therapy approaches that are used to treat clients.

I wish to thank each of the contributors for their time and work in writing these excellent chapters. My thanks also to Joan Langs for her advice and encouragement and to Mrs. Lora Textor, M.A., for her help in correcting the German contributions.

Contributors

Nicholas C. Avery, M.D.
Director of Family and Marital
  Therapy
Department of Psychiatry
Harvard Medical School
Boston, Massachusetts

Hollis Steer Brown, R.N.
Associate Director, Remarried
  Consultation Service
Supervisor, Advanced Family
  Therapy Training Program
Jewish Board of Family and
  Children's Services
New York, New York

James Coane, Psy.D.
Clinical Assistant Professor
Hahnemann University
Philadelphia, Pennsylvania

Helen M. Crohn, M.S.S.
Staff Member, Remarried

Consultation Service
Coordinator, Advanced Family
  Therapy Training Program
Jewish Board of Family and
  Children's Services
New York, New York

Ian R. H. Falloon, M.D.
Associate Professor of Psychiatry
University of Southern California
  School of Medicine
Los Angeles, California

Janice C. Goldman, Psy.D.
Clinical Assistant Professor
Hahnemann University
Philadelphia, Pennsylvania

Catherine E. Huberty, M.S.W.
Private Practice (Family and
  Chemical Dependency)
St. Cloud, Minnesota

David J. Huberty, M.S.W.,
A.C.S.W.
Certified Chemical Dependency
    Practitioner
Central Minnesota Mental Health
    Center
St. Cloud, Minnesota

Curtis Janzen, Ph.D.
Associate Professor
School of Social Work and
    Community Planning
University of Maryland at
    Baltimore
Baltimore, Maryland

Thomas F. Johnson, Ph.D.
Director, Family Intervention
    Services
Delaware County Juvenile Court
Associate Professor
Department of Psychiatry and
    Human Behavior
Thomas Jefferson University
Philadelphia, Pennsylvania

Robert P. Liberman, M.D.
Professor of Psychiatry
University of California at Los
    Angeles Medical School
Chief, Rehabilitation Service
VA Medical Center at Los Angeles,
    Brentwood Division
Director, Clinical Research Unit
Camarillo State Hospital
Camarillo, California

Evelyn Rodstein, M.S.W.
Private Practice
former Staff Member, Remarried
    Consultation Service
Jewish Board of Family and
    Children's Services
New York, New York

Clifford J. Sager, M.D.
Director, Remarried Consultation
    Service
Director, Family Psychiatry
Jewish Board of Family and
    Children's Services
Clinical Professor of Psychiatry
New York Hospital—Cornell
    Medical Center
New York, New York

G. Pirooz Sholevar, M.D.
Clinical Professor and Director
Division of Child, Adolescent, and
    Family Psychiatry
Jefferson Medical College
Thomas Jefferson University
Philadelphia, Pennsylvania

Martin R. Textor, Dipl.-Paed.
Research Fellow
Konrad Adenauer Foundation
Bavarian Julius-Maximilians
University of Würzburg
Würzburg, West Germany

Elizabeth Walker, M.S.W.
Private Practice
former Staff Member, Remarried
 Consultation Service
Jewish Board of Family and
 Children's Services
New York, New York

Edward M. Waring, M.D.,
D.Psych., F.R.C.P.(C), F.A.B.P.N.
Assistant Dean, Continuing

Medical Education
Director of Psychiatric Education
University of Western Ontario
London, Ontario

Michael White, B.A.S.W.
Private Practice
Editor, Australian Journal of
 Family Therapy
Unley, South Australia

❧ 1 ❧

Treating Schizophrenia in a Family Context

Edward M. Waring, M.D.

A schizophrenic person in the 1940s faced a gloomy future. Analytic thinking suggested that a transference relationship was impossible, and thus psychoanalytic psychotherapy with schizophrenics was not indicated. A genetic or biological breakthrough was energetically pursued. The majority of the profession and schizophrenics (the latter in custodial institutes) waited, and therapeutic pessimism prevailed.

It was in this atmosphere that the concept of the cold, aloof, and dominating *schizophrenogenic mother* appeared (Fromm-Reichmann 1939). This malevolent creature, like the "ambivalence" she was assigned in relation to her child, brought a mixed blessing to the study of her schizophrenic offspring. Her appearance stimulated the initial studies of the *schizophrenic family*. The humanistic approach of her creator, Fromm-Reichmann (and other analysts, such as Sullivan and Searles), brought the psychotherapist back in contact with the schizophrenic (Green 1964). Unfortunately, the schizophrenics' mothers and families were believed to be culpable, and their shame and guilt became part of the problem (Appleton 1972). Perhaps this schizophrenogenic mother now can be laid to rest, but first let us examine the early studies that this concept stimulated.

Fromm-Reichmann used a psychoanalytic framework to organize the character structure of the mothers of schizophrenics, as described by her patients in analysis. Lidz, Fleck, and Cornelison (1965) improved the methodology by actually interviewing the families of schizophrenics, focusing on quality of emotional ties and relative power. They found the fathers to be no less disturbed in their character structures and behavior than the mothers were and therefore introduced the terms *schism* for families in which open conflict was observed between the parents and *skew* for the subtle battle for dominance that involved the children on one or the other parental side. Their continuing studies revealed many other, equally important phenomena, including *psychic contagion* to describe the transmission of irrationality and disturbances of sexual-role identification and separation of generations. Their work focused on interaction, but their framework remained psychoanalytic and lacked proof of specificity to these families of schizophrenics.

Wynne and associates (1958) made two important methodological changes: a standardized, repeatable, and reliable method of sampling schizophrenic family behavior and control groups. They suggested that the thinking of the family members of a schizophrenic person could be blindly differentiated from neurotic and normal families on their Rorschach protocols. *Pseudomutuality*, an overriding preoccupation with a sense of relatedness, rather than the accurate perception of changing expectations, was introduced as a concept unique to the families of schizophrenics.

Bowen and his colleagues (1959) reported on their work with these families who were admitted to hospital. Clinically, Bowen and his associates gradually shifted to the family unit as their focus for study and therapy, using *emotional divorce* to describe the parents' interaction that set the stage for the development of schizophrenia.

Finally, two perspectives, sociological and existential, concentrated on communication in this type of family. Bateson and colleagues (1958) introduced the concept of the *double bind* as contributing to the pathogenesis of schizophrenia. Bell and Vogel (1960) suggested that the schizophrenic child acted as a scapegoat, a type of role function that maintained a precarious family harmony. But because of the existential and poetic nature of his later work, it is often forgotten that Laing (1965) was the first to assert that the communication of the schizophrenic becomes understandable in the context of the family, and he also introduced the term *mystification*.

In summary, one has to admire the creative thinking of these pioneers who helped return empathy to the clinical care of schizophrenics, but their observations were neither objective, repeatable, nor controlled, with the exception of Wynne and associates (1958), whose work was replicated. It is interesting to follow the fate of these concepts in the work that these scientists stimulated.

NEW FINDINGS

We shall not review the family interactional research as it relates to schizophrenia, as methodological and substantiative reviews are available elsewhere (Jacobs et al. 1974, Leff and Hirsch 1975). Rather, we shall consider representational studies that used acceptable experimental designs, reliable measures, and control groups and have particular relevance to both the previous concepts reviewed and family therapy with schizophrenics.

Studies of parents of normal and nonschizophrenic patient controls reveal that there is no one type of character structure, psychodynamics, or attitudes that can be used to describe the parents of schizophrenics. In his studies, Alanen (1970) suggested that some mothers were clearly schizophrenic and some borderline, and compared with normal controls and neurotics, a greater proportion of a third group demonstrated "very accentuated constriction of affective life, poor self-control and an inability to feel themselves into the inner life of other people" (p. 227). Alanen felt that the fathers' disorders were no less marked and suggested that "warm, over-protective mothers" were associated with schizophreniform and "cold, dominant mothers" with process schizophrenics. Despite his finding greater psychiatric disturbance in schizophrenic mothers and his postulated relationship of overprotectiveness to hostility, the studies of Gardner (1967) and others show that a cold, dominating, and threatening mother is found more commonly in control groups.

It is surprising to note the conspicuous failure of studies using personality tests (such as the Minnesota Multiphasic Inventory [MMPI]) to demonstrate any differences between the parents of schizophrenics and the parents of other psychiatric patients and controls (Cohler et al. 1972, Zuckerman et al. 1958). In reevaluating the literature, a consistent finding in the research on parents of schizophrenics is that their mothers are overprotective, an observation introduced by Kasanin and colleagues in 1934, prior to the appearance of the schizophrenogenic stereotype. Waring and Ricks (1965), avoiding the problem of retrospective bias, observed children who later became schizophrenic and found that they were often more overprotected than controls were, as shown by their being isolated from their peers, not being allowed privacy, and being bathed by their mothers even in adolescence. Even more surprising is that the studies of O'Neal and Robins (1958) of cases who later became schizophrenic and those of Pollin and associates (1966) comparing schizophrenics with their nonschizophrenic identical twins suggest that preschizophrenic children show themselves to be biologically and/or psychosocially disadvantaged at an early age compared with normals. Thus the overprotective behavior pattern may be the mother's reaction to her handicapped child.

Finally, one cannot ignore the finding of Wender and colleagues (1971) that parents who reared their own biological children who developed schizophrenia were more disturbed than were adoptive parents who had schizophrenic children, implying a strong genetic predisposing factor. Their study also showed, however, that adoptive parents whose offspring developed schizophrenia were also more disturbed than were adoptive parents whose offspring did not develop schizophrenia. This finding points to the existence of a parental predisposing factor, but along with Heston's (1966) finding that being raised in foster homes, foundling homes, or in an adoptive family had no influence on development of schizophrenia, it also suggests that the environmental predisposing factors may not be necessary or sufficient causes for the development of schizophrenia.

Using small-group interactional methodology, the concepts of dominance and sex-related role disturbance as postulated by Lidz and associates (1965) have elicited only little support. Cheek (1964) found no association between the dominance of either parent and either the diagnosis of schizophrenia or the sex of the child who develops schizophrenia. Ferreira and Winter (1965) found fathers equally dominant in families of schizophrenics, other patients, and controls. Similarly, a study by Ringuette and Kennedy (1966) demonstrated that the experts could not even agree on what a double bind was, and in two separate studies using responses to stimuli that were contradictory in tone and content, Loeff (1966) and Mehrabian and Wiener (1967) produced conflicting and contradictory results. The concepts of scapegoating and mystification have resisted efforts to be operationally defined in order to study their relevance.

Only the theory of emotional divorce, as postulated by Bowen (1960), has received any empirical support, although it has not been specifically experimentally examined. Waring and Ricks (1965) showed in their research a mutual withdrawal in parents whose offspring later developed schizophrenia. In my experience, the parents often perceive their marriages as well adjusted and deny specific incompatibilities, but on closer evaluation a lack of interpersonal intimacy and the absence of self-disclosure are revealed (Waring 1981). I also have observed that these children's delusions often reveal ideas and assumptions held by the parents which could be reasons for their lack of marital intimacy. For example, the parents often present their offspring for help at the stage of intimacy development. Thus, a major clinical feature of adolescent onset of schizophrenia is the overt expression of rejecting intimacy with members of the opposite sex.

This finding is the most consistent and frequently replicated finding comparing families of schizophrenics with families of other patients and controls: specifically that the parents of schizophrenics show more marital disharmony, as indicated by open or tacit conflict, expressed hostility, opposition of spontaneously expressed attitudes, and difficulty in reaching agreement (Caputo 1963, Cheek 1964, Farina 1960). Sharan (1966) also demonstrated that the parents were less supportive and more critical of each other in the presence of the schizophrenic offspring than they were with their normal children.

The foregoing reinforces the dramatic demonstration of Brown and associates (1972) that schizophrenics exposed to more than 35 hours per week of parental criticism have a high relapse rate. This study, recently replicated, clearly shows that parental behavior can precipitate and perpetuate schizophrenic symptomatology. Thus, the failure by parents of schizophrenic offspring to develop interpersonal intimacy may be a necessary but not necessarily sufficient etiological variable in the development of schizophrenic illness (Russell et al. 1980).

In summary, I agree with Leff and Hirsch (1975) that the following statements are "reasonably supported by the experimental evidence": (1) More parents of schizophrenics are psychiatrically disturbed than are parents of normal children, and more of the mothers are schizoid. (2) Mothers of schizophrenics show more concern and protectiveness than do mothers of normals, both in the current situation and in their attitudes toward the children before they became ill. (3) The preschizophrenic child more frequently manifests physical ill health or mild disability early in life than does the normal child. (4) The parents of schizophrenics show more conflict and disharmony than do the parents of other psychiatric patients. (5) The work of Wynne and associates (1958) strongly implies that the parents of schizophrenics communicate abnormally, but their concept of pseudomutuality has not been tested. (6) Schizophrenics having close relationships with their relatives or spouses are more likely to have a relapse than are those whose relationships are less close. Obviously, research has failed to find a single family variable that constitutes a necessary and sufficient cause for the development of schizophrenia.

IMPLICATIONS FOR THERAPY

The absence of definitive empirical evidence supporting any etiological hypothesis continues to relegate the clinical management of schizophrenic patients to the consensus of professional opinion and the individual bias of the clinician (Bellak 1979b). As a result, the clinical management of a schizophrenic individual remains an attempt by the clinician to identify that person's strengths and weaknesses and to develop a treatment that often combines medication, psychological support, and efforts at social assistance.

Many clinicians continue to involve the families of schizophrenics in family assessment interviews and occasionally to recommend specific family therapy, usually as an adjunct to other forms of intervention in the management of schizophrenic patients (Lidz et al. 1965). Research shows that all new referrals or admissions should have at least one family assessment. Langsley and colleagues (1968) compared a traditional emergency service with a service in which all individuals entering the system had a family assessment. The family-oriented service had fewer admissions and fewer readmissions, and the admitted patients spent less time in hospital. This initial contact not only prevented the detrimental effects of hospitalization, as studied by Wing and Brown (1970), but also made the treatment team available to the family, an important variable in maintaining the schizophrenic in the community by means of easing the family burden, as described by Grad and Sainsbury (1968). The initial assessment of family criticism and exposure as described by Brown and associates (1972) allows rational decisions to be made regarding going home or alternatives such as halfway houses. The initial assessment could also be used to identify the six predisposing factors previously discussed.

A theory of interpersonal dyadic relationships was developed by Schutz (1966) that suggests that there are three major independent variables of interpersonal relationships, which he calls *inclusion variables*, *control variables*, and *affection variables*. Schutz found that in dyadic relationships that last over time (i.e., marital relationships), the affection variable is the major determinant of the dyad's satisfaction. This theory is in keeping with Bowen's theory regarding emotional divorce, suggesting that any intervention that decreases the amount of expressed hostility between the parents (or conversely increases supportive statements or closeness) and decreases criticism of the schizophrenic will lead to an improvement in the schizophrenic offspring's symptomatology. The theory is simple, leads to action, offers hope, and can be verified by treatment success and failure.

Based on Schutz's and Bowen's theories, we developed Cognitive Family Therapy (CFT) which can be used in the management of schizophrenic patients. CFT is a new technique of brief psychotherapy founded on evidence that *self-disclosure* is the major determinant of a married couple's level of intimacy (Waring 1980, Waring and Russell 1980a). Self-disclosure is the process of making one's personal thoughts, attitudes, feelings, and needs known to another person through verbal behavior. Cognitive self-disclosure refers to the intentional revelation of personal thoughts, attitudes, beliefs, and assumptions, as well as the development of self-awareness of relationships (Waring and Chelune 1983). Cognitive self-disclosure to a supportive listener regarding thoughts, assumptions, and beliefs about one's motivation for marriage and one's parents' level of intimacy can, reciprocally, facilitate intimacy (Waring and Russell 1980a). Papers presenting the clinical course and effectiveness of cognitive family therapy are presented elsewhere (Waring 1980, Waring and Russell 1980a).

Cognitive family therapy begins with an evaluation interview with all family members present. The focus of the evaluation is to elicit each family member's "theory" of why the presenting problem or symptom has appeared. The children and the parents are asked to explain why the family is not functioning optimally, and a developmental history of the parents' and grandparents' courtship, marriage, and family life cycle is obtained.

Interviewers should ask only "why" or "theory" questions and avoid and suppress affective interchange and/or behavioral interpretation or confrontation. The interviewers also evaluate the eight dimensions of marital intimacy according to the Victoria Hospital Intimacy Interview: affection, cohesion, expressiveness, compatibility, conflict resolution, sexuality, autonomy, and identity (Waring et al. 1981).

The interviewers then explain to the entire family the theory on which CFT is based and offer the parents (only) ten one-hour sessions to increase their intimacy (or improve one of the eight areas of marital intimacy) and, as a result, improve family functioning and, one hopes, the symptomatology of the schizophrenic offspring. The parents are informed that the schizophrenic child will also receive from another therapist whatever individual therapeutic help is indicated. Then a specific treatment contract is made.

Only the parents are involved in the CFT sessions. The first session begins with the therapist stating, "We are here to understand why you are not close." As the therapy proceeds, each session commences with the major "why" question left unanswered from the previous meeting. Each session follows these rules: (1) No communication is allowed between the couple during the session. (2) Each member of the dyad must talk only to the therapist. (3) The therapist discourages any emotional display during the session. No feeling or behavior is identified, confronted, or interpreted. (4) One spouse initiates discussion, and the therapist asks questions about the problem at hand, such as "What is your theory?" or "Tell me more," and discourages or does not ask questions about the spouse's feeling, but only about his or her thinking. (5) When a spouse cannot answer the "why" question or has exhausted the topic, the therapist turns to the other member of the dyad and asks, "What were you thinking when your spouse was talking?" or "What is your answer to this question?" The therapist may discuss various theories. This procedure is followed throughout the sessions.

The couple alternates in talking about any biographical material they think is relevant to answering the "why" question. The content focuses on the couple's reasons for marrying, their observation and experience of their parents' marriages, and the differences of opinion and assumptions that have produced distance. Although the description of the above sounds tedious for the therapist, the material and revelations are fascinating, and clinical skills develop through the perceptiveness of the therapist's "why" questions.

The rationale for this form of intervention includes the following: (1) As only the parents are included in the therapy session, other family members are theoretically excluded from the emotional system between the parents, thus removing the schizophrenic offspring from the emotional system and allowing more cognitive control. (2) Therapists should attempt to prevent any emotional interaction between themselves and the couple and thus model a different form and method of communication. (3) The therapy may work by increasing the amount of listening by the spouses to each other, the amount of time they spend together, and their understanding of each other and therefore decreasing the use of emotional control and displays of hostility and criticism leading theoretically to an increase in closeness and a decrease of anxiety.

Using cognitive self-disclousure with these couples has led to a reported increase in their closeness and reduced tension in the home and concern about the schizophrenic offspring.

REFERENCES

Ackerman, N. W. (1958). *The Psychodynamics of Family Life.* New York: Basic Books.

Alanen, Y. O. (1970). The families of schizophrenic patients. *Proceedings of the Royal Society of Medicine* 63:227–230.

Appleton, W. S. (1972). Importance of psychiatrists telling patients the truth. *American Journal of Psychiatry* 129:742–745.

Bateson, G., Jackson, D. D., Haley, J., and Weakland, J. (1958). Towards a theory of schizophrenia. *Behavioral Science* 1:251–264.

Beels, C. C., and Ferber, A. (1969). Family therapy: a view. *Family Process* 8:280–318.

Bell, N., and Vogel, E. F. (1960). *The Family.* Glencoe, Ill.: The Free Press.

Bellak, L. (1979a). Introduction: an idiosyncratic overview. In *Disorders of the Schizophrenic Syndrome*, ed. L. Bellak, pp. 3–22. New York: Basic Books.

—— (1979b). The schizophrenic syndrome: what the clinician can do until the scientist comes. In *Disorders of the Schizophrenic Syndrome*, ed. L. Bellak, pp. 585–590. New York: Basic Books.

Bowen, M. (1960). A family concept of schizophrenia. In *The Etiology of Schizophrenia*, ed. D. Jackson, pp. 346–372. New York: Basic Books.

—— (1971). Family therapy and family group therapy. In *Comprehensive Group Psychotherapy*, ed. H. I. Kaplan and B. J. Sadock, pp. 384–421. Baltimore: Williams and Wilkins.

——, Dysinger, R. H., and Basamania, B. (1959). The role of the father in families with a schizophrenic patient. *American Journal of Psychiatry* 115:1017–1020.

Brown, G. W., Birley, J. L. T., and Wing, J. K. (1972). Influence of family life on the course of schizophrenic disorders: a replication. *British Journal of Psychiatry* 121:241–258.

Caputo, D. V. (1963). The parents of the schizophrenic. *Family Process* 2:339–356.

Cheek, F. E. (1964). The "schizophrenogenic mother" in word and deed. *Family Process* 3:155–177.

Cohler, B. J., Weiss, J. L., Grunebaum, H. U., Lidz, C., and Wynne, L. C. (1972). MMPI profiles in hospitalized psychiatric patients and their families. *Archives of General Psychiatry* 26:71-78.

Farina, A. (1960). Patterns of role dominance and conflict in parents of schizophrenic patients. *Journal of Abnormal Social Psychology* 61:31-38.

Ferreira, A. J., and Winter, W. D. (1965). Family interaction and decision making. *Archives of General Psychiatry* 13:214-223.

Fromm-Reichmann, F. (1939). Transference problems in schizophrenia. *Psychoanalytic Quarterly* 8:412-426.

Gardner, G. G. (1967). The role of maternal psychopathology in male and female schizophrenics. *Journal of Consulting Psychology* 31:411-413.

Grad, J., and Sainsbury, P. (1968). The effects that patients have on their families in a community care and a control psychiatric service: a two year follow-up. *British Journal of Psychiatry* 114:265-278.

Green, H. (1964). *I Never Promised You a Rose Garden*. New York: Holt, Rinehart and Winston.

Haley, J. (1977). Research as a handicap to the therapist. In *Beyond the Double Bind: Communication and Family Systems, Theories, and Techniques with Schizophrenics*, ed. M. M. Berger. New York: Brunner/Mazel.

Hames, J., and Waring, E. M. (1980). Marital intimacy and non-psychotic emotional illness. *Psychiatric Forum* 9:13-19.

Henderson, S. (1980). A development in social psychiatry—the systematic study of social bonds. *Journal of Nervous and Mental Disease* 168:63-69.

Heston, L. L. (1966). Psychiatric disorders in foster home reared children of schizophrenic mothers. *British Journal of Psychiatry* 112:891-925.

Hirsch, S. R., and Leff, J. P. (1971). Parental abnormalities of verbal communication in the transmission of schizophrenia. *Psychological Medicine* 1:118-127.

Jacob, T. (1975). Family interaction in disturbed and normal families: a methodological and substantive review. *Psychological Bulletin* 82:33-65.

Jacobs, S. C. et al. (1974). Recent life events in schizophrenia and depression. *Psychological Medicine* 4:444-453.

Kasanin, J., Knight, E., and Sage, P. (1934). The parent-child relationship in schizophrenia. *Journal of Nervous and Mental Disease* 79:249-263.

Laing, R. D. (1965). Mystification, confusion, and conflict. In
    Intensive Family Therapy: Theoretical and Practical Aspects,
    ed. I. Boszormenyi-Nagy and J. L. Framo. New York: Harper
    and Row.
Langsley, D. G., Pittman, F. S., Machotka, P., and Flomenhaft, K.
    (1968). Family crisis therapy—results and implications. *Family
    Process* 7:148–159.
Leff, J. (1978). Schizophrenia and sensitivity to the family
    environment. In *Annual Review of the Schizophrenic Syndrome*,
    ed. R. Cancro, p. 467. New York: Brunner/Mazel.
——, and Hirsch, S. R. (1975). *Abnormalities in Parents of
    Schizophrenics*. New York: Oxford University Press.
Lewis, J. M., Beavers, W. R., Gossett, J. T., and Phillips, V. A.
    (1976). *No Single Thread: Psychological Health in Family
    Systems*. New York: Brunner/Mazel.
Lidz, T., Fleck, S., and Cornelison, A. (1965). *Schizophrenia and
    the Family*. New York: International Universities Press.
Loeff, R. G. (1966). Differential discrimination of conflicting
    emotional messages by normal, delinquent, and schizophrenic
    adolescents. Ph.D. Dissertation, Indiana University.
Mehrabian, A., and Wiener, M. (1967). Decoding of inconsistent
    communications. *Journal of Personality and Social Psychology*
    6:109–114.
Meltzer, H. Y. (1979). Biochemical studies in schizophrenia. In
    Disorders of the Schizophrenic Syndrome, ed. L. Bellak,
    pp. 45–135. New York: Basic Books.
Minuchin, S. (1974). *Families and Family Therapy*. Cambridge,
    Mass.: Harvard University Press.
Mishler, E. G., and Waxler, N. E. (1968). *Interaction in Families:
    An Experimental Study of Family Processes and Schizophrenia*.
    New York: John Wiley.
O'Neal, P., and Robins, L. N. (1958). Childhood patterns
    predictive of adult schizophrenia: a 30-year follow-up study.
    American Journal of Psychiatry 115:385–391.
Pollin, W., Stabenau, J. R., Mosher, L., and Tupin, J. (1966). Life
    history differences in identical twins discordant for
    schizophrenia. *American Journal of Orthopsychiatry* 36:492–509.
Reiss, D. (1971). A theory for relating family interaction to
    individual thinking. *Family Process* 10:1–27.
—— (1976). The family and schizophrenia. *American Journal of
    Psychiatry* 133:181–185.

Ringuette, E., and Kennedy, T. (1966). An experimental study of the double-bind hypothesis. *Journal of Abnormal Psychology* 71:136–141.

Riskin, J., and Faunce, E. E. (1972). An evaluative review of family interaction research. *Family Process* 11:365–455.

Russell, A., Russell, L., and Waring, E. M. (1980). Cognitive family therapy—a preliminary report. *Canadian Psychiatric Association Journal* 15:64–67.

Schaefer, M. T., and Olson, D. H. (1981). Assessing intimacy: the PAIR inventory. *Journal of Marital and Family Therapy* 7:47–60.

Schutz, W. C. (1966). *The Interpersonal Underworld.* A reprint edition of *FIRO: A Three-Dimensional Theory of Interpersonal Behavior.* Palo Alto, Calif.: Science and Behavior.

Sharan, S. (1966). Family interaction with schizophrenics and their siblings. *Journal of Abnormal Psychology* 71:345–353.

Waring, E. M. (1976). Family therapy and schizophrenia: the application of research to practice. Paper presented at the Canadian Psychiatric Association Convention, Quebec City.

——— (1980). Family therapy and psychosomatic illness. *International Journal of Family Therapy* 2:243–252.

——— (1981). Cognitive family therapy in the treatment of schizophrenia. *Psychiatric Journal of the University of Ottawa* 6:229–233

———, and Chelune, G. J. (1983). Marital intimacy and self-disclosure. *Journal of Consulting Psychology,* forthcoming.

———, McElrath, D., Mitchell, P., and Derry, M. E. (1981). Intimacy and emotional illness in the general population. *Canadian Psychiatric Association Journal* 26:167–172.

———, and Russell, L. (1980a). Cognitive family therapy. *Journal of Sex and Marital Therapy* 6:258–273.

———, and Russell, L. (1980b). Family structure, marital adjustment, and intimacy in patients referred to a consultation-liaison service. *General Hospital Psychiatry* 3:198–203.

Waring, M., and Ricks, D. (1965). Family patterns of children who became adult schizophrenics. *Journal of Nervous and Mental Disease* 140:351–364.

Wells, R. A., Dilkes, T. C., and Trivelli, N. (1972). The results of family therapy: a critical review of the literature. *Family Process* 11:189–208.

Wender, P., Rosenthal, D., Zahn, T., and Kety, S. (1971). The psychiatric adjustment of the adoptive parents of schizophrenics. *American Journal of Psychiatry* 127:1013–1018.

Wesley, W. A., and Epstein, N. B. (1969). *The Silent Majority.* San Francisco: Jossey-Bass.

Wild, C. M., Shapiro, L. N., and Abelin, T. (1974). Sampling issues in family studies of schizophrenia. *Archives of General Psychiatry* 30:211–215.

Wing, J. K. (1974). *The Measurement and Classification of Psychiatric Symptoms.* New York: Cambridge University Press.

——, and Brown, G. (1970). *Institutionalism and Schizophrenia.* New York: Cambridge University Press.

Wynne, L. C. (1969). Family research on the pathogenesis of schizophrenia: intermediate variables in the study of families at high risk. Paper presented at the International Symposium on Psychosis, Institut Albert-Prevost, Montreal.

——, Ryckoff, I. M., Day, J., and Hirsch, S. I. (1958). Pseudomutuality in the family relations of schizophrenics. *Psychiatry* 21:205–220.

——, Toohey, M. L., and Doane, J. (1979). Family studies. In *Disorders of the Schizophrenic Syndrome,* ed. L. Bellak, pp. 264–288. New York: Basic Books.

Zuckerman, M., Oltean, M., and Monashkin, I. (1958). The parental attitudes of mothers of schizophrenics. *Journal of Consulting Psychology* 22:307–310.

❧ 2 ❧

Family Therapy with Hospitalized and Disabled Patients

G. Pirooz Sholevar, M.D.

Family therapy with hospitalized and institutionalized patients is a significant challenge to family system theorists, as it tests the extent and the limits of their systemic approach. The interaction between the family and hospital systems can be either enlightening or confusing.

In this chapter we shall consider the family unit as a social subsystem consisting of individuals interacting with one another according to certain rules (Shapiro 1980, Sholevar 1980, Stanton 1980). The family is seen as having homeostatic properties that attempt to balance its interacting parts. It utilizes a variety of negative and positive feedbacks to regulate the basic, adaptive, and defensive needs of different family members. The family of procreation is psychologically bound to the extended families (families of origin), and the behavior and inter-actions of the different family members have homeostatic and loyalty implications on the nuclear and extended family levels.

In this chapter we shall describe the contributions of family therapy to hospitalization and the treatment of emotional and physical disabilities:

1. Psychiatric hospitalization of patients with chronic, acute, and recurrent disorders
2. Family therapy in general hospitals
3. Physical disabilities

PSYCHIATRIC HOSPITALIZATION OF PATIENTS WITH CHRONIC, ACUTE, AND RECURRENT DISORDERS

Sholevar (1980) described the dynamics and patterns of families who institutionalize children in psychiatric hospitals or residential treat-ment centers. He defined institutionalization as the by-product of long-standing family dysfunctions in which the family attempts to reestablish homeostasis by extruding a member. The successful extrusion of a member is thought to bring harmony and stability to a family threatened by a serious imbalance caused by the increasing ineffectiveness of the long-standing defensive family patterns. Most of these dysfunctional and defensive patterns have been present in three generations, which has allowed them to attain sufficient intensity, chronicity, and lack of perspective to facilitate, rationalize, and justify a dramatic action such as the extrusion of a member from the family unit. The presence of similar relational and behavioral patterns in previous generations is necessary for the family to feel justified and syntonic about extruding a member as the end point of the long-standing family conflicts.

In many of the families who hospitalize and institutionalize their children, one of the parents, as a child, had been placed in a foster home (Sholevar 1980). In one of the cases reported, the genetic roots of the decision for psychiatric hospitalization revealed that the mother was repeating her early-life experience when she was extruded from her family of origin. The mother was identifying with the aggressor (her own mother), projecting guilt on her own child, and extruding him from the nuclear family. The mother stubbornly adhered to the decision for hospitalization until she was made to realize the impact of her own foster-home placement and extrusion from her family of origin. She then reversed her decision to hospitalize her son, reduced her covert rejection of him, and searched for more adaptive solutions. The above changes were achieved in two intensive family sessions with dramatic behavioral changes in the mother and child.

Strategic and Technical Aspects of Therapy

In addition to the techniques applicable to family therapy in general, there are specific strategic considerations for the family therapy of hospitalized patients. The following describes briefly some of the principal issues.

Family therapy has helped reduce the length of hospitalization for psychiatric patients, even though the therapists were generally trainees with little experience.

A staff person should be assigned to work with the family of the patients. Family therapists should be available for personal and phone contact with different family members, gather family information gained by other hospital staff, conduct family therapy sessions, and participate in the overall management and discharge planning. Staff members should offer to all family members an equal opportunity to help resolve problems, rather than putting the burden on the identified patient.

Even though only one member of the family (the patient) is in the hospital, the family must not be allowed to shirk its responsibility to help resolve the family's problems or to blame solely the patient for causing them. It is generally considered more effective to focus on the problems encountered by the family in the management of the patient's behavior rather than to discuss that behavior itself. The therapist should encourage the family to join in the problem management (Anderson 1977). This will usually reveal the basic familial role conflicts and help restructure the family system. For example, the reduced tension in the family unit may help reduce the scapegoating and enhance cooperative problem solving by the family.

The "enactive" style of communications in treatment is preferable with certain severely disturbed families for which a more abstract level of exploration is less successful. Suggestions such as "try to talk to your son now" or "go fishing with him this weekend" may be more fruitful than exploring the historical pattern of father-son distance. This mode, however, should not be used with all families.

Neglectful parents who feel deprived and desperate themselves are frequently reluctant to take any concrete actions to improve their parenting or perform assigned therapeutic tasks in a meaningful fashion. With such families, exploring the historical roots of inadequate parenting can result in dramatic changes during the family sessions. This can occur only if the therapist can establish an empathic atmosphere in which emotions can be exhibited and are welcomed. A phenomenon akin to the "corrective or operational mourning" described by Paul and Grosser (1965) can then take place in single or multiple family sessions. For example, the therapist can empathically and actively establish that the mother felt deprived in her own family of origin and has continued to feel so, even in the recent past. The mother's present lack of appropriate emotional response to her own daughter thus can be understood within such a perspective and point up the mother's inability to recognize her daughter's assets. This recognition can dramatically break down the old familial patterns and establish new ones in very few sessions. Its importance has escaped many of the "communicational" family therapists who have failed to recognize the essence of successful psychodynamic family therapy. Labels such as "historically oriented family therapies" ignore the focus of the psychodynamic therapists on resolving destructive family roles that maintain long-standing, unresolved family conflicts.

The most important aspect of family therapy with hospitalized patients is recognizing the state of decompensation and disintegration of the family. Members of the family may avoid, or even be openly hostile to, one another by refusing to attend family sessions. This is similar to the Absent Member Maneuver described by Sonne, Speck, and Jungreis (1962). It is important to recognize, therefore, that at the outset of the hospitalization the most significant members of the family are unlikely to attend family sessions simultaneously or will try to mislead the therapist about the conflicts among them. The most helpful information may appear on the least expected occasions, such as family visits with the patients. For example, the reluctant father who has never attended the family therapy sessions may appear in the hospital drunk and abuse his son. This may be the most important aspect of the family evaluation and diagnosis, but such information may not reach the family therapist. Furthermore, the family therapist assigned to the case may discourage hospital staff from reporting such information. The situation is then complicated, as many of the line hospital staff do not attend clinical conferences or team meetings.

I suggest, therefore, that the family therapist in the hospital be viewed as the final conduit for familial information rather than its sole repository. Following this model, the information obtained by the staff is channeled to the family therapist, who in turn uses it to evaluate and treat the family. Likewise, most of the interventions with the family should be carried out by different hospital staff at the time of hospital visits, physical therapy sessions, and the like. The informed staff will then be prepared to encounter the various behaviors expected from different family members and deal with them effectively. The diagnostic and therapeutic reach of the family therapist will thereby be expanded to include all the hospital staff.

Often the most effective negotiation with the family comes at the moment the patient enters the hospital, but many family therapists avoid discussing significant issues at this time, considering the family too acutely stressed. This is unfortunate, for this may be the point of lowest resistance to family therapy, when crucial relational information can be obtained and a treatment contract established. Later on, the resistance of the family is mobilized, and the prestige of the hospital staff is on the decline. At such later times, it may be impossible to overcome the resistance of family members to family therapy. The patient's admission to the hospital, then, is the best time to establish the family's participation in the diagnostic and treatment plan.

Acute and Recurrent Disorders

Family theory has contributed significantly to the understanding of psychiatric patients in acute or recurrent crises. The acute psychiatric disorder is not only a decompensation of the identified patient, the patient is also a part of a family unit that is disintegrating and decompensating under stress. This stress can affect any member of the nuclear or extended family. For example, the father's losing his job may bring tension and despair to the whole family, which may result in the acute psychotic breakdown of an adolescent son. Likewise, vaginal bleeding in the mother, arousing the fear of her death, can result in family tension and the psychotic breakdown of an offspring who may be unaware of the mother's physical symptom but is affected secondarily by the anxiety emerging in the relationship of the parents. Family theory can help clinicians recognize single or multiple points of stress affecting extended and nuclear family members. Such stresses are more easily recognized and treated by working with nuclear and extended family members than focusing on the hospitalized patient alone.

The social network of severely and chronically disturbed and psychotic patients is noticeably more constricted than that of less disturbed people (Speck and Attneave 1973), and this becomes more apparent with the chronicity of the illness. The impoverishment of the social network is particularly significant, as it limits the family's external resources and input, making the family particularly vulnerable to breakdown and disintegration in stressful situations. The therapeutic intervention at such times should help reestablish the family's relational ties and social network.

The following case illustrates the role of an impoverished social network in recurring psychiatric hospitalization:

> Mrs. L. is a 40-year-old divorced woman who was hospitalized because of anxiety, depression, a suicide attempt, and excessive drinking. The hospitalization occurred after her father rejected her endeavor to reestablish ties with him. Mrs. L.'s mother and grandmother died when she was in her early and late adolescence.
>
> In the hospital, Mrs. L. appeared to be a pleasant and attractive woman exhibiting extreme self-centeredness and very low self-esteem. An exploration of the composition of her family and social network revealed that her total social support system consisted of her father, with whom she had had no contact in the past several years because of his disappointment in her drinking. She viewed him as critical and rejecting. The other members of Mrs. L.'s network included her boyfriend, K., an alcoholic whose brief encounters with Mrs. L. had been followed by severe fights and prolonged periods of avoidance. The other two members

of Mrs. L.'s network were an expatient from her previous hospitalization and an old co-worker. But she avoided seeing them at times of stress, as she did not want them to see her in a state of decompensation. Although a competent worker, Mrs. L. managed to work in her home, therefore depriving herself of the opportunity to develop a social network. She longed to reestablish a relationship with her father, although she felt pessimistic about it. She blamed her father's stubbornness for their relational breakup and took no responsibility for her role in it. She also wanted to see her only son who lived with her exhusband, having seen him on only one occasion in the recent past.

The therapeutic attempt was to reestablish the ties between Mrs. L. and her father. The father was in a very vulnerable position, however, as he was the only person demanding an alteration in Mrs. L.'s drinking and general behavior. The therapeutic plan, therefore, included the expansion of Mrs. L.'s social and familial network, by encouraging her to establish relationships with her neighbors, her father, her father's new family, and her son and to obtain a job in a small company. The enlargement of her familial-social network enabled her to reveal more freely different aspects of her personality, as she was not plagued with the fear of losing her few friends. Her self-revelation also enabled the people in her social network to give appropriate feedback in a manner that heightened her level of functioning rather than supporting her frequently self-destructive behavior.

The hospitalization of a family member generally occurs when a conflict between the nuclear family and one or more significant members of the social network results in the family's exclusion of the latter. Frequently, the significant person in the social network who is "cut off" is the source of support for the patient's ego functions, although this may not be recognized or acknowledged by the family. A deterioration in the patient's ego functioning occurs following the deprivation from the ego support by the significant person in the social network. This is particularly important, as the patient's remaining social network operates according to the principle of pseudomutuality (Wynne et al. 1958). Such pseudomutual relationships in the small and close-knit network can result in extreme distortion in the family's reality-testing ability. Thus, the person excluded from the social network prior to the hospitalization may have been the only source of support of such ego

functions as self-reliance and reality testing. The restoration of the
relationship with the excluded member of the network can improve
these functions and lead to the discharge of the patient from the
facility. The following example illustrates this:

> John, 15 years old, was admitted to a psychiatric unit
> following several outbursts of temper tantrums resulting in
> the destruction of furniture and the threat of bodily injury.
> In family therapy sessions during the first week of
> hospitalization, it was discovered that John's mother and his
> four adolescent siblings believed that a man, possibly John's
> estranged father, entered their house at night and injected
> some substance under their scalps that gave them headaches
> the following morning. It was then found that John's temper
> outbursts were a reaction to the collective delusional thoughts
> shared by the rest of his family. John felt helpless and
> frightened by his family's delusional belief and reacted with
> temper tantrums.

The consultant to the family therapist could not explain the reason
for John's unexplained deviation from the family's delusional system.
The therapists also did not know the immediate reason for the decompensation of the family unit resulting in John's hospitalization.

In the family session arranged at this time, the consultant noticed the
mother's frequent inquiries about the passage of time. As it is unusual
for a severely disturbed family to be preoccupied with such a matter,
the reason for the mother's impatience was explored. Reluctantly, the
mother revealed that her older sister had given them a ride to the
hospital and was sitting in the car on the street with the car engine
running, waiting to drive the family home. Eventually the older sister's
resistance to join the group was overcome, and she was included in the
session. A significant familial conflict was then uncovered between the
mother and her oldest sister, with the older sister acting as a messenger
and go-between. The oldest sister considered the whole family—except
John—crazy and had stopped associating with them shortly prior to
John's hospitalization, though she had maintained indirect input into
the family through contacts between the older aunt and John. The
older aunt used her contacts to inform John of the craziness of his
family, which resulted in his temper outbursts. Later, the older sister
proved to be a major asset in reestablishing the relational ties between

the mother and the oldest sister. With the inclusion of the two older sisters in the family sessions, the family's delusional belief was soon cleared up, and John's ability to control his behavior improved.

FAMILY THERAPY IN GENERAL HOSPITALS

Physical disorders can put stress on families and destroy their equilibrium. The impact is particularly noticeable with serious and life-threatening disorders, such as terminal illnesses that threaten the integrity of the family unit. A life-threatening illness can produce various reactions, including anticipating loss, assuming death as a foregone conclusion, treating the dying person as if he or she is already dead, or denying death up to the last moment. In any case, the mourning reaction in the family will be incomplete, resulting in long-standing familial dysfunction and personality changes in its members, such as partial withdrawal of the family members from one another, withdrawal of the family as a unit from the larger social system, or other defensive or restitutive activities, such as delinquency or unplanned pregnancy in adolescent family members.

The inability of the family as a unit to mourn a loss can leave the children unprepared to face the vicissitudes of human relationships, including future losses. This may create disturbed communicational and relational configurations, such as pseudomutuality or social isolation, which can limit the role adjustments in the family after the death of a family member. The surviving family members may have difficulty establishing future relationships or may rush prematurely into inappropriate and unsatisfactory ones.

Dying Patients

Although impending death is, obviously, highly stressful for the patient, it can be even more stressful for the family. After all, the patient's suffering will end with death, whereas the family will continue to struggle with the loss of their member, the need for altering familial roles during the terminal illness and after the loss, and the challenge of future adjustment.

The challenge imposed by a patient's dying from cardiovascular illnesses, such as myocardial infarction, may be more formidable, as the death can occur suddenly and without prior warning. The great shock to the family may result in their using the least adaptive defenses, such as denial or projection of blame on the dying patient or the health professionals. But usually there is more time available to deal with the death of patients suffering from cancer or chronic illnesses, as many such patients can live for several months or years. This allows the family to communicate their feelings to one another and possibly to resolve immediate or long-standing relational conflicts.

The most maladaptive familial response is withdrawing from the dying patient. This defensive isolation of the dying patient occurs when the family is overwhelmed by the anticipated loss and is particularly pronounced when the family knows little about the patient's diagnosis. And it is exacerbated if the hospital staff also avoids the patient.

Patients' reactions to their impending death have been described vividly and systematically by Elisabeth Kübler-Ross (1969, 1974, 1975, 1981). The five stages in this process are denial, protest, bargaining, depression, and acceptance.

In the first stage, patients assume that it cannot happen "to me." This stage follows the initial shock of receiving the unpleasant news and is particularly prolonged in patients who have used denial throughout their lives. The use of denial is increased when the physician also uses it. In the second stage, patients exhibit protest and anger, particularly rage, envy, and resentment. They become demanding and inquire constantly why the illness had to happen to them. This stage is particularly prolonged in patients who are used to repressing their anger. In the third stage, bargaining, patients regress to an infantile position by expecting a reward for good behavior. The fourth stage is depression. Reactive depression is the reaction to losses caused by the patient's illness, such as the loss of job or position in the family. Preparatory depression anticipates future losses. The reactive depression does respond to an attitude of "cheer up" by the family and hospital staff, but the preparatory depression does not respond to such attempts. In the depressive stage, the patient sleeps for long hours. In the fifth stage, patients assume an attitude of acceptance. They appear to be void of feeling and, again, sleep long hours. They like their visits to be short and the TV turned off. In this stage, the communications among the patient, the family, and the hospital staff are mainly nonverbal. There is much touching and sitting together in silence. Unable to fight any longer, the patient seems resigned.

Any of these stages can be prolonged if they coincide with the long-standing defenses used by the patient. For example, patients who have felt victimized throughout their lives would go through a prolonged and protracted stage of protest.

The families of dying patients react in many ways. They suffer from loneliness, even while overburdened by assuming responsibilities previously assigned to the dying patient. The change of role is generally harder for husbands than it is for wives, who can adjust to a change in their familial role more readily. The feeling of guilt and self-blame is a common reaction by the family to the news of serious illness of one of their members. The family feels they should have "known it sooner" and have taken preventive measures.

It is often not realized that the family's reaction to the dying patient goes through stages similar to those described by Kübler-Ross. The physician and other health care professionals should recognize the different stages of the family's reaction to their anticipated loss and deal with them sensitively. The information about the patient's diagnosis and prognosis should be shared openly with the family, and they should be encouraged to discuss them openly with the patient. The hospital staff should try to be available to the dying patient and family and discourage the family from avoiding the patient. The family's adaptive responses, such as partial denial of the grave news, should be respected, and the information should not be forced on them when they indicate that they have reached the limits of their tolerance. Repeated forcing of the unpleasant news on the family of the dying patient may only strengthen their denial or despair. It is important to allow the family to remain hopeful about the patient's condition. Partial denial by the family members, such as wishing for "miracle drugs" or equating temporary remissions with permanent cure, may be adaptive defenses and should be respected by the hospital staff. In this regard, it is essential that the physicians refrain from specifying how much time the patient has to live, as it will drive the family into despair and may forfeit the physicians' credibility if they are proved wrong. It is generally more fruitful to talk in general terms, indicating the declining health of the patient and encouraging the family to prepare for the anticipated loss or resolve long-standing conflicts. Many families report the resolution of life-long relational conflicts at this final stage, accompanied by feelings of relief and closeness to one another.

Dying children arouse the strongest feelings of protest in the family and the hospital staff, as their lives have been short and they have not had the opportunity for self-fulfillment.

Spinal Cord Injuries

As an example of significant disability resulting in familial stress, I shall examine the alterations in family dynamics and roles following spinal cord injuries and how family therapy can help the family resume functioning.

The most disabling aspect of an injury that limits the family adjustment to the unexpected tragedy is not understanding the nature and extent of damage and disability. Additional stresses are the need for multiple surgical and rehabilitative procedures, the high and continued cost of treatment, the lower productivity of the affected person and the need for alteration in family role assignments. The physician and other members of the medical team can best serve the family by explaining these problems. This information alone can help the family assess the situation, explore solutions, and attempt to rehabilitate itself. But a premature exploration of family relationships can appear irrelevant, insensitive, or intrusive to the family members. Even though the dynamic relationship among family members and its historical roots are significant, this information will emerge as the family struggles to adjust to its new circumstances. For example, the family needing a physically active child will reveal this in its mourning of the lost health and physical ability of their offspring.

The impact of a disabling physical illness forces the family to seek support from their families of origin and the members of their social network. At such times, the latent and long-standing conflicts with the families of origin can be reactivated, resulting in the maladaptive infantilization of a mature offspring, the intensification of one parent-child relationship, and the weakening of marital bonds in the families of origin. The worst effect of such realignments is the weakening of the marital ties of the offspring who is regressively claimed by his or her family of origin. At this point, the family therapist can help mobilize support for the affected person and family on the nuclear, extended, and social level, while at the same time countering the tendency for regressive-unadaptive realignments. The role of the family therapist is of paramount importance, as the fear of abandonment by one's family following the accident and the hardship of readjustment of long-standing familial roles are the most difficult challenges to the family. One should keep in mind, however, that there are many players on the team, and the physicians, physical therapists, and nurses are also important. The family therapist can also help by straightening out any misunderstandings between the family and other professionals too. Competition between the family therapist and other professionals can develop easily and should be avoided.

The following case example illustrates some of the typical situations encountered by the family of a person who has had a spinal cord injury:

Bob is a 23-year-old married man, born, raised, and residing in the eastern United States. His wife, Bonnie, is from Seattle. The couple moved to the East Coast two years ago when they married. The couple became attracted to each other particularly because of their physical characteristics. Their marriage has been a happy one, owing partly to Bob's love of sports which dispelled Bonnie's slight inhibitions regarding physical activities. Under Bob's influence, Bonnie developed a love of new experiences, as Bob was active and interested in new adventures. The couple particularly enjoyed rapid-water rafting and dancing. They had not seriously considered having children, as the bulk of Bonnie's energy was devoted to saving money to buy a house and establishing herself as a paralegal professional. Meanwhile, Bob was exploring the possibility of convincing his boss to establish another sporting-goods store as a joint venture under Bob's management.

The family's happy days came to a sudden end when Bob suffered a serious neck injury in an accident while riding his motorcycle home from work. There was no apparent neglect on Bob's part, and the accident seemed to have been caused by a slippery item on the road.

The family's initial shock was immeasurable, particularly when they learned that Bob might be bedridden for the rest of his life and might not recover any mobility in his arms, legs, or even his fingers. In a few days, Bob became seriously suicidal, saw no meaning in life, and openly expressed feelings of despair and depression. The family needed much information and patient support in order to understand the nature of the insult to the spinal cord and the possible extent of Bob's future disability. With the emotional support of Bob's parents, the family assumed an attitude of wait-and-see. Bob 's mother provided much of the support and nurturance to Bob.

In a few weeks and after two operations, the appearance of movement in Bob's fingers and wrists heralded the possibility of full recovery in his upper extremities, though with little hope for any eventual movement in his legs. Bob felt demoralized and feared Bonnie's leaving him. He saw himself as a worthless burden. Bob's fears were partly in reaction to Bonnie's psychological withdrawal from Bob after the accident, which was caused mainly by her own feeling of isolation and lack of a social support system. Her family was in Seattle, and Bonnie was emotionally distant from her older sister, who lived in a town nearby. In the past, Bonnie had reacted to the overprotectiveness of her mother and family by assuming a prematurely self-sufficient and overly independent attitude. Her attitude was now interfering with her receiving any support from her family.

Bob's fear of losing Bonnie was based on his assumption that Bonnie's primary interest in him was based on his physical attractiveness and his active life-style. He thus felt that she would not be interested in a "worthless piece of junk" who could not get around. His fears were particularly heightened by Bonnie's withdrawal and her rigid, unhappy demeanor.

Their marriage entered a new phase when Bob's family rallied around him, welcoming him back to his family of origin. Bob's grandfather, who had been depressed because of his retirement and recent loss of his wife, was revived instantly after Bob's accident, finding new meaning in life, building an addition to Bob's parents' house for Bob to live in, and constructing a ramp for his wheelchair to have access to different parts of the house.

Bob, reassured by the loving support of his family of origin, recovered rapidly from his feeling of worthlessness and depression. But he then started to experience a strong conflict of loyalty between his family of origin and his wife. The attractiveness of the regressive pull to his parents was countered by strong feelings of guilt for failing Bonnie. Bonnie's unhappiness and isolation served as a reminder that he would be unable to produce a family or respond sexually to his attractive young wife.

Bonnie was overwhelmed by the lack of support from her family of origin, the threat of losing her defensive overindependence, and particularly the feelings of jealousy over losing Bob to his mother. This jealousy had worsened with a sudden revival of oedipal strivings in Bob's mother and the subtle competition between the two women. The mother's move toward Bob was coupled with a subtle push by her to drive Bob's father away from the family.

The therapeutic strategy and plan included work with Bob's family of origin to extend their support to Bonnie and adopt the young couple rather than reclaiming only Bob. This reduced the competition between Bonnie and Bob's mother. Bonnie was encouraged to reestablish a more communicative, open, and supportive relationship with her sister, which met with some initial resistance because of the tendency of her centrifugal family (Stierlin 1974) to remain isolated from one another. Correspondence between Bonnie and her parents in Seattle was also necessary to encourage her family to show some interest in supporting the young couple.

Once a new method of mastering the difficulties created by Bob's disability was adopted, the communicational channels among the newly established family, their families of origin, and the staff of the medical and rehabilitation centers were opened. The family members helped Bob utilize the many hours of physical therapy for his rehabilitation. The mourning of happy days prior to the disability appeared periodically intertwined with incomplete mourning for the death of Bob's grandmother.

The family thus had started on the long road of planning their future, readjusting the familial roles of its members, and addressing the sexual issues between Bob and Bonnie.

Throughout the many months of treatment with this family, the family therapist functioned as a member of the total treatment team to help the family members obtain the necessary information, formulate questions about the disability, treatment cost, and so forth. The information gained enabled the family to bring about the long-term necessary changes in the familial roles in order to enhance their adaptation to their hardships.

Physical Disabilities

Blindness and deafness greatly alter family communicational systems. Blindness interferes directly with nonverbal channels of communication in the family, which are important means of relatedness. Deafness interferes with both verbal and nonverbal channels of communication, development of language, development of abstract thinking, and higher levels of empathy and problem solving in the family. Indirectly, both visual and hearing losses result in changes in family relational patterns, such as rejection of the child, denial of the illness that can expand into general denial of reality, and affective lability. The most common reaction to handicapping conditions is overprotection of the disabled child by one of the parents, which eventually results in the rejection of the healthy siblings and the weakening of the marital ties. It is not surprising that the incidence of divorce in families with handicapped children is greater than generally expected.

Temporary handicapping conditions can alter family dynamics, even after the temporary handicap disappears. The family therapist should be able to recognize the genetic aspects of the family patterns in such conditions, as illustrated by the example below.

In the first two family sessions, the rejection by Linda, a 31-year-old mother, of her older adolescent daughter was apparent and contrasted with her overprotective attitude toward her younger, preadolescent girl, Debbie. Linda readily acknowledged this discrepancy in her attitude. In the second session, Debbie's difficulties in playing lacrosse were described by the family with a fair amount of emotion. At that point, the therapist inquired about the reason for Debbie's lack of proficiency and was told of her difficulty with perceptual-motor coordination. Linda then revealed that Debbie was born with severe strabismus requiring multiple corrective operations in the first few years of her life. During the session, Linda dramatically recounted the pain and trauma of the operations and hospitalizations. The therapist interpreted the strabismus and the corrective surgery as the genetic factor in Linda's overprotectiveness toward Debbie, an interpretation that Linda accepted and that led to the revelation of other, long-repressed feelings; Debbie's facial expression was one of disbelief, and Linda's face became white. A rapid change in Linda's relationship with her two children followed. Linda became less protective of Debbie and more accepting of her older daughter, which allowed Debbie to improve her relationship with her peers and sister.

Deaf Children and Adults

Family therapy with deaf children and adults was described by Shapiro and Harris (1976), who indicated the limited vocabulary and syntactical skills of deaf children who have severe difficulties with the development of language and abstract cognition. For example, a 5-year-old deaf child may have a limited vocabulary that does not even include the names of the food that she eats every day, in contrast to that of a hearing child who may have a vocabulary of 5,000 to 20,000 words. These language and cognitive difficulties continue and only 5 percent of the deaf achieve a tenth-grade or higher educational level. The clinical traits of deaf people include the lack of understanding or concern for the feelings of others, limited awareness of their behavior's effect on other people, an egocentric view of the world, an absence of thoughtful introspection, and coercive demands to have their needs and wishes satisfied. Their reactions to frustration, tension, or anxiety are typically of a primitive motoric nature rather than self-control and constraint. Hearing parents have more difficulties in dealing with the problems of deaf children than do deaf parents with a deaf child. Families of deaf children harbor strong feelings of guilt, rage, and depression. Their family relationships are marked by an extreme dependence of the deaf child on one of the parents, along with an imbalance in the parental marital relationship resulting in a higher parental divorce rate.

Few parents of deaf children learn sign language or finger spelling in order to communicate with their children. Rather, they try to force oral speech and lip reading on their deaf child, as part of society's unrealistic expectations for handicapped youngsters. The deaf children generally become the scapegoats in the family, becoming the target for familial problems.

The goals of family therapy with deaf children are to facilitate communication between parents and child, introduce early manual communication between parents and child, and help the parents' expectations be consistent and realistic (Mindel 1969, Mindel and Vernon

1971). For the treatment to be adequate, the family should be able to vent repressed feelings of guilt, rage, and depression and to change its defensive familial patterns, such as denial of deafness, overprotection, and parental conflict.

It is helpful in such sessions to use therapists who know sign language or to include an interpreter proficient in sign language and finger spelling. Often the parents of deaf children resist learning sign language, and so using it in the therapeutic sessions may encourage the parents to learn it.

Attention Deficit Disorders (Hyperactivity)

Attention Deficit Disorders (ADD) is a new diagnostic label for the behavioral syndrome previously described as Hyperactivity or Minimal Brain Dysfunction. The behavioral symptoms of ADD include short attention span, poor concentration, distractibility, emotional lability, and impulsivity. An overwhelming majority of children with ADD are hyperactive, as manifested by poorly organized motor activity that is not directed toward achieving specific goals. Learning disability and lowered self-esteem are commonly found in children with ADD. Children suffering from anxiety frequently have the same clinical symptoms as those with ADD, but their hyperactivity is situational and not pervasive.

The impact of children with ADD on their families and vice versa is great and can best be understood by evaluating the whole family. Such children generally disorganize their families, who respond to them with reactions ranging from confusing and contradictory communications to outright rejection. This can further lower the children's self-esteem and aggravate their emotional difficulties. But conversely, poorly organized family systems can exacerbate the hyperactivity and behavioral disorganization of children with ADD. A vicious cycle is thus initiated in which the child and family disorganize each other's behavior and lower each other's self-esteem, eventually producing a hostile-dependent relationship between the child and the mother, with the father emotionally abandoning the family.

Family intervention with ADD should be initiated by clarifying the diagnosis, emphasizing the improvement of the disorder in time and under favorable conditions. The effect of secondary hostile intrafamilial relationships by prolonging and fixating the disability should be described clearly. The importance of establishing structure and control for the child with ADD should be emphasized, and the parents should be advised to follow a strict regimen. This is generally impossible unless the father remains emotionally involved with the family unit and supports the mother and children. Strengthening of the parental-marital relationship, therefore, is necessary. In addition, siblings should be helped to recognize the task facing the family so that they do not feel neglected and abandoned.

In working with families of children with ADD and other similar syndromes, it is important to recognize the existence of hereditary-familial factors in the genesis of such disorders. ADD is often an undiagnosed condition in the history of the parents. Affected parents may have suffered many or all of the negative social consequences of ADD, leading to many unresolved conflicts and feelings. For example, they may think of themselves as "stupid" because of their learning disability and overreact to the manifestations of ADD or learning disability in their children.

The parents' overreaction to unresolved conflicts can complicate the already difficult tasks facing a child with ADD, and so uncovering the roots of the parental behavior can help resolve conflicts that are interfering with effective management of the present problems. The unaffected parent should be helped to recognize and correct the unadaptive behavior of the affected parent.

The intergenerational aspects of the parents' negative and rejecting attitude toward their child should be kept in mind in families with a history of ADD in one of the parents. Similar dysfunctional parental attitudes can be found in other behavioral syndromes with a familial-genetic pattern, such as enuresis and encopresis. For example, the father who rubs the nose of his soiling son in his feces is likely to have been a soiler himself as a child and to have encountered such sadistic responses. His present behavior can be a repetition of his painful past experience.

REFERENCES

Anderson, C. M. (1977). Family intervention with severely
disturbed inpatients. *Archives of General Psychiatry* 34:697–702.
Kübler-Ross, E. (1969). *On Death and Dying.* New York:
Macmillan.

—— (1974). *Questions and Answers on Death and Dying*. New York: Macmillan.

—— (1981). *Living with Death and Dying*. New York: Macmillan.

——, ed. (1975). *Death: The Final Stage of Growth*. Englewood Cliffs, N.J.: Prentice-Hall.

Mindel, E. D. (1969). Studies of the deaf child. In *Psychiatric Diagnosis, Therapy, and Research on the Psychotic Deaf*, ed. R. R. Grinker. Washington, D. C.: Department of Health, Education, and Welfare.

——, and Vernon, M. (1971). *They Grow in Silence—The Deaf Child and His Family*. Silver Spring, Md.: National Association of the Deaf.

Paul N., and Grosser, G. (1965). Operational mourning and its role in conjoint family therapy. *Community Mental Health Journal* 1:339–345.

Shapiro, R. (1980). Psychodynamic approaches to family therapy. In *Emotional Disorders in Children and Adolescents*, ed. G. P. Sholevar, pp. 135–158. Jamaica, N.Y.: Spectrum.

——, and Harris, R. (1976). Family therapy in treatment of the deaf: a case report. *Family Process* 15:83–96.

Sholevar, G. P. (1980). Families of institutionalized children. In *Emotional Disorders in Children and Adolescents*, ed. G. P. Sholevar, pp. 181–190. Jamaica, N.Y.: Spectrum.

Sonne, J., Speck, R. V., and Jungreis, J. E. (1962). The absent member maneuver as a resistance in the family therapy of schizophrenia. *Family Process* 1:44–62.

Speck, R., and Attneave, C. (1973). *Family Networks*. New York: Pantheon.

Stanton, D. (1980). Systems approaches to family therapy. In *Emotional Disorders in Children and Adolescents*, ed. G. P. Sholevar, pp. 159–179. Jamaica, N.Y.: Spectrum.

Stierlin, H. (1974). *Separating Parents and Adolescents*. New York: Quadrangle.

Wynne, L. C., Ryckoff, I. M., Day, J., and Hirsch, S. I. (1958). Pseudomutuality in the family relations of schizophrenics. *Psychiatry* 21:205–220.

❧ 3 ❧

Psychosomatic Problems

Michael White

The application and efficacy of family therapy to various psychosomatic conditions presenting in childhood and adolescence are well documented (Liebman et al. 1976; Minuchin et al. 1975, 1978). This thorough documentation is largely based on the relatively easy measurement of psychosomatic conditions, including their duration, frequency and intensity of symptoms, degree of incapacity, and so on. Although there have been many contributions in this area, Minuchin and his associates from Philadelphia appear to have been the most consistent and systematic in their application of structural family therapy to various psychosomatic conditions.

Minuchin and his associates formulated a map of *psychosomatic families* as well as specific approaches to treatment according to a structural systems orientation. They proposed five major structural characteristics or patterns of relationship of psychosomatic families that they believe provide context for psychosomatic symptoms. These characteristics are enmeshment, overprotectiveness, conflict avoidance, conflict detouring, and rigidity.

In psychosomatic families, these patterns of relationship and the specific psychosomatic symptoms are said to fit together in a way that is mutually perpetuating: The relationship patterns perpetuate the symptoms, and the specific symptoms perpetuate the patterns of relationship. This is a theory of circular rather than linear causality, and speculation about certain initial conditions or root causes of psychosomatic illness is not considered relevant.

According to this circular theory, the goal of therapy is to disrupt such self-perpetuating cycles by challenging the family system's specific structural characteristics and modifying the symptoms' transactional significance. Minuchin and his colleagues (1978) then recommended specific interventions.

The characteristics of enmeshment, overprotectiveness, conflict avoidance, conflict detouring, and rigidity can be considered relative. At their most intense they represent extremes along certain dimensions of family life. For example, intense enmeshment can be considered to lie close to one pole on the dimension of cohesion, whereas the polar opposite on this dimension would be extreme disengagement.

The following family-rating system places the above characteristics on a series of dimensions of family life. I developed this system as a teaching aide and later adapted it for use in research on chronic asthma (the Adelaide Children's Hospital Chronic Asthma Research Project). Although this rating system is relatively crude and lacks operational definitions, the interrater reliability was demonstrated to be high on the research project and on the numerous occasions during which the scheme was presented to various groups. The rating system is composed of the dimensions of cohesion, support and concern, conflict resolution, and adaptability. Simple bar scales are used for dyadic, triadic, and overall ratings.

FAMILY CHARACTERISTICS

Cohesion

Russell (1979) defined cohesion as "an emotional, intellectual and/or physical oneness that family members feel toward one another. This variable ranges from extremely high family cohesion, resulting in over-identification, or enmeshment within the family, to extremely low family cohesion, which results in isolation, or disengagement within the family" (p. 31).

1. **Extreme enmeshment:** an extreme proximity and intensity in family interactions, weak and diffuse subsystem boundaries, and poor interpersonal differentiation. Evidence of extremes of family loyalty or patriotism.
2. Strong enmeshment.
3. Moderate enmeshment.
4. Mild enmeshment.
5. **Balanced cohesion:** a degree of intimacy and sharing but with clear boundaries and interpersonal differentiation. A capacity for subsystems (including individuals) to belong yet remain separate.
6. Mild disengagement.
7. Moderate disengagement.
8. Strong disengagement.
9. **Extreme disengagement:** an extreme distance and aloofness of family relationships and highly rigid subsystem boundaries (including individuals), conveying a sense of interpersonal isolation and absence of family loyalty or patriotism.

Support and Concern

This dimension evaluates the family's support of and concern with the growth, development, and differentiation of subsystems (including individuals). This "support and concern" ranges from extremes of overprotectiveness, in which individuation is undermined, to neglect, in which support for individual growth and development appears absent.

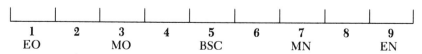

1. **Extreme overprotectiveness:** excessively high mutual concern for each subsystem's welfare (including individuals); hypersensitivity

to signs of distress, tension, and conflict; and retardation of development of competence and investment in extrafamilial involvement.

2. Strong overprotectiveness.
3. Moderate overprotectiveness.
4. Mild overprotectiveness.
5. Balanced support and concern: a supportive and encouraging atmosphere that allows subsystems (including individuals) to explore developmental potential and allows for general movement in the direction of subsystem (including individuals) competence and differentiation.
6. Mild neglect.
7. Moderate neglect.
8. Strong neglect.
9. Extreme neglect: an absence of concern for each subsystem's (including individuals) welfare and a lack of support necessary for subsystem growth, development, and elaboration. Also, a prevailing atmosphere of nonsensitivity to signs of distress.

Conflict Resolution

This dimension evaluates the family subsystem's (including individuals) ability to struggle with and resolve conflicts. This dimension includes extremes of conflict avoidance and conflict escalation.

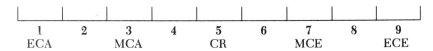

| 1 | 2 | 3 | 4 | 5 | 6 | 7 | 8 | 9 |
| ECA | | MCA | | CR | | MCE | | ECE |

1. Extreme conflict avoidance: apparently low threshold for conflict, rigid traditions and ethical codes, and conflicts that remain unacknowledged, unresolved, and denied. Frequently evidence of explicit conflict detouring (see Conflict Detouring).
2. Strong conflict avoidance.
3. Moderate conflict avoidance.
4. Mild conflict avoidance.
5. Effective and appropriate conflict resolution: a capacity to introduce problem-solving techniques early and effectively in order to

resolve family conflicts. Emphasis on direct approaches with accommodation and negotiation strongly featured.

6. Mild conflict escalation.

7. Moderate conflict escalation.

8. Strong conflict escalation.

9. Extreme conflict escalation: an absence of accommodation and negotiation and apparent escalation of vicious circles of "intoxicating," self-righteous anger, a repetitive feature. Polarization of viewpoints and attitudes evident. Original conflicts usually exacerbated by problem-solving attempts. Problem-solving energy often spent on unchangeable situational difficulties.

Conflict Detouring

Conflict detouring is a mechanism by which conflict is avoided. For effective detouring, it is necessary that a third party become involved with the dyad in conflict. This third party monitors and controls the level of direct explicit conflict within the dyad, ensuring that it does not exceed the threshold level. Thus conflicts remain unacknowledged, unresolved, and denied. There are various patterns of third party involvement. Child centeredness, fixed coalition, and triangulation are three such patterns (see Minuchin et al. 1978).

1. Child centeredness: An example of child centeredness is a couple uniting in protective concern for one of their children. When, and if, explicit conflict threatens the marital partners, their response is to invest increasing amounts of energy in protective concern for their child. A child who accepts such a devoted role can acquire an entrenched "sick" status.

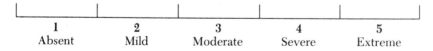

1	2	3	4	5
Absent	Mild	Moderate	Severe	Extreme

2. Triangulation: An example of triangulation is a child being "triangled" into the parents' chronic conflict by their attempts to enlist the child as a comrade in their conflict with each other. Such parents are often locked in a rigidly symmetrical relationship. In these situations there is evidence of a vicious circle of

guilt and blame. Frequently the parents escalate their self-sacrifice and place a tremendous burden of responsibility on the child. Here conflict is not resolved outside the triangle.

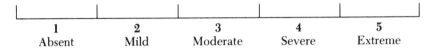

1	2	3	4	5
Absent	Mild	Moderate	Severe	Extreme

3. Fixed coalition: Fixed coalitions frequently occur when spouses have relationship problems regarding dominance and submission. When one partner is dominant and the other submissive, there is little basis for conflict resolution, as this necessitates some equality of power. Hence, conflict remains submerged and becomes chronic. In such situations a third party, such as a child, can be engaged in coalition with the submissive partner in an attempt to equalize the power balance and to provide a mechanism through which chronic conflict can be detoured. Such coalitions remain fixed over time and are denied by the partners of the coalition. These coalitions are further reinforced by any indirect attacks on behalf of the triangle's peripheral member.

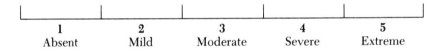

1	2	3	4	5
Absent	Mild	Moderate	Severe	Extreme

Adaptability

Russell (1979) defined adaptability as "the family's ability to shift its power structure, role relationships, and relationship rules in response to situational and developmental stress. Adaptability ranges from extreme change which results in chaos, to limited change which results in system rigidity" (p. 31).

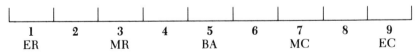

1	2	3	4	5	6	7	8	9
ER		MR		BA		MC		EC

1. Extreme rigidity: heavy commitment to maintain status quo, insistence on retaining accustomed methods of interaction to deal with all contingencies, and repression and denial of the need for

change. Family alliances overly rigid and usually ambivalent. Because of such rigidity of alliances, family members not allowed to draw on family resources to complete tasks. Can be defined as "forced morphostasis" (Wertheim 1973).
2. Strong rigidity.
3. Moderate rigidity.
4. Mild rigidity.
5. Balanced adaptability: a flexible accommodation to the demands for change and firmly structured to provide a sense of continuity with the past. Can be defined as a state of "consensual morphostasis" (Wertheim 1973). Prevailing supportive atmosphere of flexible working alliances that maximize options available to family members to complete tasks.
6. Mild chaos.
7. Moderate chaos.
8. Strong chaos.
9. Extreme chaos: an absence of sense of continuity and lack of overt leadership. Overresponsiveness to all external and internal demands for change. Little sense of limit or rule setting and no capacity to persevere. Nonsupportive atmosphere. Completion of tasks frustrated by the absence of flexible working alliances.

Discussion

This scheme provides a structural perspective on family systems. The therapist's principal task is to challenge specific structural characteristics and any symptoms that contribute to their perpetuation and to assist the family in developing alternative patterns of relationship.

Interventions based on a structural perspective appear to be effective for many presenting problems, including most psychosomatic symptoms. But in the treatment of certain psychosomatic families that score at the extreme pole of these dimensions (e.g., severely anorectic families), my clinical experience has been that it is more useful to move more explicitly to a level transcending the structural level. This is the level that incorporates the family's implicit belief system. A family's belief system contains specific values, traditions, customs, prescriptions for specific roles, rules, and attitudes concerning relationships in areas that include sexuality and intimacy and guidelines for the general management and expression of feelings. Such beliefs are acquired mainly through a transgenerational process, passed on from one generation to the next, and are more or less implicit and rigid.

I have argued elsewhere (White 1982) that extraordinarily resistant and overly cross-joined family systems are constrained by rigid systems of implicit beliefs and that these beliefs preclude the development of structural alternatives. Direct attempts to alter family structure in rigid systems, moreover, not only will complicate the goals of therapy but also will be unsuccessful in provoking change.

In this chapter I shall confine my discussion to psychosomatic families that score in the mild-to-strong range on the above dimensions. Such families clearly have some capacity to accommodate change without compromising their system of implicit beliefs. Directly challenging family structure and assisting in the search for and struggle with alternative structures require some flexibility in the family's system of implicit beliefs. The more flexible the system of implicit beliefs is, the more readily and effectively a direct structural intervention can be applied.

The following intervention program has been useful with a broad range of psychosomatic disorders and illnesses that have complicating psychosomatic components (e.g., psychogenic pain, psychogenic vomiting, chronic asthma, skin disorders, and the like). It has also been effective with a variety of conversion disorders. Although the program was developed for children or adolescents presenting with a psychosomatic condition, it may be generalized to adults presenting with a psychosomatic illness. This program offers ideas and strategies divided into specific stages of therapy, though in practice these stages may not be so clearly defined. When applied systematically, these stages of therapy offer rapid symptomatic relief; most psychosomatic families in the previously defined group can be treated in five sessions. If the symptoms do not begin to disappear in the short term, notwithstanding a brief and immediate deterioration in some cases, then the therapist should consider reevaluating the family structure according to the dimensions outlined above and reassessing possible physiological causes.

Usually therapy is initiated with an engagement phase of one and one-half to two hours, followed by a meeting one week later to begin the actual therapy, with meetings at two-week to monthly intervals.

Stages of the Intervention Procedure

Engagement

In the first stage, engagement, it is the therapist's task to join the family members and map the presenting problem onto the family system. Much has been written about this stage elsewhere (e.g., Haley 1976, Minuchin 1974).

At the outset, family members are told that the meeting has been convened to enable the therapist to elicit everyone's opinion of the problem so that an accurate map can be drawn. They also are advised that their assistance may be enlisted to help resolve the dilemma that is posed for the family by the illness or symptoms. The therapist then gathers information from family members in order to test his or her hypothesis regarding the structural characteristics of psychosomatic families (i.e., degrees of enmeshment, overprotectiveness, conflict avoidance, conflict detouring, and rigidity). In this process it is useful for the therapist to consider the following systems questions:

1. How are family patterns of relationship perpetuating the symptoms?
2. How are the symptoms perpetuating the family patterns of relationship?
3. What are the likely consequences to the patterns of relationship of resolving the symptoms?

Because the relationship patterns and symptoms are mutually causative, the answers to these three questions provide essentially the same information. However, as the relatively inflexible organization of psychosomatic families tends to render its members oblivious to the presence of relationship and as direct comment on relationship tends to provoke blame or guilt reactions, the explicit activation of the first and third questions is usually experienced as abrasive by family members. Therefore, the application of the second question tends to be more successful in gaining information and also in enabling the therapist to gain access to the system in the first place. In the later stages, when organizing particular tasks for family members, the third question can be made more explicit.

The information collected in this way usually includes opinions relating to the onset, duration, and frequency of the symptom and the effect that this symptom has had on various family members. It is essential during this stage that the therapist accept the family members' definition of the problem while at the same time placing this definition in a broader context. Analysis of the organization of family relationship patterns in response to recent crises or acute episodes of the symptoms, or when chronic symptoms are the most intense, can prove enlightening. At times of stress, the rigid aspects of family organization are most apparent, and information relating to the mutual perpetuation of specific relationship patterns and symptoms is readily available.

The "gossip" method is also useful for broadening the family member's perspective and testing hypotheses. This method has the therapist ask members about their observations of the way in which other members are organized in relation to one another regarding the symptomatic behavior.

Dodging the Impasse

It is important that before the engagement stage any physiological causes of the symptoms or problems be thoroughly evaluated by reasonable and appropriate medical examinations. Even if no physiological causes are found, however, it is not unusual to find vigorous and crippling debate among family members and between family members and members of the health professions over the cause of the symptoms. Such debate is paralyzing to family members, who frequently feel unable to take any positive action until the debate is settled and the impasse resolved.

The wise therapist will avoid taking sides in this debate. Attempts by the therapist to convince the family that the symptoms have psychological, emotional, or interactional origins will often provoke family members to argue more strongly for a physiological cause.

The therapist can help resolve such an impasse by commenting on this debate, explicitly identifying the opposing arguments, and then drawing attention to how such an impasse blocks family members from taking constructive action. This often provokes a moratorium on the debate during which family members are better able to evaluate possibilities for constructive action (Lang and Lang 1981).

Alternatively, the therapist may sidestep the issue by stating that such debate is likely to remain unresolved for some time and that in the interim there should be a concerted effort to reduce the pain and distress associated with the symptoms, regardless of their origin. The therapist can suggest that the symptoms may be worse than they need to be and that it may be worthwhile to attend to any issues complicating the symptoms.

The therapist may then ask family members whether they are prepared to try some small experiments that could reduce the intensity of the symptoms by addressing any such complicating factors, while leaving options open regarding causation. Such an approach is indicated for conditions such as chronic asthma in which numerous causative factors are posited and considered to contribute to acute episodes.

It is usually unwise for the therapist to suggest that the parents abandon their skepticism about psychological, interactional, or emotional root causes of their child's illness. But if this skepticism is considerable, the therapist may suggest that family members preserve their doubts about the causes of their child's illness. For example, when asked to coach his son in bringing on an abdominal pain, Mr. Ball expressed his profound conviction that such an approach would not work. He did not believe the pain was anything other than physiological in origin, despite the negative medical findings. Rather than argue with Mr. Ball about this, the therapist praised the strength of his conviction, indicating that what was being asked of him was not a change in belief but his participation in a simple experiment. In fact, he should not change his belief until something altered his son's abdominal pain. The therapist suggested that Mr. Ball's skepticism would give him a degree of objectivity necessary to carry out the task in the most considered fashion and that under these circumstances his skepticism could only be helpful.

Such an approach effectively undermines any unhelpful symmetrical struggle between the therapist and family members.

Establishing a Theme: Sensitivity

If the information collected during the engagement stage supports a hypothesis relating to the various characteristics as described by Minuchin and his colleagues, then there should be ample support for introducing the theme of the symptomatic family member's sensitivity and the notion that he or she is a secret worrier. During the introduction of this theme the therapist can draw attention to instances of apparent hypervigilance of the child or adolescent toward other family members, particularly toward the parents. Specific sequences of interaction that appear related to the escalation of symptomatic behavior, as identified in the engagement stage, can be used here. For example, in the Harris family, the adolescent daughter's various psychosomatic symptoms escalated after her mother's birthday. Incident analysis revealed that Mr. Harris had forgotten his wife's birthday and had also been oblivious to her hint about what she would like for a present. Even though Mrs. Harris "understood" her husband's memory lapse, she developed a headache and found the day something of an ordeal. The daughter responded to the events by pursuing Mrs. Harris throughout the day, inquiring endlessly about her well-being. The following day the daughter suffered a relapse of her symptoms. In this case, family members accepted the explanation that the daughter's sensitivity to the preceding events had led her to worry about her mother's health and welfare.

During the sensitivity stage the therapist does not ask for confirmation of the child's capacity for sensitivity and "other directedness," although it is frequently given by family members. Instead, the therapist systematically explains the events in a way that is difficult for the family to reject (see Watzlawick et al. 1974).

After introducing this theme the therapist is in a position to discuss the positive aspects of such sensitivity as well as the pitfalls associated with it. Although such a capacity for sensitivity is a valuable asset in that it enables the child to understand the needs of others, such sensitivity can produce a denial of and a total exclusion of self for the sake of others. If mischanneled and turned inward toward other family members, this sensitivity can become an overwhelming worry and anxiety for the child. This burden is clearly complicating, and channeling sensitivity in this way depletes the resources required for the child's growth and development and it is possible that such children can worry themselves sick. Further, such a burden is likely to complicate various conditions, such as asthma, and thus increase the child's discomfort and the number of acute episodes.

Apart from these undesirable consequences such misdirected sensitivity can become a mechanism by which the child inadvertently becomes the family worrier and thus stalls important activities and the completion of certain tasks in family life. For example, this condition frequently makes it difficult for the parents, as they become organized by and around their child's difficulties, to practice their marital relationship.

During this discussion the therapist should be careful to address the child and praise the caring and nurturing behavior but suggest that it is possible for such a desirable attribute to get out of control.

The Battle for Control of Symptoms

During the battle for control of symptoms the therapist poses a split between the child and the symptoms and identifies the symptoms as a target for combat. The therapist explains that the child has expended much attention and concern on other family members and thus is unfamiliar with his or her own affliction and has little control over it.

With such little attention to self-monitoring, the child has been largely oblivious to the symptoms' incremental gains. These symptoms have become a controlling force in the child's life, dominating and constraining in unsuspecting ways. Following the introduction of this idea, the therapist can invite family members to speculate as to what degree the symptoms control the child and to what degree the child controls the symptoms.

The therapist can then ask the parents about how their child's capacity for monitoring the distress of others could be refocused toward becoming more sensitive to his or her own psychosomatic symptoms. The therapist can encourage family members to think of practical ideas that would enable the child to monitor the pattern of the symptoms, including their onset, frequency, duration, and intensity. The therapist can also assert that with the child's clearly demonstrated abilities in the area of hypervigilance, it should not be too difficult for him or her to chart accurately the symptoms' various aspects.

Because the first task is to map the nature and extent of the symptoms, there initially should be no effort to reduce or override the symptoms. All acute episodes are opportunities to map the symptoms and become familiar with them before instituting a program to help the child take control of the symptoms.

The therapist should explain to family members that an interim step toward ridding oneself of symptoms is to take control of them and that a program to take control of the symptoms needs to be thoroughly planned before they can be resolved. One effective method of taking charge of the symptoms is to practice inducing them at predetermined times. A daily schedule of symptom practice can be instituted, perhaps varying the duration and intensity, but with an average for the week. Structure is particularly important here, and the time for practice should be specific, in fact, to the second. Analogies in sport can be used; for example, it is clearly impossible for any football player to kick the ball exactly where he wants to without considerable practice beforehand in ball handling.

Common sense should prevail, and the symptom practice should be screened to rule out any serious consequences. For example, with asthma, deep-breathing practice should substitute for the induction of an acute episode. Family members are assured that once the child is in charge of the symptoms, he or she can more easily and effectively combat them.

Usually, symptom practice also establishes a rationale for challenging some of the enmeshment in particular family relationships. Participation in structuring the task and supervising the monitoring of the task is assigned to the more distant parent, if there is a fixed coalition between the other parent and the child. The more involved parent is instructed to ascertain developments in the status of the symptoms from the previously more distant parent and to resist any communication directly from the child in regard to the status of the symptoms. In turn the child's cooperation is enlisted to help the overly involved parent to break his or her habitual monitoring of the symptoms.

As it is not unusual for these interventions to precipitate a brief and immediate intensification of the symptoms as the family struggles with the demands requiring reorganization and as this can weaken the resolve of family members if unexpected, the therapist should predict that it is likely that symptoms will become more apparent for a short time as they fight back to stay in charge.

Restructuring the Family: Breaking the Cycle

The successful construction of a reality relating to sensitivity lays the foundation for the fifth stage of therapy. The desirability of channeling the child's sensitivity in certain directions is questioned, and the therapist collects opinions from family members as to whether this is a mis-directing of sensitivity or is appropriate.

Usually parents argue that it is absurd and unnecessary for their daughter or son to misdirect her or his energies in this way. The therapist supports their indignation and agrees that although the idea sounds absurd, this in fact appears to be the case and that it does not matter whether their daughter or son is responding to real or imagined anxieties or worries.

As the parents argue that such sensitivity is misdirected and that their child's overconcern is misguided, the therapist can respond, "Well, you don't need to convince me of this; the task is to convince your daughter (son) that you could cope if she (he) stopped mother (father) watching. She (he) is going to take some convincing. What can you tell her (him) about how you intend to rearrange things to stall her (his) behavior, and how will you prove that all this is unnecessary?"

In the ensuing debate the parents often come up with a number of ideas that will enable them to prove, beyond any shadow of a doubt, that it is unnecessary for their daughter or son to fit with them in this way. The therapist can assist the parents in their determination by recommending various tasks. I have discussed such tasks elsewhere (White 1979) and will restrict my discussion here to the triad-based "fail-safe" task. The fail-safe task prescribes a role for each of the members of the triad. Each role challenges specific structural charac-teristics and precipitates a reorganization of family relationships. The task is termed fail-safe because if only one or two participants perform the task, then a crisis is generated as the triad becomes unstable and no longer viable. This crisis in itself precipitates change, as it is impossible for the relationship patterns to persist in the same way as previously. Such crises provide excellent opportunities for the therapist to become involved in restructuring family relationships.

Nonetheless, at times the fail-safe task does fail and is not to be confused with the paradoxical, "no-lose" task. The introduction of the fail-safe task is preempted by the notion that mere words are not enough to convince family members that certain adjustments in rela-tionships are necessary. The need for action can be further emphasized by the therapist's stating that certain things can be demonstrated to the children in a way that cannot be achieved by words alone. This tends to undermine the parents' use of reason that often perpetuates certain structural arrangements, as it tends to intensify enmeshment and patterns of conflict avoidance in psychosomatic families.

In the fail-safe task each member of the primary triad (usually the mother, father, and symptomatic daughter or son) is given a task aimed at achieving the same overall goal. This idea is evident in the work of Minuchin and his colleagues and many other structural therapists. I shall illustrate the fail-safe task by applying it in three moves to a common configuration in psychosomatic families in Western society; that is, when there is a fixed coalition between one parent and the child, with the other parent relatively disengaged from both.

Move 1. Having identified certain signals that indicate that the child is engaging in mother-watching behavior, the therapist requests that when aware of such behavior, the mother refer the child to her husband in the following manner: "I am aware of your vigilance. If you are concerned about me for a particular reason, either you should talk with your father about this, or I will ask him to come and talk with you. It is his job to care for me in this way, and not yours." If there is evidence that the child is attempting to keep the mother central to his or her life by bringing certain worries or problems to her, the mother should block this by saying, "Save it for your father." There are many possible variations, and the task can include a request that the mother refer the child more frequently to her husband in regard to various issues to which her part is not essential, such as signing a school diary on a daily basis. In the first move, the responsibility for the restructuring is assigned to the parent more involved with the child, in this case the mother.

Move 2. The therapist requests that the father become vigilant in regard to his child's mother-watching behavior. Whenever he becomes aware of such behavior, he should block it in some way. He may do this physically but always gently and should include an explanation to the effect, "It is not your job to take care of your mother in this way; she's married to me, and not you. It is your job to look after your own life and grow up. Your mother and I will talk together about what you might be worrying about." The parents are told that it does not really matter what they talk about, as this task is for the sake of their child. Before beginning the second move, it is essential for the parents to agree on what constitutes mother-watching behavior. In the second move the more distant parent is made responsible for a part designed to produce the same structural rearrangement as the part given to the more involved parent.

Move 3. In the third move the child is requested to approach the father whenever believing that the mother is anxious or worried about something and ask the father to take care of it. The child is also frequently asked to help the mother break her habit of monitoring the child's symptoms by responding to questions from that parent about the status of the symptoms with "Hold it; you are not supposed to ask me those questions." Of course, permission for this must be granted by the more involved parent.

In families in which both parents are highly child centered, a modified form of the fail-safe task can be devised that enlists the help of someone outside the triad.

After this task has been introduced, the therapist should discuss with family members what might prevent its successful implementation. Any circumstances or events likely to complicate the task should be considered, and the therapist can assist with contingency planning. Speculation by the therapist about possible obstacles often helps head off difficulties. For example, the therapist can predict that each member of the triad will struggle with certain feelings as he or she attempts to accommodate to the changes required for the task's successful implementation. Members may feel overwhelmed by despair, threatened by abandonment, or crushed by new demands. The intensity of these feelings may make it impossible for family members to continue with the task.

Usually the family members discount the possibility of such experiences, and the therapist can express eagerness for the next session in order to check with the family about these predictions.

Encouraging a Relapse

Relapses are not uncommon in psychosomatic families for a variety of reasons, including the family's tendency to resort to characteristic or habitual patterns of behavior when confronted by stress related to new developmental phases or situational crises. Such relapses, if taken out of context, can halt the progress made by the family members in reorganizing their relationships. It is helpful for such relapses to be considered as a test of the family members' resolve. Framed in this way, a relapse can be considered a signal to the parents to do whatever is necessary to encourage their child to channel his or her sensitivity in more creative directions.

A relapse's negative aspects can also be treated if the relapses are prescribed. The therapist can encourage the symptomatic child to have a spontaneous relapse whenever he or she feels insecure about the relationship rearrangements, his or her and other family members' ability to cope with new demands in developmental stages, and whether the parents can cope if the child turns outward from the family and invests less sensitivity in the parents.

The therapist may also explain to the symptomatic child that he or she may have second thoughts about abandoning these symptoms and that there may be important aspects relating to these symptoms that the child may wish to keep. Such a relapse will provide an opportunity for review. This approach to relapses places them under the control of family members, and as they trigger responses that are likely to consolidate structural rearrangements, they can only be considered helpful.

What If the Task Fails?

If careful attention is paid to the various stages outlined in this program, the therapist will rarely have the fail-safe task fail with psychosomatic families that score in the mild-to-strong range along the dimensions outlined earlier. If all family members persist with the task, then rapid changes will take place, and I have found that the symptoms are quickly resolved. If only one or two members persist with the task, then the collusion over the "fit" of family members within the triad breaks down, thereby precipitating a crisis. This crisis provides opportunities for the therapist to address issues of closeness and distance, dominance and submission, symmetrical struggles, and other triadic and dyadic phenomena. This effectively places the family system at a crossroad and presents dilemmas that cannot be ignored and must be resolved. If all of the members partially or completely fail to undertake the task, this will provide an opportunity to introduce paradox. A discussion of the use of paradox, springing from the failure of direct tasks, is beyond the scope of this chapter, though such discussions can be found elsewhere (e.g., Haley 1976, White 1980).

REFERENCES

Haley, J. (1976). *Problem Solving Therapy*. San Francisco: Jossey-Bass.

Lang, M., and Lang, T. (1981). Debbie and her slurping stomach. *Australian Journal of Family Therapy* 3:3–26.

Liebman, R., Minuchin, S., Baker, L., and Rosman, B. (1976). The role of the family in the treatment of chronic asthma. In *Family Therapy: Theory and Practice*, ed. P. Guerin, pp. 309–324. New York: Gardner Press.

Minuchin, S. (1974). *Families and Family Therapy*. Cambridge, Mass.: Harvard University Press.

———, Baker, L., Rosman, B., Liebman, R., Milman, L., and Todd, T. (1975). A conceptual model of psychosomatic illness in children. *Archives of General Psychiatry* 32:1031–1038.

———, Rosman, B., and Baker, L. (1978). *Psychosomatic Families: Anorexia Nervosa in Context*. Cambridge, Mass.: Harvard University Press.

Russell, C. (1979). Circumplex model of marital and family systems III: Empirical evaluation with families. *Family Process* 18:29–45.

Watzlawick, P., Weakland, J., and Fisch, R. (1974). *Change: Principles of Problem Formation and Problem Resolution*. New York: Norton.

Wertheim, E. (1973). Family unit therapy and the science and typology of family systems. *Family Process* 12:361–376.

White, M. (1979) Structural and strategic approaches to psychosomatic families. *Family Process* 18:303–314.

——— (1980). Systemic task setting in family therapy. *Australian Journal of Family Therapy* 1:171–182.

——— (1982). Anorexia nervosa: a trans-generational system perspective. *Family Process*, forthcoming .

❧ 4 ❧

Alcoholism

Curtis Janzen, Ph.D.

There is evidence that many families are in treatment programs for alcoholism. There are many ways of including family members in treatment and many reasons for doing so. Programs differ in their reasons for involving the family, in their conception of how the family is related to the problem of alcoholism, and whether the service is primarily for the benefit of the family or the alcohol abuser. Programs differ also in their modes of involving the family, whether to include all or some family members, whether conjointly or in separate groups, and whether as inpatients or outpatients. They differ also in treatment theory and technique.

This chapter is an overview of the developments in conception, method, and technique and the potential to the alcoholic and the family in treatment. The predominant concern of treatment programs, as shown in literature reports, has been the family situation in which the adult male is the alcohol abuser. Our primary reference will be to this category of family. We shall not discuss in detail the required differences in approach if the primary patient is either the adult female or an adolescent or if both adults are alcoholic, but we shall address the differential consequences for the family and for treatment.

No one questions that alcoholism is a family problem. The family may be viewed as causal, participant, or victim, but there is no doubt that all members experience the problem in some way. Evidence suggests that family inclusion in the treatment program tends to enhance outcomes for the alcoholic, in terms of both reduced drinking and improvement of the alcoholic's relationship to the family. For every alcoholic, however, there are three to four family members who also suffer the consequences of the drinking problems. Even if there are no positive outcomes for the alcoholic as a result of the family members' participation in treatment, the tasks for the family posed by the alcoholism are a sufficient basis for including all family members in a treatment program.

We shall demonstrate that the family functions as social organization and that events or changes in any part of the organization influence the other parts. The alcohol abuser's behavior affects the family, whether that behavior is increased or reduced drinking, and the family members' response in turn affects the alcoholic, either to promote or reduce the drinking behavior. In this conception, the search for the causes of drinking becomes secondary. It is not a question of whether alcoholism causes family problems or whether the family problems cause the alcoholism (though much investigation has approached the situation in this way). Rather, it is understanding how particular kinds of interactions between the alcoholic and the family have perpetuated the problems for both. The ways that the family members and the alcoholic have attempted to deal with one another in regard to the alcoholism become the focus of concern. It is assumed that the alcoholic and family members are searching for means of dealing with the discomfort of their relationship with one another and that the means they use encourage rather than relieve the discomfort. And if either the family or the alcoholic can obtain some relief, it is likely that the other will also improve. In a review of treatment programs, Janzen (1977) concluded that there are data to support the idea that when there are change and positive outcomes for the family, there will also be improvement in the alcoholism.

We shall also show that the conception of family treatment is a broad one and includes a variety of interventive modalities. It includes conjoint sessions between the alcoholic and one or more other family members, couples' therapy, separate individual sessions or groups for spouses or children, and couples' or family groups. This conception assumes that however or wherever change is initiated, its repercussions will be felt and new responses will occur. The helping personnel must be able to predict and monitor the consequences in the family or in the alcoholic of a particular kind of change when it is proposed. For our purposes, the definition of family treatment lies more in the helper's conception of the alcoholic family as a system than in the particular modes of including its members.

FAMILY RELATIONSHIPS AND ALCOHOLISM

In tracing the relationship between family problems and alcoholism, we have found three different, but interrelated, positions. Using those cases as a reference in which the adult male is the alcoholic, the first position defines the spouse as the aggravating cause of the alcoholism, a view that the alcoholic himself is likely to take. It is thought that the wife's need for dependency, feelings of inadequacy, sexual anxiety, and emotional disturbance all prompt her to relate to the alcoholic in an aggressive, controlling way, behavior that bolsters her feelings of adequacy and gives her some sense of control over her life. Her behavior "causes" her husband's alcoholism by fostering his sense of inadequacy and meeting his needs for a protected, dependent relationship.

There is considerable disagreement regarding this point of view. Other studies (Fox 1968, Krimmel 1971, Rae 1972) suggest that if the wife is disturbed, the disturbance arose as a consequence of the alcoholic's behavior and was not the first cause of the drinking. Several sources (Bailey 1968, Cohen and Krause 1971, Kogan and Jackson 1965) report that the spouse's behavior improves as the drinking decreases. In a review of all the literature pertaining to this issue, Edwards, Harvey, and Whitehead (1973) similarly concluded that there is little substantiated evidence that wives of alcoholics are always aggressive and domineering or that there is long-term deterioration in their functioning.

Wives of alcoholics are not a particular personality type, but their personalities do vary with fluctuations in their husbands' alcohol usage. There is support, however, for the view that the drinking behavior and the spouse's response clearly affect each other and perpetuate both sets of problems.

A second position regarding the relationship beween family problems and alcoholism is that family problems exist independently of the alcoholism. Ballard (1959) concluded that marital conflict was more likely to develop in alcoholic couples than in control-group couples, even if no problems of alcoholism existed. Similarly Al-Anon states, "Troubled wives and alcoholics often take it for granted that their marital discords are due entirely to alcoholism, whether the alcoholic is sober or is still drinking. Yet alcoholism itself rarely creates all these problems and sobriety itself usually does not cure them" (Al-Anon Family Group 1967, p. 3). Esser (1968) also confirmed that it is difficult for spouses in alcoholic relationships to admit the existence of marital problems. In his experience, drinking serves as a means of avoiding the task of dealing with difficult marital problems. Treatment sessions in which marital issues are raised are often followed by drinking episodes, and thus the drinking becomes the focus of the next treatment session. This position suggests that even though the two sets of problems may have an independent origin, there is a functional relationship between them.

A very different illustration of such a functional relationship comes from Steinglass, who observed families in a number of drinking and nondrinking sessions. He noted that "a family that claimed drinking by their 'identified alcoholic' caused depression, fighting and estrangement was observed to show increased warmth toward each other, increased caretaking, and greater animation when the alcoholic was permitted to drink" (1976, p. 105). Carter (1977) made a similar observation. Obviously such reactions by the family are not standard, but they do question the approach that would not go beyond discontinuance of the drinking behavior alone. Other aspects of family functioning also need attention so that the drinking behavior is no longer necessary.

The third position on the relationship between the alcoholism and family problems focuses less on personality and more on the transactions among the participants. This is basically my position, which I shall discuss in regard to role relationships between family members, the struggle to maintain power and position, and the payoffs for the role takers. Interwoven into these emphases is the idea that role relationships vary over the time that the alcoholism persists and according to the family members' changing view of the behavior and their own predicament (Jackson 1956).

The alcoholic and the spouse have reciprocal roles (cf. Black 1980, Strausner et al. 1979, Wegscheider 1981). During the early phases of the drinking problem, the spouse collaborates with the alcoholic in denying the drinking problem, thus enabling it to continue. The spouse thus supports the continued role enactment. At this stage the wife typically excuses her husband's drinking as a response to stress, as something that will pass, or excuses it in order to avoid embarrassment, to save the alcoholic's job and thus ensure family support, or to ensure that the children will have a father. At later stages, when the wife no longer denies the seriousness of the drinking behavior, she may attempt to regulate and moderate the drinking behavior by drinking with the alcoholic or limiting money or alcohol supply. The alcoholic husband resists this new role behavior in an attempt to maintain his independence and deny her control over his behavior. The more she tries to assume responsibility for his behavior, the more he needs to resist. In either role, denying or controlling, the wife unwittingly becomes an actor in an ongoing transaction that enables the situation to continue without change.

Several independent investigations support this position. From his testing of alcoholic and nonalcoholic spouse pairs, Gorad (1971) found that spouses in alcoholic marriages are more competitive than are spouses in nonalcoholic marriages. Sharing and self-revelation are less common than among other couples. Though the dependent, irresponsible behavior of the alcoholic is not usually seen as controlling, such behavior requires a response from others and in that sense serves to control. Thus, even though the wife may seem dominant and strong, she does not dominate the alcoholic any more than he dominates her. As each spouse tries to control the other, the control efforts are resisted. The relationship does not change except for variations in the conflict's intensity.

Drawing a similar conclusion, Wiseman (1976), in a study of Finnish alcoholic couples, also documented that the spouse's tactics of persuasion, crying, pleading, and threats, which may be viewed as efforts to control the drinking, have no durable effect and produce no long-standing change. Thus, whether the spouse's collaboration occurs by denial or by efforts to control, the drinking persists. If the alcoholic does not begin independently to change, efforts to induce the spouse to dispense with such an enabling role will be needed to bring change.

The efforts by the alcoholic and the spouse to control each other imply that each views the other in the relationship as having no separateness or autonomy. The other is viewed as an extension of self. Al-Anon noted the destructiveness of the idea that "being married to a man puts us in charge of him. We are so deeply involved that we treat those closest to us as though they were a part of ourselves" (Al-Anon Family Group 1967, p. 118). Bowen (1974) views such behavior as evidence of the participants' failure to differentiate their personalities. As one partner in the relationship becomes less responsible, the other compensates by taking on more responsibility. One underfunctions, and the other compensates by overfunctioning. The relationship continues in that form. Since, in Bowen's view, it is easier for the overfunctioning spouse to change by assuming less responsibility than for the underfunctioning alcoholic to assume more, treatment efforts are initially directed to the nonalcoholic spouse.

Steiner observed that repetitive behavior sequences are transacted between the alcoholic and other family members and that the motive for engaging in these "is the production of certain interpersonal payoffs" (1969, p. 922). Ward and Faillace provided a useful example:

> If the wife is forgiving, the husband has learned that forgiveness for being drunk can be obtained, provided he is appropriately remorseful and very sick. If she punishes him for his behavior by criticizing him, his guilt and shame are relieved and he feels considerably less anxious. In either case the pattern cannot be understood except in terms of the total sequence and, in either case, the sequence recurs because the outcome is re-enforcing to both. (1970, p. 686)

Our discussion until now includes only one other person in the relationship with the alcoholic. Though it has not yet been demonstrated, other persons, including children, may take similar roles. Other roles develop in the family that can serve to maintain the alcoholic role.

Children in Alcoholic Families

The effects of parental alcoholism on children have been widely documented. Beginning with Cork (1969) and continuing with Auger and associates (1973), Chafetz and colleagues (1971), Cohen and Krause (1971), and many others, various effects have been found, including the tendency for the children themselves to become alcoholics or to marry alcoholics (Bosma 1972). Depending on age, they may manifest a variety of symptoms, including stuttering, fears, bed wetting, tantrums, fighting, school problems, or other forms of psychosocial pathology. El-Guebaly and Offord (1979) reviewed all these studies and reported that deficiencies in the research made it difficult to conclude definitively that the children of alcoholics suffer more than do the children from other problem families, but there is no doubt that they do suffer. It is also not certain whether the alcoholism alone is responsible for these children's difficulties, since other problems, such as poverty and family disorganization, may also be present.

Children are upset by their parents' unhappiness, quarreling, and fighting, and they suffer from their lack of interest in them (Clemmons 1979). When the parents do pay attention to their children, the children see them as inconsistent, ranging in responsiveness from spoiling to neglect or punishment. Children are faced with uncertainty and unreliability, and the denial of the alcoholism causes confusion and loss of adequate reality testing. Both the nonalcoholic and the alcoholic parent perform inadequately in the parental role because of their own unmet needs (Clinebell 1968), resulting in inadequate structure, discipline, and nurturance. This becomes worse if both parents are alcoholic and the children are left to assume responsibility for themselves or parenting roles for one another.

The formation of family triangles that include the children is another aspect of the children's involvement in the problem. Both the alcoholic and the nonalcoholic spouse exploit the children by seeking their support (Krimmel 1971, Press 1975). For example, the nonalcoholic parent may induce the child to collaborate in denying the alcoholism or, once it is no longer denied, in attempting to control and moderate the drinking behavior. In this sense the child also helps maintain the problem. Or the alcoholic may complain to the child that he or she is misunderstood and abused by the nonalcoholic spouse. The child is confused about who is right and loses one parent's support, no matter which side he or she takes. Or, the child may experience increased power or security, and seek these through alliance with one parent or the other. Whichever side the child takes, the choice locks both the child and the parents into their previous role relationships. If the child attempts to mediate or break up parental conflict, the child may, in addition to the psychological suffering, be subject to the physical abuse intended by the parents for each other. If the parents cannot carry out their parental responsibilities, the child often has to assume parental roles. The phenomenon of another family member overfunctioning to compensate for the underfunctioning of the alcoholic appears again, enabling and preserving the system's homeostasis. In effect, the child is both the victim of these transactions and an unwitting participant in perpetuating the problem, in much the same way the nonalcoholic spouse helps perpetuate the problem.

We should not assume that the consequences for all the children in an alcoholic family are the same. It is likely that age, sex, and sibling rank all help determine the response, though the influence of these factors has received limited comment except by El-Guebaly and Offord (1979). Others (Black 1980, Strausner et al. 1979), however, have identified the various family roles that the children may take. Besides the role of primary enabler, usually the spouse, other roles are those of hero, scapegoat, lost child, and mascot (Wegscheider 1981). These roles are seen as secondary enabling roles, in that in their own way they help maintain the alcoholism. Each role has different consequences for the role player, as suggested by the role label.

The hero child may also be seen as a parental child, in that he assumes a great deal of responsibility for himself, and in some ways also for the parents and the family and is thus heavily involved in a triangle with the parents. He does not get into trouble, achieves in school, and in other ways is successful, enabling both parents to continue denying the alcoholism's impact on the children. The role continues to be carried beyond the child's experience in the family into successful adulthood. To the extent that it is accompanied by a denial of dependency feelings and a compulsion to achieve, it serves to create problems in adjustment.

The scapegoat child engages in negative behaviors, some of which may be similar to those of the alcoholic, drawing attention to herself because she is not included, as is the hero child, in the triangle with the parents and away from the alcoholism and the problems the parents have with each other. This helps maintain the parents' denial of the alcoholism, keeps the family together by keeping the attention—albeit negative—on the child, and pushes the child into delinquent role behavior. This behavior too is carried into adult adjustment, with the usual negative consequences.

The lost child is the unnoticed and neglected child in the family interaction and adapts by becoming a loner and staying out of the way. Since he causes no trouble for the parents, their denial of problems is facilitated, and the child is not drawn into their conflicts. The danger in this role lies in the extent to which the child retreats into isolation and fantasy.

The mascot role is that of family clown. The child relieves her own and her family's tension by humor, antics, and distraction. This role is continued to the extent that the distraction succeeds. Although humor and distraction are useful qualities in some situations, the long-term emotional and role consequences of being locked into such a role are often negative.

This definition of the consequences for the children of alcoholic parents is clearly a systems definition. The role serves a function for both the person taking the role and the family system. It is both an adaptation for the individual and a homeostatic mechanism for the system. As long as the roles are performed, the system stays the same, and neither the family relationships nor the drinking problem changes.

Beyond the Nuclear Family

The extended family network also has a role in relation to the current problem of alcoholism in the nuclear family. Wolin, Bennett, and Noonan (1979) considered the role of family ritual during mealtimes, anniversaries, and holidays. In general they concluded that the continuation of rituals reduces the likelihood that alcoholism will be transmitted into the succeeding generation. Although these events and relationships are largely historical in regard to the present alcoholic and family, these same ritual occasions may provide one medium for current contact among three generations of family members. Extended family members are frequently drawn into the conflicts between members of the nuclear family, taking sides with one or the other in much the same way that the children side with either the alcoholic or the nonalcoholic parent.

Members of the extended family are, to varying degrees, unable to separate themselves and stand apart from the problem. Bowen (1974) viewed this as a failure of both the alcoholic and the nonalcoholic spouse and their parents to achieve a sufficient degree of differentiation from one another, while at the same time disclaiming any dependency.

TREATMENT

An analysis of the association between the alcoholism and the family's problems leads to certain conclusions about the treatment required for the alcoholic family system. It suggests that any change that begins with any member of the family is likely to affect the rest of the family and that such a change may be produced by various means. Any treatment that changes behavior in a family member is viewed as a treatment for the family, in that the family members must somehow react or adapt to it.

In an earlier review, Janzen (1977) noted that several means had been used to treat alcoholics and family members. Some programs are intended primarily for family members and serve the alcoholic only secondarily (Cohen and Krause 1971, McDowell 1972). Many programs are for outpatients alone and include alcoholics who may or may not have been hospitalized previously (Preston 1960, Woggon 1972). Some family treatment services are offered during the alcoholic's hospital stay, and others require the residence of key family members during all or part of the residential phase (Binder 1971, Brown-Mayers et al. 1973, Catanzaro et al. 1973, Corder and Laidlaw 1972). And a few programs treat the family at home (Esser 1968, 1971; Pattison 1965).

In some programs, the spouses are seen separately, either individually or in groups, whereas others provide service only in groups (Smith 1969). In other programs, both spouses are seen together or occasionally with other couples (Berman 1966, 1968; Burton and Kaplan 1968). Many programs use several treatment methods (Ewing and Fox 1968,

Preston 1960). In some instances, the children are included in the family treatment interviews (Esser 1968, 1971; Meeks and Kelly 1970). Bowen (1974) and Esser (1968) recommended that if possible, members of the extended family should be included in the treatment as well.

Gerard and Saenger (1966) showed that even one contact with the spouse may determine whether the alcoholic will continue in treatment. Wright and Scott (1978) and Berger (1981) found that the more family members that participated in the treatment and the longer that they participated increased the likelihood that the alcoholic would continue treatment and recover.

The impression conveyed by the preceding paragraphs suggests that there are extensive services for families. But a study by Regan (1978) noted that though many treatment programs offer service to the family, the service is limited in scope, especially for children. For the most part, the family is not treated as a unit, and treatment services assume no responsibilities for the family's needs. My own data (preliminary analysis) confirm this impression of limited service to the family, limited understanding of the family members' needs, and limited understanding of the relationship of the family to the drinking problem. It is evident that in many programs the alcoholism is viewed as a problem of the alcoholic apart from the family.

In earlier work I have cited the advantages to the alcoholic and the family of the family's participation in treatment. All the various treatment procedures, although numerous, have been successful. On the basis of the available studies, it is not possible to state unequivocally that family treatment is better in changing the alcoholic than are other forms of treatment. It is clear, however, that family treatment can bring about some growth and change in both alcoholic and family that may not be possible with treatment of the alcoholic alone. There is, however, only little evidence that individual programs take a comprehensive view of the relationship between family problems and alcoholism or that they rely solely or draw fully on any of the major family treatment approaches.

Various family treatment approaches have been tried. Ward and Faillace (1970) used transactional analysis which, though not a theory of family treatment, is useful in understanding family relationships. Bowen (1974) used for alcoholic families the theory he applies to all problem families. Berenson (1976) followed Bowen's theory, as did Carter (1977), who also incorporated in the early stages of treatment the procedures of structural family therapy. Esser (1968, 1971) used Satir's (1967) communications approach to treatment. More recently, Wegscheider (1981) worked with Satir in developing her approach. But specific family treatment theories have been applied to alcoholic families only to a limited, noncomprehensive extent. I would now like to present my own synthesis of several theories, of the necessities and variations in approaching both the alcoholic and the family.

It is essential, whatever the means of family participation, to help the family members discontinue behaviors that maintain the drinking behavior. Only when they no longer deny the existence of the problem or when they do not feel responsible for it and have abandoned their efforts to control or regulate it, can there be relief for them and the possibility of change for the alcoholic.

Several approaches have been used to accomplish this end. An educational approach that simply teaches the nonalcoholic spouse that alcoholism is a disease for which he or she cannot provide a cure has been useful. In this sense the spouse is relieved of guilt and responsibility for what happens and can stop trying to control the drinking behavior. Though the disease concept is useful, a project by Cohen and Krause (1971) found that the same results can be gained without it. A group of social workers was trained to use the disease concept and teach it to the nonalcoholic spouse. This helped the spouse function more effectively and draw the alcoholic into treatment. A comparison group of social workers was not trained in the disease concept but used their usual practice theory that individuals cannot regulate the behavior of others and that they can be responsible only for their own well-being. This approach achieved similar success. Thus, by whatever means, the wife (usually the nonalcoholic spouse) needs to recognize that

> . . . she did not cause the illness and that she is not capable of or responsible for curing it. Once freed of that burden, she can drop her ineffective coping and rescue operations. She can learn to stop nagging, making threats without carrying them out, and protecting her husband from the consequences of his drinking. . . . Her consequent lack of action should not emanate from anger and retaliation but rather, so far as possible, from a sense of objectivity and detachment . . . surrender and release. (Mueller 1972, p. 82)

The essential point here is that the family members, in particular the nonalcoholic spouse, learn that they cannot control one another's behavior and are not responsible for it. This implies, according to Bowen's (1974) terminology, differentiation of the nonalcoholic from the alcoholic and a reduction in the former's overfunctioning. In Minuchin's (1974) structural terms, it is a strengthening of the individual subsystem within the family.

The approach being described here arises out of concern for the well-being of the spouse or family as well as that of the alcoholic. Success may be achieved in both individual treatment and family sessions or group approaches as long as all involved therapists are aware of the repercussions that individual role changes may have on the role taking of others. One of the likely repercussions is that the alcoholic may see the changed behavior of the spouse and family as a loss of interest and love, which may initially motivate him or her to greater dependency or belligerence. At this point the family must be encouraged to persist in their new ways and to view the alcoholic's behavior as a transitional response. No longer being able to accuse the family of trying to run his or her life, the alcoholic must assume that responsibility. This, in turn, may produce a sense of responsibility and freedom that the alcoholic has not experienced before.

Referring the spouse and other significant adults to Al-Anon also helps reinforce and support such professional approaches (Gorman and Rooney 1979). Al-Anon groups believe that family members suffer if they can only react to the alcoholic's behavior. They learn that being so reactive does not alleviate the drinking, that they can be responsible only for themselves and their own well-being, and that they are justified in such "selfish" behavior. Self-help groups, probably more than the therapeutic groups run by professionals, often have the advantage of long-term members whose experience can provide the long view and the support needed for new members to persist in their newfound ways.

Although these approaches may indeed be helpful to the family, they may not change the alcoholic or encourage treatment. Some reports (McDowell 1972, Cohen and Krause 1971) suggest, however, that change in the family will result in the alcoholic's changed drinking behavior or search for treatment. This may be more likely if the family seeks help early in the alcoholism career and less likely if the drinking history is of long duration. In the latter event, additional family pressure seems warranted and useful. This may come in several forms.

In one approach (cf. Wegscheider 1981), work with the family prepares them for direct confrontation of the alcoholic. Family members, including spouse and children, are helped to acknowledge rather than deny the problem and to identify instances in which they have been hurt by the drinking behavior and how it has affected them. Lack of money, aggression and inconsistency, lack of love and relationship, isolation, alienation of friends, and shame all are revealed. When the family is prepared to confront the alcoholic with their own pain, arrangements are made for them to do so. Simultaneously, preliminary plans are made for the alcoholic's immediate admission to a treatment program, should he or she decide on treatment.

Such an approach is predicated on the nonalcoholic spouse's wish to continue the relationship. But the spouse may need to be willing to consider separation and divorce, and the threat of this may be sufficient to produce change in the alcoholic (cf. Finlay 1966, 1974). Her ability (if the nonalcoholic is the wife) to do this depends on her confidence in her ability to survive independently, both psychologically and financially. The treatment described here speaks to the development of psychological resources. If financial resources are lacking, treatment will necessarily include their acquisition as well. Such last-resort measures are required in some instances before the alcoholic will change. Such an approach will be effective in changing the alcoholic only if he still values his relationship with the family. If the family acts too late in his alcoholism career, both his addiction and his dissatisfaction with the family may have grown to the extent that continuance of a relationship no longer interests him. Thus it is evident that, for the sake of the family and the alcoholic, early intervention and change are desirable.

If through family change or voluntarily the alcoholic begins treatment or stops drinking, the situation has changed, though work on family problems continues to be important (cf. Jackson 1956). Amid the alcoholic's efforts to resume a responsible role in the family and the family members' doubts that he can do so, every family member will be required to make role adjustments and to communicate constructively in order to do this. Family sessions (cf. Esser 1968, Meeks and Kelly 1970) can help in this during the recovery stage, as can multiple family or couples' groups. Many of the same feelings that the alcoholic and family members have about one another's behavior and that were revealed in persuading the alcoholic to seek treatment should be dealt with during the recovery phase. A simple decision by the nonalcoholic spouse, for example, one that she has become accustomed to making, about allowing the children an evening out may leave the now-recovering alcoholic feeling excluded and result in further conflict. The renewal of sexual relations will be accompanied by strain, and it will take time for the partners to trust and to feel trusted in the rebuilding of their relationship, for each to be able to rely on what the other says he or she will do. Training in communication skills and resolving disagreements and misunderstandings are essential for all family members during this recovery phase.

Children in Family Treatment

Our discussion has focused primarily on the wife of the adult male alcoholic with passing reference to the children in the treatment plan. Since the children, as presented here, are both victims of the alcoholic's behavior and unwitting participants in enabling it to continue, both aspects of their experience require their involvement in treatment. Much of what has been said about treatment for the spouse applies to them also. They need to be freed of their anxiety about what will happen to them as a result of the alcoholic's behavior. This can come in part through changes in the wife and her ability to assume the new roles suggested above. The children also need to be relieved of their sense of guilt and responsibility for the alcoholic's behavior, for their parents' conflicts, or for compensating for their parents' inability to maintain parental leadership within the family. Children can be helped to understand the uselessness of either rescue or persecution behaviors, and their efforts can be directed toward more constructive goals of personal growth and development. Emancipation from the hero, scapegoat, lost child, or mascot roles requires considerable time in treatment and, again, is based on the concept that the children are not responsible for others, only for themselves, that they and their parents are separate individuals. Obviously this emphasis will vary with the age of the children. Family communication needs to be more open so that the children can ask questions, get clarification, air complaints, and enunciate their own needs. Family-oriented therapists will see that these things happen. For the growth of both parents and children, this can best happen in family sessions; however, referral to Al-A-Teen or separate group treatment also serves these ends. Richards (1979), however, documented many disadvantages in individual treatment. Further, the achievement of any of these ends will be more difficult if both parents are alcoholics. Extra supportive measures will be needed, and in severe instances the children may need to be removed from the home.

Social-Situational Issues

We have considered mainly the family's interpersonal aspects and have only briefly touched on the many social problems that the family has as a consequence of the alcoholism. The family's needs are often neglected by the emphasis on the alcoholic's behavior, but their needs for safety, food, shelter, financial support, personal growth, and life satisfaction are often what bring them to social agencies (cf. Flanzer 1978). In the early stages the nonalcoholic wife may have temporarily removed herself and the children from the alcoholic's presence when he began drinking, but in response to belligerent and abusive behavior she may need to seek the support of extended family, friends, or social agencies for shelter and support. In the early stages she may seek outside employment simply to give herself something else to think about or to provide extra resources. Although both kinds of actions affect the family dynamic, they are congruent with the theory presented here that the nonalcoholic spouse is not responsible for the alcoholic, but only for herself. If she can accomplish these moves with a reasonable sense of detachment, they may produce the desired effect on the alcoholic. Just as the additional relationships enable her to meet her own and her children's needs, they are in many instances also available to the alcoholic when he recognizes the changes and begins to consider change for himself. But there must be services available to help the family, as well as the treatment services for the alcoholic. Simple moves such as those mentioned above, though extremely difficult to execute, do more to evoke change in the alcoholic than do collaboration and tolerance of the drinking.

Treatment for Alcoholic Females and Their Families

Space limitations and my own experience preclude extensive discussion of families in which persons other than the adult male are the identified alcoholic. Furthermore, the research on the family situations of and family treatment for female alcoholics is sparse. The literature does, however, offer disagreements about the male spouse of the female alcoholic that are similar to the ones offered about the female spouse of the male alcoholic. It has been customary to think that the male spouse is less apt to try to control the drinking behavior of the wife and that he is more prone either to passive acceptance or earlier departure from the scene. Some recent data refute the view that male spouses are more likely to abandon the female alcoholic (Corrigan and Anderson 1978, Dahlgren 1979). Fox (1968) showed that the husbands of alcoholic women vary in personality. Some are long suffering and controlling; some are ambivalent and vacillate between leaving and begging to return; some are extremely dependent; and still others are hostile and sadistic. Others have noted that in as many as one-third of the cases of alcoholic wives, the husband was also alcoholic. Wolin (1980) noted that women alcoholics are frequently married to men with psychiatric problems but that there is no single personality type among the husbands. Wolin found that such couples often have unsettled arguments, communication patterns that are more disturbed and less successful than in nonalcoholic marriages, and a poor match in the spouses' self-perceptions. These differences are evidence that role interactions, needs for separateness and individuation, and control struggles are similar to those that occur with the male alcoholic and spouse. Though it is not certain that there is a basic power differential between men and women—in favor of men—in marriages generally, the control struggle here may be even more difficult. Therapists should assume that the female alcoholic's reduced power position will need differential attention in treatment.

Similarly, it is not clear how different the situation of the children of alcoholic mothers is. Many alcoholic women, perhaps as many as three-fourths, live with and care for their children in some way. Again, it seems likely that the effects on the children vary with their age, sex, sibling rank, and time of the drinking behavior's onset. Since the husbands of alcoholics differ in their responsiveness to their wives' alcoholic behavior, it seems likely that these husbands' abilities to meet their children's needs will also vary. Social agencies, particularly children's protective services, are well acquainted with the damaging effects of situations in which both parents are alcoholic and those in which the nonalcoholic parent is inadequate for other reasons. But there is little literature, and no research, that compares the children's situation in the two types of alcoholic households. Davis and Hagood (1979) did describe inhome help to alcoholic women and their children.

Family Treatment for Adolescent Alcoholics

Again, the literature and my own experience preclude specific commentary on treatment, though I have mentioned that the children of alcoholics often become or marry alcoholics. Those who do become alcoholics have obviously suffered from deficient parental role modeling and their parents' failure to provide nurture, structure, direction, and discipline for the adolescent's behavior. Adolescent alcoholics do not necessarily have alcoholic parents but may suffer from the same deficiencies of parental leadership. In any case, it is clear that the parents should be involved in the treatment of the adolescent's alcoholism. The many approaches to family treatment of child behavior problems probably would also be relevant to the adolescent alcoholic. Family treatment for adolescent alcoholics is another subject that needs extensive investigation, reporting, and trial before we can determine how different it needs to be and how useful it is.

REFERENCES

Al-Anon Family Group (1967). *The Dilemma of the Alcoholic Marriage.* New York: Al-Anon.
Auger, R., Bragg, R., Corns, D., and Milner, R. (1973). Preliminary assessment and prognostic indicators in a newly developed alcohol treatment program. *Newsletter for Research in Mental Health and Behavioral Sciences* 15:21–24.
Bailey, M. B. (1968). Alcoholism and marriage: a review. *Quarterly Journal of Studies on Alcohol* 22:81–97.

Ballard, R. G. (1959). The interaction between marital conflict and alcoholism as seen through MMPI's of marriage partners. *American Journal of Orthopsychiatry* 29:528-546.

Berenson, D. (1976). Alcohol and the family system. In *Family Therapy: Theory and Practice*, ed. P. Guerin, pp. 284-297. New York: Gardner Press.

Berger, A. (1981). Family involvement and alcoholics' completion of a multiphase treatment program. *Journal of Studies on Alcohol* 42:517-521.

Berman, K. (1966). Multiple family therapy: its possibilities in preventing readmission. *Mental Hygiene* 50:367-370.

—— (1968). Multiple conjoint family groups in the treatment of alcoholism. *Journal of the Medical Society of New Jersey* 65:6-8.

Binder, S. (1971). Newer therapeutic procedures for alcoholics. *Zeitschrift fuer Psychotherapie und Medizinische Psychologie* 21:239-247.

Black, C. (1980). Children of alcoholics. *Alcohol Health and Research World* 4:23-27.

Bosma, W. (1972). Children of alcoholics: a hidden tragedy. *Maryland State Medical Journal* 21:34-36.

Bowen, M. (1974). Alcoholism as viewed through family systems theory and family psychotherapy. *Annals of the New York Academy of Sciences* 233:115-122.

Brown-Mayers, A., Seelye, E., and Brown, D. (1973). Reorganized alcoholism service. *Journal of the American Medical Association* 224:233-235.

Burton, G., and Kaplan, H. M. (1968). Group counseling in conflicted marriage where alcoholism is present: client's evaluation of effectiveness. *Journal of Marriage and the Family* 30:74-79.

Cadogan, D. A. (1973). Marital group therapy in the treatment of alcoholism. *Quarterly Journal of Studies on Alcohol* 34:1187-1194.

Carter, E. (1977). Generation after generation. In *Family Therapy: Full-Length Case Studies*, ed. P. Papp, pp. 47-68. New York: Gardner Press.

Catanzaro, R. J., Pisani, V. D., Fox, R., and Kennedy, E. R. (1973). Familization therapy. *Diseases of the Nervous System* 34:212-218.

Chafetz, M., Blane, H., and Hill, M. (1971). Children of alcoholics. *Quarterly Journal of Studies on Alcohol* 32:687-698.

Clemmons, P. (1979). Issues in marriage, family and child counseling in alcoholism. In *Women Who Drink*, ed. V. Burtle, pp. 127–144. Springfield, Ill.: Chas C Thomas.

Clinebell, H. J., Jr. (1968). Pastoral counseling of the alcoholic and his family. In *Alcoholism: The Total Treatment Approach*, ed. R. Catanzaro, pp. 189–207. Springfield, Ill.: Chas C Thomas.

Cohen, P., and Krause, M. S. (1971). *Casework with Wives of Alcoholics*. New York: Family Service Association of America.

Corder, R. F., and Laidlaw, N. D. (1972). An intensive treatment program for alcoholics and their wives. *Quarterly Journal of Studies on Alcohol* 33:1144–1146.

Cork, R. M. (1969). *The Forgotten Children*. Toronto: Addiction Research Foundation.

Corrigan, E., and Anderson, S. (1978). Training for treatment of alcoholism in women. *Social Casework* 59:42–50.

Dahlgren, L. (1979). Female alcoholics IV: marital situation and husbands. *Acta Psychiatrica Scandinavica* 59:59–69.

Davis, T., and Hagood, L. (1979). In-home support for recovering alcoholic mothers and their families: the family rehabilitation coordinator project. *Journal of Studies on Alcohol* 40:313–317.

Edwards, P., Harvey, C., and Whitehead, P. (1973). Wives of alcoholics: a critical review and analysis. *Quarterly Journal of Studies on Alcohol* 34:112–132.

El-Guebaly, N., and Offord, D. R. (1979). On being an offspring of an alcoholic: an update. *Alcoholism Clinical and Experimental Research* 3:148–157.

Esser, P. H. (1968). Conjoint family therapy with alcoholics. *British Journal of Addiction* 63:177–182.

—— (1971). Evaluation of family therapy with alcoholics. *British Journal of Addiction* 66:86–91.

Ewing, J., and Fox, R. (1968). Family therapy of alcoholism. *Current Psychiatric Therapies* 8:86–91.

Finlay, D. (1966). Effect of role network pressure on an alcoholic's approach to treatment. *Social Work* 11:71–77.

—— (1974). Alcoholism: illness or problem in interaction? *Social Work* 19:390–405.

Flanzer, J. (1978). Family management in the treatment of alcoholism. *British Journal on Alcohol and Alcoholism* 13:45–59.

Fox, R. (1968). Treating the alcoholic's family. In *Alcoholism: The Total Treatment Approach*, ed. R. Catanzaro, pp. 105–115. Springfield, Ill.: Chas C Thomas.

Gallant, D. M., Rich, A., Bey, E., and Terranova, L. (1970). Group psychotherapy with married couples: successful techniques in New Orleans' alcoholism clinic patients. *Louisiana State Medical Society Journal* 122:41–44.

Gerard, D. L., and Saenger, G. (1966). *Outpatient Treatment of Alcoholism: A Study of Outcome and Its Determination.* Toronto: University of Toronto Press.

Gliedman, L., Rosenthal, D., Frank, J. D., and Nash, H. T. (1956). Group therapy of alcoholics and concurrent group meetings of their wives. *Quarterly Journal of Studies on Alcohol* 17:655–670.

Gorad, S. L. (1971). Communicational style of alcoholics and their wives. *Family Process* 10:475–489.

Gorman, J. M., and Rooney, J. F. (1979). The influence of Al-Anon on the coping behavior of wives of alcoholics. *Journal of Studies on Alcohol* 40:1030–1038.

Jackson, J. K. (1956). The adjustment of the family to alcoholism. *Marriage and Family Living* 18:361–369.

Janzen, C. (1977). Families in the treatment of alcoholism. *Journal of Studies on Alcohol* 38:114–130.

Kogan, K. L., and Jackson, J. K. (1965). Stress, personality, and emotional disturbance in wives of alcoholics. *Quarterly Journal of Studies on Alcohol* 26:486–495.

Krimmel, H., ed. (1971). *Alcoholism: Challenge for Social Work Education.* New York: Council on Social Work Education.

McDowell, F. K. (1972). The pastor's natural ally against alcoholism. *Journal of Pastoral Care* 26:26–32.

Meeks, D. E., and Kelly, C. (1970). Family therapy with the families of recovering alcoholics. *Quarterly Journal of Studies on Alcohol* 31:399–413.

Minuchin, S. (1974). *Families and Family Therapy.* Cambridge, Mass.: Harvard University Press.

Mueller, J. F. (1972). Casework with the family of the alcoholic. *Social Work* 17:79–84.

Pattison, E. M. (1965). Treatment of alcoholic families with nurse home visits. *Family Process* 4:74–94.

Press, L. (1975). Treating the family. *Maryland State Medical Journal* 24:32–35.

Preston, F. B. (1960). Combined individual, joint, and group therapy in treatment of alcoholism. *Mental Hygiene* 44:522–528.

Rae, J. (1972). The influence of wives on the treatment outcome of alcoholics. *British Journal of Psychiatry* 120:601–613.

Regan, J. M. (1978). Services to the families of alcoholics: an assessment of a social support system. Ph.D. Dissertation, Brandeis University.

Richards, T. (1979). Working with children of an alcoholic mother. *Alcohol Health and Research World* 3:22–25.

Satir, V. (1967). *Conjoint Family Therapy*. Palo Alto, Calif.: Science and Behavior.

Smith, C. G. (1969). Alcoholics: their treatment and their wives. *British Journal of Psychiatry* 115:1039–1042.

Steiner, C. (1969). The alcoholic game. *Quarterly Journal of Studies on Alcohol* 30:920–938.

Steinglass, P. (1976). Experimenting with family treatment approaches to alcoholism, 1950–1975: a review. *Family Process* 15:97–123.

Strausner, S. L., Weinstein, D. L., and Hernandez, R. (1979). Effects of alcoholism on the family system. *Health and Social Work* 4:111–127.

Ward, R., and Faillace, L. (1970). The alcoholic and his helpers. *Quarterly Journal of Studies on Alcohol* 31:684–691.

Wegscheider, S. (1981). *Another Chance: Hope and Health for the Alcoholic Family*. Palo Alto, Calif.: Science and Behavior.

Wiseman, J. P. (1976). The wives of alcoholics: diagnosis of alcoholism and treatment strategy involving the family. *Alkoholipolitiikka* 41:62.

Woggon, H. A. (1972). The alcoholic unit at Broughton Hospital. *Inventory* 22:18–19.

Wolin, S. J. (1980). Introduction: psychosocial consequences. In *Alcohol and Women: Research Monograph* No. 1, pp. 63–70. Rockville, Md.: National Institute on Alcohol Abuse and Alcoholism.

——, Bennett, L. A., and Noonan, D. (1979). Family rituals and the recurrence of alcoholism over generations. *American Journal of Psychiatry* 136:589–593.

Wright, M. D., and Scott, T. B. (1978). The relationship of wives' treatment to the drinking status of alcoholics. *Journal of Studies on Alcohol* 39:1577–1581.

❧ 5 ❧

Drug Abuse

David J. Huberty, M.S.W., and
Catherine E. Huberty, M.S.W.

Twenty years ago the research describing the addict's family was already in place. Early studies in the 1950s and 1960s, as summarized by Seldin (1972), focused on the addict's family of origin. Divorce, desertion, and open hostility among family members, as well as a lack of cohesiveness, was observed in 97 percent of youthful addicts (McCord 1965). Mothers were described as seductive, emasculating, overprotective, and the dominant family figure. Fathers were described as morally vague, pessimistic about life, passive and easily swayed, remote, detached, and uninvolved with the family or totally absent. Although the literature on the family of the drug abuser at that time dealt specifically with addiction to narcotics, there are similar descriptions of other types of drug abuse (Stanton 1979a).

A summation of these descriptions is that the prototypical family of a drug-dependent person or "identified patient" provided an unstable environment for emotional growth during the adolescent years when the adolescent is most apt to experiment with drugs (Huberty and Malmquist 1978). This is consistent with the affirmation that the family has a central role in creating the personality (Seldin 1972). Certainly, there are many other factors and people, particularly peers, that influence adolescent behavior and drug experimentation. Recent research, however, has verified that "peer influence appears to be of a more limited duration than family influence" (Glynn 1981, p. 375), thus adding credence that the family of origin is not only the primary ingredient in developing personality but also in developing drug dependency.

This type of family inadequately prepares the youthful family member for healthy emancipation, for it fails to instill any motivation for building his or her own family group. "This inconsistent family process was overindulging as well as overdenying" and suggested that the addict was destined to repeat the original family dynamics and relationship patterns through a flight into marriage to a "dominating, psychosexually dominant, ambivalent woman who perpetuates the addict's immature behavior patterns" only to return to mother in defeat (Seldin 1972, p. 105). Despite the descriptive family data of the time, it was not until the mid to late 1970s that the techniques for restructuring the family system of the chemically dependent client were formulated and researched.

INTEGRATING THE DRUG SCENE
WITH FAMILY TREATMENT

It is worthwhile to note that a family systems approach to drug abuse treatment is not without historical context in three areas: (1) the evolution of the drug scene itself, (2) the developing field of family therapy, and (3) the emergence of family therapy as applied to the drug abuse field.

Changes in Drug Use Patterns

The drug scene in the United States prior to the late 1960s claimed as its victims the subcultural ghettoed groupings of racial minorities or immigrants. The primary drug of choice was narcotics. But as the use of drugs grew in the early 1970s, drug use moved from narcotics to multiple-drug use; from subcultural minority groupings to the white middle class; from a primarily male urban populus to include significant percentages of both rural youth of both sexes and younger users (Stephens 1980); from essential neglect of its victims by banishing addicts to federal narcotic farms in Kentucky and Texas, over a span of 30 years prior to the late 1960s, to solid community-based programs by the end of the 1970s (Huberty 1980); and from "family," which used to mean the addict's mother and perhaps spouse, to include both parents (Huberty and Huberty 1976), siblings (Coleman 1979), and others in a two- or three-generational perspective (Stanton 1980).

This past decade in particular has seen rapidly changing patterns of drug abuse which have led to a broader family focus in federal policy toward drug treatment (Clayton 1980), and it is this family emphasis that has paralleled the developing field of family therapy in general.

Family Therapy as a Mental Health Specialty

Olson and colleagues stated that it was the decade of the 1970s in which

> . . . marital and family treatment gained credibility and emerged as a significant and separate mental health field . . . traditional distinctions between marriage counseling and family counseling have faded . . . growth of family therapy has attracted professionals interested in working with persons within a relationship context and has become a "melting pot" of therapists. . . . Viewed from a developmental perspective, the field of marital and family therapy has emerged from its infancy in the 1950s, achieved childhood in the early 1960s, adolescence in the late 1960s and has reached young adulthood in the 1970s. (1980, pp. 974–975)

The hallmark of family therapy is its emphasis on treating problems within a relationship context. This and a refinement of these techniques will increasingly preoccupy clinicians in the drug abuse field in the next decade.

Family-Focused Drug Treatment

Drug treatment has learned from its failures and has traveled a great distance from that treatment framework that focused on the strictly medical and psychiatric treatment approaches of earlier decades. Yet, in contrast with the alcoholism field, which has used family and marital treatments for years and found them effective, family approaches are relatively new in the drug abuse field (Stanton 1979b).

It was not until the early 1970s that a number of drug treatment facilities in the United States began using family therapy techniques. Since that time, there has been increased interest in family factors in the genesis and maintenance of drug abuse and dependency throughout the chemical dependency treatment field. Even therapists working in drug abuse areas that have not been primarily family focused have begun to include more relevant family information in their efforts. The literature also reflects this trend. A recent bibliography of the literature on family and drug misuse included 370 titles, of which 299 or nearly 80 percent were published since 1970, with more than one-third dealing specifically with family and marital treatment (Stanton 1978b). One survey (Coleman and Davis 1978) found that of the drug abuse programs that responded, 93 percent were providing family services for at least a portion of their clients; 69 percent noted that they provided family therapy that included the drug abuser; 74 percent felt that family treatment was highly important for the addict's recovery process; and less than 1 percent felt that such treatment was not necessary. Seventy-five percent of the facilities that had family programs tended to see both the drug abusers and their families together, with the second most common approach being marital therapy. These programs ranked Virginia Satir, Jay Haley, and Salvador Minuchin as the three most influential family theoreticians.

It is also these schools of relationship-oriented treatment—most notably structural family therapy and strategic family therapy—"which have yielded some degree of documented effectiveness" in drug abuse treatment (Olson et al. 1980, p. 980). Kaufman, a noted authority in family drug treatment, attested that "although I have used a variety of family therapy techniques for many years, it is only since I have incorporated structural treatment into my methods that I have felt the family treatment of substance abusers has fallen into place" (1979, p. 260). We, as clinicians, began from an Adlerian base and later discovered the structural model to support and refine our techniques. It is this orientation to families with drug-abusing members and their treatment that we shall describe here.

Family Systems Theory

In systems theory, the family is an open, dynamic system that functions as a basic structural unit providing a unifying nucleus, a central focus, and gravital balance for the family members. In the family unit, each subset or member affects and is affected by every other member of the system, including those on the horizontal plane (siblings) and those on the vertical plane, going back at least two generations (parents and grandparents as well as uncles, aunts, great-uncles and great-aunts) and at least one generation down the genogram to include one's children. Anything less than a three-generational perspective will not lead to an understanding of the system's dynamics.

Because the events that precede the drug use and the behavioral context in which the substance abuse occurs are important determinants of the drug's function within the family, concepts of circular causality and homeostatic balance are central to understanding the dynamics of family systems theory and the treatment of drug abuse through the restructuring of family patterns.

Circular Causality

Systems theory holds that causality is not a direct linear relationship between a cause and an effect, such as is possible with the stimulus-response model. In systems theory, causality is circular: What one person says or does is a stimulus to which another responds, and that response in turn becomes a stimulus evoking many more responses. This pattern of circular causality is more descriptive of what really happens when individuals interact, particularly within a system as stable as a family unit (Olson 1974). In circular causality, the emerging interaction cannot be traced to a single cause, and consequently it is less possible to blame a single source, and so scapegoating can be defused.

Homeostatic Balance

Homeostasis refers to the family's ability to regulate or balance and stabilize itself. In treating drug abusers and their families, it is important to understand that the family as a unit is guided by a rational desire for stability. Its behavior can be viewed as homeostatic, since it readjusts itself and continues despite reverses. As Wegscheider (1976) observed, the family is an organism, and its parts are interdependent. The body of parts works together, sometimes for peace and harmony, sometimes for destruction, and sometimes for survival. Wegscheider suggested that the family resembles a mobile—a hanging, multipart sculpture. The beauty of the mobile is in its balance and flexibility. It changes position but always maintains connections with each part, and once flicked out of balance, the whole system gradually moves itself back into equilibrium. In a family in which there is stress, the whole organism shifts to bring balance, stability, or survival, and this is the type of dynamic that families carry on throughout several generations.

Drug abuse then evolves into an integral part of the family's delicate balance. It meets the individual drug abuser's need for equilibrium within the family unit, and likewise, the drug abuse itself and the behavior that accompanies it become a part of the family's own equilibrium. Coleman (1980) stated that homeostasis is dependent on "feedback loops" that operate both within and outside the family system. She cited an example of an internal feedback loop in which a drug-using adolescent male comes home late for dinner appearing to be "high." Father confronts him with his suspicions, but son denies using drugs. Father becomes more attacking and "grounds" son. Mother intercedes and tells father that he should not punish son without more evidence. Father then begins arguing with mother, and son disappears.

When the mother entered the situation, the interaction between father and son was redirected; the conflict shifted from parent versus child to husband versus wife. The mother's intervention freed her son to return to drugs, thus restoring the homeostatic pattern which can be expected to be recycled and reenacted when the son returns home.

Family Enmeshment

Family enmeshment is a prototypical description of the drug-abusing family in action, in which the executive or parental subsystem has been disturbed. Rather than the parents' operating as hierarchical peers, the parental subsystem has been mixed with the child's subsystem. Mother and son have entered into a cross-generational coalition—a rigid, inappropriately constituted subsystem with each other and against the father. The boundaries between the generations have become diffused or blurred, and communication has become difficult. The pattern is one of the father's scapegoating the drug abuser and the mother's protecting him. The parental roles are typically reversed in cases in which the drug abuser is a daughter. Even when both parents appear unified, more often than not one parent will later violate this unity by trying to be "overly understanding" or apologizing for "dad's temper." The result is an *enmeshed family* which becomes excessively concerned with itself and its members. Contacts with systems outside the family are diminished. The boundaries between parents and children become blurred, and these subsystems merge. System "overload" occurs, and the family becomes vulnerable to stress. In enmeshed families, relatively minor problems in one family member are treated by the entire system as a crisis.

Disengaged Family

An alternative family pattern at the other extreme of the family cohesion continuum and seen far less frequently in drug-using families is the *disengaged family*. Here families become overly rigid and disengaged from one another; members communicate little with one another; subsystems become isolated; and levels of concern and adaptive-protective functions are reduced. In the disengaged family, one member's problems must reach crisis proportions before the family system will respond to them. Even here, however, the scapegoat role exists and is assigned to the drug-using family member. This "identified patient" is labeled as "sick," "bad," or "incompetent" or in some other way becomes the "sacrificial member" whose problems become the only "cause" around which the parents can unite; so in a sense he or she keeps them together (Stanton 1979b).

The above concepts provide the background for understanding the foundations and principles within which drug use becomes an expression of family structure and function.

FAMILY CHARACTERISTICS
DISTINGUISHING THE ADDICT

Certainly, a number of disorders show a pattern of overinvolvement by one parent and distance or absence by the other. This book attempts to fill a void in family therapy literature by offering a chapter-by-chapter comparison of family therapy with different medical, psychological, and behavioral disorders, and so it is particularly relevant to distinguish drug-abusing families from other symptomatic family types.

Multigenerational Chemical Dependency

Drug-abusing families have a higher frequency than do normal families of multigenerational chemical dependency, particularly alcoholism, as well as a propensity toward other compulsive disorders, for example, gambling, overeating, and the passivity of compulsive television watching (Stanton 1978b). Smart and Fejer (1972) found that if the parents used psychotropic drugs, even medically, their children were also more likely to use psychotropics. It has been estimated that approximately 52 percent of alcoholics come from homes in which one or both parents had a drinking problem (Fox 1968). It should come as no surprise, then, that one study concluded that "for young teenagers, the most frequent source of first drug experience is from drugs obtained in the home" (Bernstein 1973, p. 110). Our clinical experience supports the contention that well over 50 percent of drug-dependent youths come from families with a history of identifiable alcoholism or some other form of substance abuse.

Such practices then become models for living, handed down by the family of origin, and can also develop into family traditions with built-in rewards for carrying on the family tradition and punishments for failure to fit in.

Drug Use Tied to Individuation

Drug misuse is tied to the process of experimenting with new behaviors, growing up, and leaving home—with separation and individuation as the goal. On the systems level, the cycle of drug dependency gives the appearance of dramatic movement within the family.

But as the drug dependent shuttles back and forth between peers and home, his or her ambivalence and apparent helplessness are redefined in a dependency-engendering way (e.g., "sick," "failure") by the family, and they are further justified in rescuing the drug dependent from the consequences of his or her behavior (Stanton 1978b).

This attempted move from parental control toward independence can also stimulate conflict between the parents. What was a normal dependence-independence issue and struggle for "couple identity" in early marriage is resurrected (Barcai 1981). Themes surrounding the parents' individuation process from their own parents may be relived. If basic trust and equality between the parental partners were never negotiated, the atmosphere is ripe for the following relationship patterns to occur: The addict's mother may well have once protected her own husband from his overindulgent, overprotective mother, and now 20 years later she carries on this family tradition and maternal role with her addicted son. Without her involvement in treatment and without confronting her role directly, she will "benevolently and lov- ingly" sabotage her addicted son's efforts to free himself from these time-honored traditions. The mother's need to take care of her child often has its roots in her own family of origin—watching her mother in a care-taking position with her father or perhaps one of her dependent brothers. Even in single-parent or stepparent families, there are usually at least two adults involved in the offspring's problems, and clinicians should look for a triangle consisting of one overinvolved parent and one more peripheral parent, grandparent, boyfriend, or girlfriend. Stanton (1978b) maintains that achieving separation and independence is even more of an issue in single-parent families, since the mother may be left alone with few psychological resources if the addict departs.

Expressions of Conflict

Families with drug dependency tend to express conflict more primi- tively and directly. As one parent directly expresses anger and conflict, the alliance between the dependent and the overinvolved parent be- comes more overt and explicit (Stanton 1979b). The result is rage felt by the drug abuser, which is often expressed in one of two extremes: The anger is either deeply buried and further tranquilized through self- medicating drug abuse, or it results in angry explosions of violence.

Either way, however, the pattern is one of rebellion and acting-out behavior, usually under the influence of drugs. Any aggression or rage is thereby discounted, the drug is blamed, and the drug user comes down from his or her high with no genuine relief. Often the stormy scene is between the chemically dependent youth and an uninvolved father; the mother interrupts the process by protecting her son and thus redirecting the father's anger toward herself, and the son leaves with his anger still smoldering. The more direct expression of conflict is between the marital pair, with the addict's once again experiencing feelings of impotence.

Drug Use by Peers

Actual drug use by peers—especially a close friend—provides the drug abuser with a safe retreat from family conflict. Compared with families of schizophrenics and families in which the identified patient displays a severe psychosomatic disorder, drug abusers tend to form stronger outside relationships and are more likely to retreat to them following family conflict (Stanton 1978b). The symptom of the drug abuse itself receives reinforcement through peer support, and a corresponding temporary illusion of independence follows. This reinforcement is particularly strong when the best friend is among the illicit drug-using group (Glynn 1981). Consequently, it is nearly impossible to confront the drug-taking incident or the homeodynamic character of the family of origin without built-in program controls.

For parents, the abuser's problems and "negative" peers rationalize their involvement in the continuing overindulgent and overdependent relationship. For the family as a whole, addiction supplies an excuse for delaying attention to other family (domestic) problems (Alexander and Dibbs 1975). Treatment techniques must therefore consistently confront the family process that occurs prior to and following any drug incident. Program controls must be flexible, allowing for lengthy family sessions of two to three hours or evening sessions, and insist on the participation of both parents, siblings, and other family members or family substitutes.

Residential treatment helps short-circuit the retreat to drug use and drug-using peers when family conflict is stimulated and released in therapy. In outpatient treatment, the immediate availability of detoxification facilities following drug usage enables the parents to set limits and allows the therapist to capitalize on the crisis event before it is lost in the more familiar explosion of anger and retreats to drug-using peers and ultimate argument between parents.

Symbiotic Child-rearing Practices

Mothers of addicts prolong "symbiotic" child-rearing practices, as these mothers have greater symbiotic needs than do the mothers of schizophrenics and normals. Attardo concluded:

> Since the symbiotic relationship normally decreases as the child grows older, the indications are that the mothers of addicts and, to a lesser extent, the mothers of schizophrenics seem to be fixated at the earlier phase of the mother-son symbiosis. The symbiotic interaction in these cases persists up to the onset of the son's symptomatology in late adolescence. (1965, p. 156)

When the drug abuser finally does leave home, parents are often blaming and bitter, since they have no more opportunity to correct the child who has "abandoned" them and their dreams. They are thus left feeling that they and their parenting have been judged as failures. In other words, the addict's mother tends to have strong dependency needs that are met through the addict-mother relationship. This basic dependency thus needs redirection and fulfillment, and the most obvious available person is her husband or some other partner or close friend. Often this becomes a transfer of dependency, and the parenting function is continued within the marriage, with the object being the other partner, resulting in a transferred symbiosis rather than a partnership (Barcai 1981).

Fear of Departure Related to Incomplete Mourning

The fear that the families of addicts have for the drug abuser's departure to emancipation appears to correlate with unresolved grief over previous death themes in the family (Coleman 1980). Coleman also noted that several researchers have found an unusual number of traumatic or premature deaths, separations, and losses that occurred during critical or transitional stages of the family's developmental cycle and that were not effectively resolved.

Such losses are intensified for the family during adolescence. This fear first peaks in the adolescence of the oldest child as the "parenthood" is being "judged" by society. Another peak of fear and loss is when the youngest child leaves home and the parents begin to face their own aging and mortality (Barcai 1981). The parents may have already experienced such a loss through the death of one of their own parents, a close grandparent, or sibling at an early age. But the drug abuser may view the drug use itself as a medication to combat the pain of losing a family member, often a parent or perhaps a close peer. The family's incomplete mourning of the deceased member keeps the parents in a continuous grieving process. Because they have not mastered the loss, they make the drug abuser a substitute for the dead person and encourage him or her to stay close to the family. The drug use then keeps the abusing member helpless and dependent on the family, a process that unifies and sustains it. The drug use is thereby adaptive, functional, noble, and sacrificial, as well as self-destructive— a process of "chronic suicide." Even if the addict should die, the parents will be again united in their grief (Coleman 1980).

TREATMENT STRATEGIES

Several implications for treatment follow from the foregoing discussion, and we shall illustrate the various goals and techniques through case examples.

Shifting the Homeostasis
by Restructuring Family Patterns

In the more typical triadic relationship of mother and son versus father or father and daughter versus mother, this shift initially requires confrontation in order to disrupt the established patterns of interaction and communication as well as to strengthen the generational boundaries, notably the marital relationship between husband and wife. Restructuring direct communication is one way to begin this family-restructuring process. Much of their communication has been indirect, referring to one another in the third person and discussing issues instead of feelings. We insist that all family members speak directly to one another about their feelings and have them use time in therapy to practice.

One couple who had been seen together in several conjoint sessions came in on an emergency basis because their drug-abusing daughter had just flunked out of her freshman year at college. The familiar mother-daughter coalition was being played out, as the mother began crying and explaining, in front of her husband, that he wanted to kick her daughter out of the house. I redirected her to tell her husband how she felt. The message quickly changed: "I feel afraid for our daughter. She has no money, no place to go, and yet I am afraid for us (as a couple) if she stays!" Her husband could now respond to her fears with more sensitivity, whereas before he could only become defensive. Later in the session, as the mother, father, daughter, and I returned from the waiting room to my office, the daughter was quick to sit down first and placed herself in the middle chair, obviously between her parents. I wrote a note to the mother which she read directly to her daughter. "You will not break us up! I want you to change chairs with my husband!" To restructure further the communication patterns, it was the mother who announced the decision that she and her husband had agreed to before their daughter had joined the session: "We love you very much, but we have decided that you have to move. You may stay with us one week while you find a place to live, and we shall pay your rent for the first month, but no longer than that." The mother was no longer protecting their daughter from her father, and he was no longer the hard disciplinarian.

The family was assigned "homework" to enable them to realize further these coalitions and to encourage their having fun together.

For another family in which the 16-year-old daughter often conflicted with her father but was protected by her mother, we required the father and daughter to go horseback riding together. Because this assignment was not carried out—the father "withheld" this reward when the daughter did not do the dishes one night—we reassigned it and emphasized that he was again controlling and entering into a power struggle with the therapists rather than "disciplining" his daughter. We also assigned the mother to go to a friend's house on the daughter's dish-washing night in order to prevent her rescuing her by "helping" with the dishes. The following

week, when the mother was enjoying the freedom of an
evening out with a friend, the dishes were done with dad's
help, and the horseback riding went on as scheduled.

Treating the Marriage Relationship

In another work, we described in detail a full-length case study
in which the emphasis was on shifting the homeostatic balance
with the goal of helping salvage the marriage (Huberty and Huberty
1981). In that case study, the therapist's advocate position was primarily to treat the parents. This is essential when the addict-client
refuses to enter therapy or is unwilling or unable to stay drug-free.
Parents feel guilty and desperately need the hope and support that
comes from encouragement. In the wisdom and knowledge they have
gained from hindsight, they frequently blame themselves and each
other. The therapists play down the notion of guilt and remind the
parents that in raising their children, they did the best they could at the
time. We have often used parent support groups, either formal therapy
groups or self-help groups such as Families Anonymous. Support from
other parents who are or have been in a similar situation is the strongest
kind of support they can receive. By sharing their feelings of disappointment, frustration, and failure, these parents discover the normalcy
of their feelings and problems. They feel reassured that the anger and
the hate/love that they feel toward their adolescent (drug abuser) and
toward each other are acceptable. Through this mutual support, they
feel understood and are able to respect themselves and each other.
They also receive specific suggestions from other parents regarding
techniques to use in limit setting and phrases to use in reestablishing
communication with the drug abuser and with each other (Huberty
and Huberty 1976).

> One couple's 16-year-old adopted daughter was still using
> marijuana, speed, and alcohol after five unsuccessful
> residential programs and numerous outpatient programs. We
> saw her separately for 14 months on an infrequent basis,
> perhaps once a month. She flatly refused any sessions with
> her parents, who were seen in parallel conjoint sessions. No
> insight techniques were used with the parents, only support
> for some sense of a unified parental response—rewards,
> punishments, logical consequences—anything to strengthen

parental unity. The mother's depression lifted within two months; her feelings became spontaneous, and she felt less trapped and intimidated by her daughter. The father increasingly supported his wife, especially after he was laid off from his job as an engineer and was spending more time at home where he witnessed their daughter's intimidation of his wife. We saw the daughter with the aim of comprehending her feelings about her adopted family and thereby her feelings of abandonment by her birth mother. She still did not let up on her drug use, and we abandoned our usual requirement of drug abstinence, perhaps because she seemed genuinely interested in the family genogram process. But after discovering that she was pregnant, she spontaneously discontinued using all drugs and alcohol and then consented to sessions with her parents, remaining drug-free throughout her pregnancy.

Even when it is not possible to treat the marriage relationship directly, other techniques can support and strengthen the parental boundaries. In one parent group, a single-parent widow became very close friends with another mother whose husband refused to enter the group. Their support of each other brought partial relief from the problems of their drug-abusing children, who also refused treatment at that time. In both families, the children entered treatment programs two or three years later.

Establishing a Visual Family Map

A genogram, or a three-generation family map, describes the people in the relationship system and explores the childhood and early family relationship of the drug abuser and his or her siblings, parents and their siblings, and grandparents. The genogram should include a marking of marriages, divorces, births, deaths, and other notable events or traits such as family values and illnesses. This extended family complex is crucial to understanding the consistency and replication of family dynamics. Spontaneous insights are often gained by merely listing family events and traditions. Scapegoating roles are often revealed in each generation, and secrets may be uncovered accidentally. These insights and connections may stimulate anger over having been blamed and scapegoated for fulfilling a family scenario unknowingly prescribed by the parents and supported by siblings and possibly even grand-parents, uncles, and aunts.

In our first family session with a 30-year-old chemically dependent woman (drug-free for one year) and her parents, we began by asking the parents to list the names and ages of their four children of whom Cindy was the oldest. The next question was whether or not the mother had had any miscarriages or stillbirths. The father answered no, while at the same time the mother answered yes. The anguished look of shock and hurt on the father's face suggested much about the couple's communication. Interestingly, Cindy had always known of this miscarriage. This family map quickly showed the father that his wife had excluded him from certain vital and intimate family information. Cindy discovered that she had been mother's confidante, who was expected to keep certain family secrets from her father and thereby prevent a more open relationship with him. She found, too, that blaming her father for being distant was connected to a pattern of stifled communication, with certain areas ruled by her mother as being "off-limits" for discussion. Strongly held family values, such as education and religion, which had lasted for two generations, were revealed simply by listing the level of formal education and the vocational choices of Cindy's uncles and aunts. The fact that they were priests and nuns, physicians, a psychologist, nurses, and teachers pointed to the expectation that Cindy too must be highly educated and quite religious or else be considered a failure, unaccepted and unacceptable.

Issues of Death, Separation, and Grief

The family genogram is one way of discovering a family's death themes.

Duane, a 32-year-old teacher who established a drug users' counseling group in his school, felt overwhelmed by the many late-night telephone calls from his drug-using students asking for his immediate help; for example, driving 40 miles to rescue them when they were stranded or taking them in overnight when their parents had locked them out. As we began his genogram, we charted the suicide of his father (pill overdose) when Duane was 16 years old. Duane had found his father dead on the bathroom floor just four hours after a sensitive, close, caring talk between the two of them. As the oldest child and only son, with two younger sisters, he felt he was the "man of the family" and should take good care of his mother. Six months later his mother died suddenly of a heart attack. Although he was clearly aware of what he had told us, he did not realize that "if you express concern and get close to someone, then you had better always be there when they need you!" Therefore, he felt he must never limit his availability to his students. Because of the deteriorating effect this was having on his marriage, he discontinued his drug group for one year.

Another method of discovering a family's death themes is "early recollections," a projective technique we use extensively for several purposes (Huberty 1980). The following early recollection offers insight into one mother's clinging to her 16-year-old daughter, who had just completed a residential drug dependency treatment program.

Mother's early recollection: "At age 4, it was after I got home from four weeks in the hospital, and my 6-week-old baby sister had died from whooping cough, and I know she got it from me. The picture I have is the body of the baby lying on the dining room table. The doctor came to get the baby, and the baby was dead, and my older brother seems to be in the picture too—I'm not sure what he's doing—just observing, maybe. After the doctor took the baby, my mother went upstairs, and I went upstairs, too. She was lying on the bed crying, and I asked her why she was crying because I didn't understand what had gone on. She said her baby had died." The most vivid scene in the memory was "the baby on the table" and the emotion connected to that scene was "not understanding" and "confused." Our mutual interpretation was that she truly did not understand. She felt that she should have understood better, that if she had understood better or known more, then the tragedy somehow would not have happened. This had a similar connection in her relationship with her daughter in the present: If she (mother) is not in full control of the situation, something horrible or sad may happen. She saw women (girls, females) as fragile, easily hurt, and emotional and female children as exceptionally fragile, vulnerable, and sickly. Therefore, they need to be protected, taken care of, and treated gently and very carefully. This picture helped us understand and later confront the mother's need to control, her emphasis on education and pressure on her daughter to get A's ("to understand better"), her oversensitivity to issues of illness, and her protectiveness of her daughter. It also allowed the daughter to view her mother's protective behavior in a different light. The mother cried, and the daughter felt less need to rebel, and thus the grieving provided a release and insight.

Mock conversations with the deceased also are helpful. The family member stuck in the grieving process talks to an empty chair representing the deceased and later in the conversation changes chairs and speaks for the deceased. One family member expressed surprise and relief over how much wiser and understanding his mother had become after she had died. This allowed him to feel more angry over past rejections, since she was now more "approachable" and "listened better."

Teaching Expressions of Anger and Hate and of Love and Affection

Expressing anger constructively often requires therapist modeling and group support, not only for expression, but also for dealing with the drug abuser's guilt that follows as the injured parents recoil and retaliate with blame and shame. Residential treatment is often required, so as to separate the addict from the parents and to allow the addict to experiment and learn these new behavioral patterns away from established family expectations, sanctions, and equilibrium. Many parents become bewildered and frightened as their adolescent, while in treatment but in the absence of a crisis or a drugged state, begins to express anger, criticism, or even hate (Huberty 1975). Yet the outer layer of anger must be expressed in order to uncover the inner core of love. Likewise, when the addict is married, the spouse becomes equally fearful of the hostility targeted toward her. But because the anger and unresolved individuation are really issues between the addict and his or her parents, efforts at marital treatment seem to have limited results (Stanton 1979b).

I spent the bulk of four multiple-family therapy sessions arguing, confronting, and being angry with a mother of a

19-year-old drug abuser, as she tried to dominate the session by lecturing her son "Bobby." Rob, as he preferred to be addressed, hung his head in a passive, "mother-deaf" expression of complacency. With each exchange between his mother and me, he cautiously looked up at me as if to encourage. Gradually, the safety of the group structure and with coaching as to the exact words to recite, he began to assert himself. As he began, so as to not lose his mother in the therapy process, I moved my chair closer to hers and later held her hand while explaining that he needed to share his anger and she needed to hear it directly from him. She was a strong and formidable opponent; yet she respected someone who would stand up to her. Her husband was later confronted with his ignoring his wife, her need to be listened to, and this need having been transferred to their son. As the mother and father began their homework of spending 20 minutes at the end of each workday actively listening to each other without interruptions, the emotional flow was redirected. Rob and his mother established a comfortable relationship, and Rob and his father formed a more active and respectful relationship when Rob realized that he had resented his father for not standing up to his mother.

Therapist as Advocate for the Addict

Not all families can or should move from enmeshment or a disengaged state to a nurturing and comfortable mutuality. Some families begin disengaged and should stay disengaged! Frequently in such families, however, the drug abuser longs for a nurturing family, a sense of belonging and acceptance. Yet no matter how hard he or she tries, no matter what successes are achieved in drug abstinence, education, employment, financial status, or marriage, one or both parents wait patiently, watching the calendar, and waiting for their prediction of failure to come true. The family, usually both parents and siblings, want a permanent scapegoat to fill their need for inadequacy, perhaps so that the parents can validate their martyrdom (i.e., "she was such a difficult child to raise, and we tried so hard"), whereas the siblings may need a scapegoat to deflect parental controls and to enhance their own success and status in their parents' eyes. In such families we take sides in order to support the recovering drug abuser's process of dissolving family ties.

Mary, aged 23, heavily abusing speed, grass, and alcohol, had
run away from a state hospital in Florida where her upper
middle-class parents had committed her, "because of
depression." She hitchhiked nearly 2,000 miles to her
maternal aunt's house in Minnesota in order to gain a sense
of "freedom," only to realize that extended families tend to
share family sanctions, expectations, and traditions. After
eight months she was able to "arrange" getting kicked out of
her aunt's home (because of continued drug use) and ended
up in a drug treatment center, followed by halfway house
placement. After another year of periodic drug use, Mary
was able to express directly her intense anger toward her
aunt ("mother's representative"). Gradually she was able to
understand and accept that the extreme measure of running
2,000 miles away from her parents was a dramatic attempt to
free herself from her parents' control and blame.
Interestingly, most of her drug supply during the eight
months she stayed at her aunt's came from her two brothers,
still in Florida, who tried in this way to preserve her as the
family failure and scapegoat. In the seven years that Mary
was away, her parents never together visited her. Separately,
on four annual occasions of her repeated hospitalizations for
drug treatment or depression, one parent came "at great
sacrifice and expense" to meet with hospital staff to "be of
whatever help we can!" After Mary's hospitalization finally
ended, both parents came to Minnesota, not specifically to
visit her, but to attend a large family reunion of the maternal
side of the family. Being genuinely good people and wanting
to be "good" parents, they could not turn down the
therapist's request for a week's worth of "marathon" family
sessions (four hours per day for five days), since they were
going to be in town anyway. They had rejected earlier
requests by the therapist for both of them to come for such
family sessions when there was no crisis.

The sessions, all audiotaped for Mary's review at a later
date, with Mary and both parents present, focused on the
parents' families of origin as well as the parents' description
of each of their children. This process showed clearly that
Mary, as the oldest of four children, had been given much
responsibility for her younger siblings, and when they
misbehaved she had been held accountable and blamed. Her
parents expected her to be religious and educated and to
choose a health career—all firmly held traditional values in
both extended families, going back for two generations. They
even accepted Mary's illnesses and hospitalizations, although

with judgmental sympathy. But during one four-hour session, which began as a didactic presentation of hereditary factors in drug and alcohol abuse, the real insight was the exposure of her mother's alcoholism. We asked if there was any other substance abuse in the family tree. For one brief hour, her father painfully expressed his deep concern over his wife's daily drinking. Although there was not enough time for him to follow through, this did give Mary a sense of no longer being "crazy" and not fitting into her family. To the contrary, she began to see her position and role as scapegoat as consistent with her family's traditions and expectations. Her addiction had supplied an excuse for her father's overlooking his wife's alcoholism. Gradually, and with much sadness, she was able to break away from her parents and understand the enabling role her siblings played in trying to maintain her as the "sick" child and thereby keep their parents' attention away from themselves. Mary was able to accept her need to finish college, to enter a career in public health, and to accept her need for some spiritual orientation in her life—something she had rejected for many years. All of this followed her family's traditions; yet she was able to accept her own expression in each of these areas, as she was now free from parental pressures. The cutting of family ties has been painful and lonely for her, and her ability to develop a new "recovery family" has been slow. Her trust of friendship relationships has been minimal but has increased as she nears two years of being drug-free.

Therapy Should Be Fun

Not only do families need role models, encouragement, and direct instruction on how to express anger and hate, love and affection, and bereavement and sadness, they also often need help in having fun together, to learn how to laugh at themselves (Huberty and Huberty 1981). Although therapists must be careful not to imply that the drug abuse and family problems are not serious, they do need to help families relieve themselves from the accompanying gloom and tension. Some of the intent of this fun is to enable the families to view their problems differently.

In one family the mother had extreme difficulty handling her in-laws' rejection of her and had taken over her husband's role in dealing with them. His interest was in winning their

approval of himself, and he had never extracted himself from
the enmeshed family system. Therefore, whenever his wife
was hurt by her in-laws, she angrily reminded him of his
inability to deal with them and rubbed his nose in it in
somewhat the way one might (mistakenly) with a dog who
refused to go to the bathroom outdoors. This reminder was
administered periodically over time, well after the rejecting
events. In therapy, she was assigned the task of returning his
responsibility—his "mess"—to him. She was given clay with
which she made a facsimile of a dog mess. She then boxed
it, wrapped it with a ribbon, and in one session gave it to
him, stating that she was no longer responsible for his mess.
The reaction was hilarious but very effective in that she truly
did let go of it. With such a graphic presentation of the
return of his responsibility, he did commence a more
constructive relationship with his family.

Requiring Drug Abstinence by All Family Members

Because of the high incidence of parental and sibling substance
abuse, we ask all family members in therapy to abstain from all mood-
altering substances. In addition to detecting otherwise hidden parental
and sibling drug or alcohol abuse, such an agreement also removes the
double standard attached to the drug abuser in therapy. Parents are
thereby allowed to experience the adult peer pressures, which often
produces greater empathy. The parents' excuses are similar to their
children's and become grist for the mill of family therapy.

One father, a beer distributor, explained that all his
customers expected him to taste each keg that he was
assigned to hook up, and so he rationalized that he simply
could not comply with our request, even though he "wanted
to." After we gave him the ultimatum of removing both him
and his family, including the identified patient, from our
program, he became angry over being told what to do but
did comply. He later experienced rejection by some "business
friends," similar to the rejection, sneers, and intimidation that
his son felt with his own peers. In less than four weeks,
however, the father and son developed a mutually supportive
relationship that had previously been strained by the father's
judgmental attitude. Furthermore, he acknowledged, and his
wife verified, that his excessive drinking had been an issue
for several years, and both pointed to improvements in their
marriage as a result of his sobriety.

In a field that for years suggested poor prognosis with programs based on the individual, there is much hope for success when the emphasis in therapy is on the positive ways that families can deal with drug-related problems. This hope was summarized by Auerswald, a psychiatrist who has spent well over 20 years treating drug-abusing families:

> In all the time that I have spent working with and observing families, I cannot recall a single, openly communicating, mutually respecting, well-organized, lovingly close family in which an actively participating member had a serious and *lasting* drug habit—transient experimentation, occasional booze or pot, yes, but disabling and lasting drug use, no! . . . One conclusion that seems inescapable is that the phenomena of the family and of consistent psychoactive drug use do not mix at all. They do not even form a stable emulsion. Where one thrives the other does not. (1980, pp. 124-125)

Hope, then, comes from developing a system that will support and foster family life. And more than anything else, drug abusers, families, and even therapists need hope.

References

Alexander, B. K., and Dibbs, G. S. (1975). Opiate addicts and their parents. *Family Process* 14:499-514.

Attardo, N. (1965). Psychodynamic factors in the mother-child relationship in adolescent drug addiction: a comparison of mothers of schizophrenics and mothers of normal adolescent sons. *Psychotherapy and Psychosomatics* 13:249-255, as summarized in T. J. Glynn, ed. (1981). *Drugs and the Family: Research Issues* 29, pp. 155-156. Rockville, Md.: National Institute on Drug Abuse.

Auerswald, E. H. (1980). Drug use and families—in the context of twentieth century science. In *Drug Abuse from the Family Perspective*, ed. B. G. Ellis, pp. 117-126. Rockville, Md.: National Institute on Drug Abuse.

Barcai, A. (1981). Normative family development. *Journal of Marital and Family Therapy* 7:353-359.

Bernstein, D. M. (1973). Drugs and the adolescent. *Minnesota Medicine* 56:108-110.

Clayton, R. R. (1980). The family-drug abuse relationship. In *Drug*

Abuse from the Family Perspective, ed. B. G. Ellis, pp. 86–103. Rockville, Md.: National Institute on Drug Abuse.

Coleman, S. B. (1979). Siblings in session. In *Family Therapy of Drug and Alcohol Abuse*, ed. E. Kaufman and P. Kaufmann, pp. 131–143. New York: Gardner Press.

——— (1980). Incomplete mourning in the family trajectory: a circular journey to drug abuse. In *Drug Abuse from the Family Perspective*, ed. B. G. Ellis, pp. 18–31. Rockville, Md.: National Institute on Drug Abuse.

———, and Davis, D. I. (1978). Family and drug abuse: a national survey. *Family Process* 17:21–29.

Fox, R. (1968). Treating the alcoholic's family. In *Alcoholism: The Total Treatment Approach*, ed. R. J. Catanzaro, pp. 105–115. Springfield, Ill.: Chas C Thomas.

Glynn, T. J. (1981). From family to peer: a review of transitions of influence among drug-using youth. *Journal of Youth and Adolescence* 10:363–383.

Huberty, C. E., and Huberty, D. J. (1976). Treating the parents of adolescent drug abusers. *Contemporary Drug Problems* 5:573–592.

Huberty, D. J. (1975). Treating the adolescent drug abuser: a family affair. *Contemporary Drug Problems* 4:179–194.

——— (1980). Treating the young drug user. In *Drugs and the Youth Culture*, ed. F. R. Scarpitti and S. K. Datesman, pp. 283–315. Beverly Hills, Calif.: Sage Publications.

——— (1980). Early recollections as a projective technique in marital therapy. Paper presented at the National Alcohol and Drug Coalition, Washington, D.C., September.

———, and Huberty, C. E. (1981). Helping the parents to survive: a family systems approach to adolescent alcoholism. In *Family Case Studies in the Treatment of Alcoholism: The Power to Change*, ed. E. Kaufman. New York: Gardner Press, 1983.

———, and Malmquist, J. D. (1978). Adolescent chemical dependency. *Perspectives in Psychiatric Care* 16:21–27.

Kaufman, E. (1979). The application of the basic principles of family therapy to the treatment of drug and alcohol abusers. In *Family Therapy of Drug and Alcohol Abusers*, ed. E. Kaufman and P. Kaufmann, pp. 255–272. New York: Gardner Press.

McCord, W. M. (1965). We ask the wrong questions about crime. *New York Times Magazine* November 21, as quoted in

N. E. Seldin, (1972). The family of the addict: a review of the literature. *International Journal of the Addictions* 7:97–107.

Olson, D. H. (1974). Therapy for addicts: a family affair. In *Drug Perspectives: A Handbook of Readings in Drug Abuse,* ed. H. Brown, and T. J. Cahill, pp. 336–341. Washington, D.C.: National Institute on Drug Abuse.

———, Russell, C. S., and Sprenkle, D. H. (1980). Marital and family therapy: a decade of review. *Journal of Marriage and the Family* 42:973–994.

Seldin, N. E. (1972). The family of the addict: a review of the literature. *International Journal of the Addictions* 7:97–107.

Smart, R., and Fejer, D. (1972). Drug use among adolescents and their parents: closing the generation gap in mood modification. *Journal of Abnormal Psychology* 79:153–160.

Stanton, M. D. (1978a). The family and drug misuse: a bibliography. *American Journal of Alcohol and Drug Abuse* 5:151–170.

——— (1978b). Heroin addiction as a family phenomenon: a new conceptual model. *American Journal of Drug and Alcohol Abuse* 5:125–150.

——— (1979a). Drugs and the family. *Marriage and Family Review* 2:1–10.

——— (1979b). Family treatment approaches to drug abuse problems: a review. *Family Process* 18:251–280.

——— (1980). Some overlooked aspects of the family and drug abuse. In *Drug Abuse from the Family Perspective,* ed. B. G. Ellis, pp. 1–17. Rockville, Md.: National Institute on Drug Abuse.

Stephens, R. C. (1980). The hard drug scene. In *Drugs and the Youth Culture,* ed. F. R. Scarpitti and S. K. Datesman, pp. 59–79. Beverly Hills, Calif.: Sage Publications.

Wegscheider, S. (1976). *The Family Trap.* Crystal, Minn.: Nurturing Networks.

❦ 6 ❦

Therapeutic Interventions in Delinquency

Thomas F. Johnson, Ph.D.

Family theory is creating an important shift in the way delinquency is understood. Historically, theories of delinquency have been concerned with questions about the delinquent. The essential question, whether stated or implied, was, "What is wrong with him or her?" It has generally been assumed that the act of delinquency was prima facie evidence that something had happened to the individual to cause the delinquent behavior. That cause might be thought of as social forces, psychological forces, or biological forces, but whatever the postulated determiners, the question was how they made the delinquent act that way, with the underlying implication that a change had taken place that made the affected individual different from other people. The nineteenth century witnessed an acceleration in the sciences and scientific thought that produced theories that were both positivist and determinist. In the study of crime and delinquency the focus was, increasingly, on finding out what was wrong with the individual.

Family theory represents the first movement in a different direction, and it is in the nature of family studies to ask another kind of question. Family theorists are more likely to ask, "What is the delinquent member trying to accomplish with his or her family?" The assumption that the delinquency did something negative to the family has given way to the awareness that delinquency could also make a positive contribution to the family and that all family members have some degree of involvement in what the identified delinquent is trying to do. Theorists have traveled a path from concern about how the personality was organized, through the development of several theoretical family models, to concern for how the family was organized.

PSYCHODYNAMIC PSYCHOTHERAPY, BEHAVIOR MODIFICATION, AND SYSTEMS THEORY

Family theories tend to fall into two broad groups, those that still attempt to deal with the individual psychodynamic and behavioral modification and those that espouse some form of systems theory, for example, Bowenian, structural, organizational, and the like. The distinction is one of emphasis, since all family theorists, by definition, are concerned about the family. All, therefore, recognize the family as a system with which to reckon.

Behavioral Approaches

Most behavioral theorists working with delinquents do not include the family. Those who do, define the problem as a learning problem, also, and consider the family as forming interlocking systems with reciprocal behaviors. One of the advantages of behavioral models is the absence of labeling. No one is considered to be sick, irrational, or responsible. There is a shift from the individuals to their mode of relating to and dealing with one another, but a problem exists because there is a strong tendency to ignore the way that families are structured, and the participants tend to be treated as peers (Liberman 1970).

There seems to be no special view of delinquent behavior. This would seem to be an outgrowth of the general theoretical position that behavior is learned and that dysfunctional behavior requires new learning. The general feeling is that somehow the individual did not learn and therefore has acquired faulty patterns of behavior.

Psychodynamic Theory

Many theorists have been unwilling to abandon their psychoanalytic origins. Freud himself recognized the importance of parental influence and, in at least one instance, elected to treat the parent rather than the child (Freud 1976). Child guidance centers were organized in order to treat parents as well as children, and the papers emerging from these centers detailed the ways that delinquency related to parents (Johnson and Szurek 1952).

Ackerman (1958) continued to attempt to forge a link between the dynamic individual concepts and those of families as systems. Framo (1980) and Pearce and Friedman (1980), along with many others, continue trying to build a bridge. What they hold in common is a view of the family as the primary influence in the development of the personality and as the chief source for acculturation processes. Typically, attention is given to the influence of the family members on one another; especially to the impact of the parents on their children in the development of repressed conflicts. More recently the historical chain has been extended to the grandparents and great-grandparents (Boszormenyi-Nagy and Spark 1973). Special importance is given to understanding, and so an important part of the therapist's concern is directed toward gaining knowledge, eliciting feelings, and interpreting content.

Ackerman (1966) saw the delinquent as a scapegoat, and in serving as scapegoat, he or she helped the parents maintain a precarious relationship. Boszormenyi-Nagy and Spark (1973) extended this view, indicating that delinquency may serve to bring feuding parents together and thus divert attention from their mutual destructiveness. They pointed out that many delinquents are committed to a sacrificially negative role. Their delinquent behavior is implicitly sanctioned because the acts gratify the parents' dependent needs. Other members of the family who are overly righteous are given the opportunity to participate vicariously in delinquency and at the same time feel morally superior. Delinquency, then, may be a revolt against the parents in order to repair suffered injustice. Thus, Boszormenyi-Nagy and Spark presented delinquency as an unconscious effort to revive the family, making chastisement and punishment preferable to noninvolvement.

Bowenian Theory

Murray Bowen has been in the forefront of family theorists for many years. His efforts to develop a language appropriate to systems theory and his contributions to therapy make him unique, and his influence places him at the head of his own school.

For him, the delinquent is the result of a family projection process by which a family problem is transmitted to one family member through years of nagging pronouncements and then is fixed in place with a label (Bowen 1971). The so-labeled delinquent has been triangled in by two other family members who are trying to maintain togetherness and need the third to help them (Bowen 1978).

Communication Theory

From (and including) Bowen onward, the theorists can be identified by their view of the identified patient (IP), the delinquent, or whoever as the keys to the pathological balance of a set of ongoing relationships (Hoffman 1971). They do not try to understand the delinquent but, instead, try to understand what the scapegoated member is doing for the family as a system. Their position is that the individual view badly misrepresents the nature of scapegoating and that labeling makes the identity seem to be fixed, whereas the roles of the different family members may shift from time to time. The particular difficulty is better understood, and the therapeutic interventions can be more directly related to the difficulty when the family pathology instead of the individual is emphasized.

Communication theory is derived from the work of the group involved with Gregory Bateson in the 1950s. Watzlawick, Beavin, and Jackson (1967) and Haley (1963) who were of that group, presented the logic of communication theory, making clear that human interaction is concerned with the present relationship of family members and the rules that govern this relationship. Specific behavior, such as delinquency, is dependent on the family's current needs and the kinds of messages being sent within the system. If the system needs to improve its cohesiveness, the delinquent's behavior will help promote solidarity and highlight norms of behavior (Hoffman 1971). If the family needs external controls, the activity of the delinquent will serve to bring them to the attention of the authorities or whomever. Whether the activity of the IP takes the form of delinquency or some other form depends on the kinds of messages being sent. The messages could be as follows: "You're crazy"; "you're hopeless"; "you're incompetent"; "you're bad." If the messages are focused on badness, the action will take the form of delinquency. These messages are sent in many guises, ranging from accusation to solicitude. They may be couched in terms of what the parents cannot do; for example, "I don't know what to do about you," as well as what is expected, "Be careful and stay out of trouble."

The messages are not restricted to verbal expressions but include the full range of nonverbal statements. Careful note is made of who sits where, changes in posture and attitude, the sequences of behavioral events, and the gestures, gazes, and shifting of location in the room. As Scheflen (1968) showed, the patterns appear in relatively unvarying sequences and are very repetitive. They have a cyclic, automatic quality and represent a grammar of command to, or comment on, relationships in the group.

Structural Theory

Best exemplified by Minuchin (1974), structural theory does not abandon communication but focuses on the importance of the family's maintaining appropriate relationships. The failure to maintain appropriate closeness between spousal pairs, the overinvolvement of a spouse with a child, or any deviation from what is perceived as sound structure can breed disturbed behavior.

Minuchin also observed that in families with delinquent children, the parents' control is dependent on their presence (Minuchin and Fishman 1981). The family's communication patterns are chaotic, and the members do not expect to be heard. In such families, relationship messages per se are more important than their content. Although Minuchin's model has been criticized as being predicated on a middle-class orientation, my own experience suggests that the above patterns transcend class lines, being found throughout society, irrespective of class.

Organizational Theory

Gregory Bateson was perhaps the ultimate seminal thinker for social sciences in modern times. It was he who pointed out that delinquency is not an action or a kind of behavior, but a way of organizing behavior (Bateson 1979). This observation is profound and should be attended carefully, as it has had a revolutionary impact on the way problems are conceived. Since concepts both limit and extend thought, this is crucial.

Haley (1980) wrote on the importance of family organization and discussed the implications of organization for hierarchies. He presented hierarchies not as the consequence of family structure alone but as the consequence of communication. As communication becomes systematic, communication becomes the organization with hierarchic ordering. Youthful disturbances, which Haley subsumes under the term *madness*—which includes all forms of disturbed and disturbing behavior—are best understood as the results of a family life-stage in which reorganization is taking place. The youth's behavior is considered to be adaptive to that social context.

A theory that focuses on family organization seems to suit best the observable data on delinquency. The realm is broad enough to cover a wide range of phenomena, as there are no implications of being limited to particular social class or other demographic attributes. The concepts are flexible and imply ongoing change, and there is room for a variety of organization plans rather than a single ideal for a family.

PUTTING THE THEORY INTO PRACTICE

Psychodynamic Therapy

In their effort to help families understand their situation, therapists with psychodynamic orientations rely on interpretation. The aim of such moves is to loosen the child's pathological defenses by breaking down the parents' pathological defenses (Ackerman 1966). To weaken these defenses, therapists use a number of tactics to make the family realize their situation. The range of tools is impressive, including the use of dramatic improvisations, role playing, sculpting, videotape playback, photo albums, diaries, group tasks, one-way vision screens, and so forth.

Behavior Modifiers

The behavior modifiers' aim in therapy is to help the family members find new ways of responding to one another. Certain behaviors are identified as troublesome, and social reinforcement is used to modify the behavior. Such features as differential reinforcement and imitative learning are employed. In some instances, operant conditioning may be used.

Bowen's Therapy

Bowen's goals in therapy are to help the individual family members become system experts who become so familiar with the family system that they can correct it themselves. To do this, Bowen takes firm control of the proceedings, while at the same time defining himself as a consultant rather than a therapist. Having clearly established what he will and will not do, he sets out to help the individual differentiate himself or herself from the other family members. Bowen does this by working on the marital relationship and the relationship of each member to his or her family of origin. An important feature of this therapy is to persuade the family members that it is useless to attempt to influence, change, or depend on one another. Bowen states that he himself is not subject to being influenced, cannot be changed, and cannot be depended on in the therapy (Bowen 1971).

In helping the individual achieve an "I" position, Bowen assumes that ego-mass problems are not limited to the marital pair and their offspring but are triangulated within the family of origin as well. He therefore assigns the spouses the task of differentiating from their parents and freeing themselves of entanglements with their family of origin. It is assumed that the successful development of a higher level of differentiation from the parents will contribute to better differentiation between the spouses. And with improvement in the marital relationship, the children will be relieved of their symptoms.

The Communicators

Virginia Satir is one of the most charismatic therapists, using her great warmth and ability to lead and induce family members to work toward improving mutual esteem and communication. Satir does this by pointing out the difference between the meaning given and the meaning received; by being alert for covert, incongruent, or confused messages; and by leading the family into new ways of communicating, including demonstrating, responding, and sharing (Satir 1971). In this way respect for individual differences grows, and with it self-esteem, which Satir views as the basic problem.

The communicators focus on the need to change behavior. Jackson (1967) addresses this problem by attending to the family rules. Who has the right to do what to whom is the big question, and so the first aim of the therapist is to disturb the family system. Jackson uses two tactics to do this, relabeling and creating runaway situations by prescribing the symptom. When the family system is disturbed, it is more open to self-examination and can begin to work on developing new rules.

Structural Therapists

Minuchin and Fishman (1981) pointed out some important features of delinquent behavior. Parental control is often dependent on parental presence, and the disturbing behavior of many delinquents takes place only in situations in which they are not being supervised; they may be reasonably obedient and well behaved at home. Because this is so, it is very hard to obtain direct control over the behavior.

But in the families of delinquents, chaotic communication patterns are common; the family members do not expect to be heard. There are many tactics that may be used to help families regain proper structuring and, thereby, to relieve the children of having to act out. The basic assumptions are that when the parental relationship is sound and the relationship of the parents to the children is appropriate, with the parents setting the rules, providing limits, and guiding behavior, delinquency will disappear.

Organization Therapists

Organization theory, more than any other, emphasizes the positive contributions of delinquency. Rather than identifying the behavior as dysfunctional, organization theory points up its adaptive nature.

Organizational therapy is aimed at changing the family's social organization, since normal behavior can be appropriate only when the social organization is functioning well. For example, delinquent behavior is, by definition, irresponsible. It is important to note that such irresponsible activity is shared by the important people around the delinquent: parents, other family members, school officials, and so on. This further suggests that a therapist would ideally have to become involved with social forces beyond the immediate family. Obviously, there are limitations to what can be done about society, but there can be conferences with school officials, physicians, and others who may become involved with the delinquent. There are efforts, also, to remove the youngster from institutional settings whose social organization is such that it is beyond the therapist's ability to intervene successfully.

An important point regarding Haley's thinking about therapy is that he assumes that "the destination of the therapy will be determined by the choice of the problem . . ." (1980, p. 64). Therefore, in using therapy with disturbed youngsters, Haley tries to put the parents in charge of the problem and defines it as a "trouble-making" problem, on the grounds that that is something for which parents can assume responsibility. The parents are asked to help form a plan to deal with the specific problems, a plan with which they can work. Care is taken not to undermine parental authority and at the same time to restore normality at the earliest possible time. If behavior is adaptive to a situation, then a normal situation must be arranged in order to achieve normal behavior.

UNDERSTANDING DELINQUENT BEHAVIOR

Delinquency as a subject has so many aspects that it is hard to know where to begin. There are two important points that should be made at the outset if one is to avoid the intellectual minefields and the emotional booby traps that strew the way. Classical criminology would have no trouble with the statement that delinquency is a product of a particular time and place, but the positivists might overlook the fact that legal codes change, and as they change, new behaviors are proscribed, and others become acceptable or, at least, unpunishable. Because of these changes, the concept of delinquency may say more about the social climate of a locale than it does about the person whose status has altered.

The second point that should be made is that everyone has the capacity to act in ways that may be labeled delinquent (Johnson 1978). To ignore this is to set up a false dichotomy between delinquents who are caught in the juvenile justice system and those who are not. Those who are involved in that system and with delinquents who may or may not be in the system are aware of how meaningless such a distinction is. The principal difference is that for the delinquents who are involved with the justice system, there is the necessity of doing something about them. The youths become the concern of various agents of social control who must identify them according to their functions. If a delinquent is defined as a threat to the community, measures will be taken to minimize that threat. These measures may range from supervision by the courts to being removed from the community. Special programs may be devised, including some form of psychotherapy. What these measures do, of course, is to label the offender as different and, in some way, dysfunctional. The focus is placed on the offender and kept there. This is very comforting for the rest of us, because it assures us that we are not responsible for what has taken place. The need to feel absolved is understandable. Absolution, however, is all too often obtained at the expense of others, who are trying to make the best of a very difficult situation. In doing so, matters are made worse, not only for those who are subjected to control measures, but also for those who become locked into endless, escalating struggles to control the delinquent.

Bateson's comment on certain forms of activity as being names for ways of organizing actions included crime and, by extension, led to the recognition that delinquency is a name for a way of organizing actions, too. The important questions became questions of what the delinquents were trying to do with the situation in which they found themselves. More specifically, what were they trying to do with their families? To what were the delinquents responding?

Behavior is not organized in a particular way because the individual decides what to do; rather, behavior becomes organized as a result of the interactions among people. Since the work of Bowen, we have come to look for three people as a minimal condition for organizing behavior. Within the nuclear family we think of father, mother, and child, but the setting may also include grandparents and others. Similarly, among delinquent populations there are many single-parent families, in which case we look for relations or friends who may be triangled with the parent and child.

It is by means of the communications among these people that organization takes place. The attitudes expressed by each member toward the others and the deference, hostility, defensiveness, affection, and so on, however conveyed, all help shape the organization. Who is entitled to do what, who fills a particular role, and who is obligated to whom are established in this way. There is not only the question of what rules the family has arranged but also how they were arrived at, how they are carried out, and by whom. Such fundamental aspects of relationship as trust, confidence of being emotionally supported, and reliability are worked out here and contribute to the organization of both the family and its members' activities. When there are problems with communication, the reasons have to do with disagreements about the relationships, which create instability. It is a bid for the reorganization of the relationship, and consequently it is a time in which unsocial and antisocial behavior appears. The distressing behavior of the young may take many forms in order to cope with the situation created by disorganization or movement toward reorganization. But what is of greater importance in dealing with delinquency is how this sort of problem is labeled. Many still speak of delinquent youngsters as incorrigible. This implies both willfulness and determination on the youth's part and also suggests that nothing can be done about it. It then becomes incumbent on the state to take charge, with the expectation that the youngster will be locked up somewhere.

Another kind of labeling defines the problem as mental illness. This definition requires the development of treatment plans aimed at helping the delinquent youngster acquire healthier patterns of behaving. This implies that delinquent acts are symptomatic of a disordered psyche, a proposition that is very hard to support when one examines the broad spectrum of juveniles who have been adjudicated delinquent.

What these two types of definitions do is make very clear that delinquency is the result of something going on inside the delinquent that makes him or her behave in a certain way. These definitions assume that the behavior is dysfunctional, to the extent it is disturbing to others. The consequences of any definition are that it determines the ways in which the problem is understood and the manner in which the solutions to it are devised. And identifying delinquent activity as either incorrigibility or mental illness has not corrected it. It is time to pursue another course. If delinquency is seen as a way of organizing acts in order to cope with a problem in family organization, it is immediately possible to begin to search for the organizational problems and to devise ways for correcting them. This is not to claim the task is simple, for it is not. But the efforts will be guided rationally.

Complex as the organizational problems may be, identifying them may be the easiest part of the job. Helping a family improve its organization is a much more difficult task. Some delinquents act against their parents. One or both parents seem to be locked into a protracted and exhausting struggle to persuade their child(ren) to be respectful, to adhere to parental rules and expectations, and to behave responsibly. In these situations the organization problems can usually be quickly recognized, and corrective action can be planned. Most of the explanations of delinquent behavior fall into this group. The behavior may be intended, among other things, to bring the parents together for joint action, to provide the family with an excuse for external control, to revolt against the parents in order to repair injustices, or to force the parents into care-taking activities.

But many delinquents are relatively respectful, cooperative, and obedient at home. Nevertheless, when they are beyond their parents' physical reach, the rules no longer hold. It is more difficult to discover the nature of the organization problems when this condition exists, because the parents are not dissatisfied with the child, are puzzled by the events in which their child has become involved, and are at a loss as to what to do about it. Among children such as these are delinquents whose activity vicariously satisfies the parents' and other family members' desires to be delinquent. In this class, also, may be found delinquents who are avenging their parents for losses they are believed to have suffered at the hands of society.

Parents of many delinquents do not desire to work as a family, but their pain and exhaustion may make them amenable to participating in family therapy. They may take the position that they are at a loss as to what may be done. They have, in their view, "tried everything," and so they pose a great challenge to a therapist's skill and ingenuity. These parents do not admit to a problem that in any way involves them, nor do they see how they could exert control beyond the distance that they can see, hear, or reach. Their passivity is often insurmountable.

One of the dilemmas posed by carrying out therapeutic interventions with delinquents is the question of whom one is representing. If one is representing the court, this can be an especially difficult problem. Presumably, the court is the employer and, therefore, is entitled to the therapist's expert knowledge. If the courts are more sophisticated, they are sometimes willing and able to support therapeutic services for those brought before the court without asking for information about the therapy. This allows the therapist the freedom to serve the court by serving the court's clients as well as he or she is able.

There remains one more important problem to be solved, the matter of how one conducts therapy with involuntary clients. Not all clients who are referred by the courts are unwilling to take part, but there are many who would not present themselves for therapy if it were not for their legal problems. Although there are parents who have been seeking help for a long time and are glad of this opportunity, many youngsters want no such service because they suspect that they are "it," and they reject this role. Other parents do not want to be involved, because it is their child who is in trouble. Besides, requiring their presence implies that their child's behavior is both their responsibility and their fault, and they do not wish to accept either responsibility or blame. But many families accept service so as not to annoy the court and bring further action against themselves or their child. They come with reservations, if not with the intent of superficial compliance.

The initial therapeutic task is to engage these clients. It is important to treat them considerately and with respect. To begin by informing parents that they have problems that are affecting their offspring and that, therefore, they are part of the problem is not only poor therapy but is also downright rude. The introduction to therapy should begin with a social period, sometimes referred to as *joining*, or some similar name. Moving along toward the business at hand, the family is advised that they have been assembled to participate in finding ways to keep their identified patient (IP) from further involvement with the court. Their ideas, knowledge, and judgments should be valued, since they know more about their IP's problems than anyone else is likely to. The process of engagement is continued by asking each of the family members about the presenting problem(s). Care is taken to head off scapegoating and to encourage personal statements of the range of thoughts and feelings that were experienced when they learned of the IP's involvement. Usually delinquents begin such meetings with either a proper air of contrition and shame or one of surly resistance. But as their parents and siblings voice their concerns and share their personal distress and sometimes important family struggles, the delinquents' chins rise, their bodies straighten, and the hangdog, dejected, or defiant attitudes disappear. They become participants in examining family problems rather than scapegoats for the family's distress.

The presence of the entire family is diagnostically important. The family meeting lets the therapist observe the members' interaction, the parents' parenting style, and other valuable information about the family's organization.

After the exploratory phase, the parents are asked to identify the problem(s) that most concern them. Which parent is approached first may depend on what the therapist already has surmised about the cultural norm for that particular family, the power balances within the family, the therapist's wish to convey a message to the family or to a particular member, and so on. In my experience, the problems are usually stated in relation to the delinquent behavior, and one of them can be selected as a starting point. One of the parents is asked what he or she would like to do about the problem and, from the ensuing discussion, is encouraged to work on a plan of action. The other parent is brought into the discussion, and a negotiation between the parents is begun while at the same time maintaining the focus on what to do about the child. The therapy may cover a whole range of family problems, though concentrating on handling the delinquency.

Some families have trouble resolving their problems, and so they may wish to talk about their child's not wanting to get up in the morning, teasing the cat, not doing homework, and the like. In doing so, they ignore the serious behavioral problems of their children who have been engaged in crime. These parents are advised that the problems they present may need attention at some point but that there are other problems (e.g., rape, assault, arson, or whatever) that have priority.

Some families express hopelessness and the conviction that all is beyond them. They not only do not respond to efforts to involve them in working out a problem but also loudly assert their unwillingness to act. Although it is important to maintain a respectful and supportive stance, it is also important to be clear and firm about the outcome of the decision to do nothing. Such parents are advised that they may be correct about their inability to function; their limitations are recognized as important; and they are given a sketch of the alternatives. It is made clear that the choice is theirs, and their readiness to live with one or another of the alternatives is examined in some detail.

Clarity and firmness at such times are essential. Some families attempt to produce chaotic situations to cut off the therapist's efforts, and so tactics for settling chaos need to be part of the therapist's arsenal. When one or more children behave inappropriately or disrespectfully or ignore rules or whatever, the therapist should be ready to establish limits either directly or by appealing to the parents' authority. These situations provide excellent opportunities for not only judging parental effectiveness, motivation, and the like but also initiating changes in the family organization.

The key to understanding delinquency and to developing appropriate responses to it, I believe, lies in the understanding that delinquency is a name for a way of organizing action. Those actions that are known by the name of delinquency are themselves a form of communication resulting from problems in organization. And the level at which we have elected to work is the level of family organization.

REFERENCES

Ackerman, N. (1958). *The Psychodynamics of Family Life.*
New York: Basic Books.
—— (1966). *Treating the Troubled Family.* New York:
Basic Books.
Bateson, G. (1979). *Mind and Nature: A Necessary Unity.* New
York: Dutton.
Beels, C., and Ferber, A. (1969). Family therapy: a view. *Family
Process* 8:280–318.
Boszormenyi-Nagy, I., and Spark, G. (1973). *Invisible Loyalties.*
New York: Harper and Row.
Bowen, M. (1971). The use of family therapy in clinical practice.
In *Changing Families*, ed. J. Haley, p. 169. New York:
Grune and Stratton.
—— (1978). *Family Therapy in Clinical Practice.* New York:
Jason Aronson.
Framo, J. (1980). Introduction. In *Family Therapy: Combining
Psychodynamic and Family Systems Approaches*, ed. J. K. Pearce
and L. J. Friedman, pp. vii–xi. New York: Grune and Stratton.
Freud, S. (1976). Analysis of phobia in a five-year-old boy. In
The Complete Psychological Works of Sigmund Freud, Vol. 10,
ed. J. Strachey, pp. 5–148. New York: Norton.
Haley, J. (1963). *Strategies of Psychotherapy.* New York: Grune
and Stratton.
—— (1976). *Problem Solving Therapy.* San Francisco: Jossey-Bass.
—— (1980). *Leaving Home: The Therapy of Disturbed Young
People.* New York: McGraw-Hill.
——, ed. (1971). *Changing Families.* New York: Grune and Stratton.
Hoffman, L. (1971). Deviation amplifying processes in natural
groups. In *Changing Families*, ed. J. Haley, pp. 285–311. New
York: Grune and Stratton.
Jackson, D. (1967). The eternal triangle. In *Techniques of Family
Therapy*, ed. J. Haley and L. Hoffman, pp. 174–264. New
York: Basic Books.
—— (1968). *Communication, Family and Marriage.* Palo Alto,
Calif.: Science and Behavior.
Johnson, A. M., and Szurek, S. A. (1952). The genesis of antisocial
acting out in children and adults. *Psychoanalytic Quarterly*
21:322–343.

Johnson, T. F. (1978). A contextual approach to treatment of
   juvenile offenders. *Offender Rehabilitation* 3:171-179.
Liberman, R. (1970). Behavioral approaches to family and couple
   therapy. *American Journal of Orthopsychiatry* 40:106-118.
Minuchin, S. (1974). *Families and Family Therapy.* Cambridge,
   Mass.: Harvard University Press.
————, and Fishman, H. C. (1981). *Family Therapy Techniques.*
   Cambridge, Mass.: Harvard University Press.
Pearce, J. K., and Friedman, L. J. (1980). *Family Therapy:
   Combining Psychodynamic and Family Systems Approaches.*
   New York: Grune and Stratton.
Satir, V. (1971). The family as a treatment unit. In *Changing
   Families,* ed. J. Haley, pp. 127-132. New York: Grune and
   Stratton.
Scheflen, A. (1968). Human communications: behavioral programs
   and their integration in interaction. *Behavioral Sciences* 13:44-55.
Speck, R., and Attneave, C. (1973). *Family Networks.* New York:
   Pantheon.
Watzlawick, P., Beavin, J., and Jackson, D. (1967). *Pragmatics of
   Human Communication.* New York: Norton.

✕ 7 ✕

Behavioral Therapy for Families with Child Management Problems

Ian R. H. Falloon, M.D.,
and Robert P. Liberman, M.D.

This chapter discusses the clinical application of behavioral family therapy in cases of parents who have problems managing their children. Training parents as behavior therapists is much more difficult than it might at first seem to be, and it is an indirect way of modifying the whole family interaction system. The parents are trained as behavior therapists, or as "stand-ins" for the professional. Since the explicit focus

This chapter was supported in part by NIMH Grants MH-33138 and MH-30911, and in part by NIHR Grant G-008006802.

is on the child, and changes in parent behavior are "to manage the child," there tends to be much less resistance and defensiveness by the parents. The parents' behavior toward the child and other family members is changed in order to modify the child's behavior, and these changes in the parents' behavior may have lasting importance on the child's development.

Parent training as a way of modifying family behavior has many practical features to recommend it. First, there are not enough qualified therapists to treat all the problem children who need help. So, not only can parent training relieve therapists from having to treat children directly, but it also can build competence in the parents, who can be the first to intervene when new problems first present themselves. Such early intervention can greatly reduce the costs and difficulties in correcting a behavior problem, since well-trained parents are likely to stop it before it becomes serious enough to invest the money and energy to consult a professional. Thus, parent training is a way of moving child mental health from intervention to prevention.

It is much easier for a parent than for a mental health consultant to prevent behavior problems, because the parent naturally controls the child's main reinforcers. Many reinforcers, such as social reinforcement from a parent, simply and obviously are not transferrable to another person, such as the therapist. Also, training parents makes it much easier for children to use the new behaviors they learn, because they do not have to transfer stimulus control from a therapist to the people they have to respond to on a day-to-day basis.

Since transferring training is a major problem in generalizing any new learned behavior, avoiding the issue pays off handsomely in quicker and more durable changes in family behavior. Training the parents as behavior therapists also serves to modify their behavior toward the child, and not just the child's behavior. Therefore, parent training is also a way of intervening in the family contingency system at more than one point, and this increases the probability that the intervention will last after the mental health consultant has withdrawn, because more than one person has intervened in the system.

There are many approaches to training parents, each with its own advantages and disadvantages. For our discussion purposes, these can be divided into modeling versus didactic approaches and office versus home implementation.

We organized in community mental health centers groups of up to

12 parents who participate in eight- to ten-week workshops in child management led by paraprofessionals and social workers. Over 4,000 parents have obtained training during the past ten years, and the Parent Training Workshop has become a mainstay of mental health centers' programs and their first line of service for child psychiatry. The great majority of the deviant children's problems can be diagnosed as "adjustment reaction of childhood," "unsocialized aggressive reaction of childhood," and "hyperkinetic reaction of childhood."

FAMILY TRAINING

Since a principal part of this parent training effort is to remedy the presenting problems, our workshop format includes approximately one hour of general didactic material and one hour of individual case consultation and intervention for each meeting. Both general and spe-

Table 7-1

BEHAVIOR PROBLEMS REPORTED AS "SEVERE" BY PARENTS
PARTICIPATING IN THE WORKSHOP

BEHAVIORAL PROBLEM	PERCENTAGE RATING AS "SEVERE"
Disobedience; difficulty in disciplinary control	52
Disruptiveness; tendency to annoy and bother others	49
Fighting	45
Talking back	43
Short attention span	42
Restlessness; inability to sit still	40
Irritability; easily aroused to intense anger	37
Temper tantrums	35
Attention seeking; "show-off" behavior	35
Crying over minor annoyances	33
Lack of self-confidence	33
Hyperactivity; "always on the go"	33
Distractibility	33
Specific fears; phobias	17
Bed wetting	16

cific interventions are presented through a combination of lecture, discussion, and behavior rehearsal with modeling and feedback.

The general curriculum is outlined in Table 7-2. At the first meeting, the social learning model of child behavior is presented and compared with other orientations, or schools, of psychotherapy. The concept of a behavior is described, and the parents are taught how to observe their children's behavior. Parents also learn that normal and abnormal behaviors are on a continuum and have similar causes and explanations in the social learning model.

Parents are instructed to specify a behavior that not only is of major concern to them but that they also can correct. If possible, the parents identify an appropriate behavior that they would like to encourage, since this will require a positive parent-child interaction rather than criticism, ignoring, or punishment.

In subsequent workshop sessions, parents bring in a daily count of the behavior that they have identified and are observing. After one or two weeks of record keeping, the leader suggests ways for the parents to redirect this behavior into a desired direction. The parents continue their observations and data records on a daily basis until they find a successful intervention strategy. When the parents are satisfied with the behavior change, they identify a second behavior problem and begin the intervention process again.

In the workshop, parents cover the antecedents and consequences of behavior, the importance of reinforcing consequences for behavior, the types of reinforcers available to parents, reinforcer fading, bribes versus rewards, social modeling, shaping, role punishment, kinds of punishment, and how to use each.

For all these topics, parents read homework assignments from a text on child management (Eimers and Aitchison 1977).

At the beginning of each meeting, a brief quiz on the reading assignment is given in order to encourage the parents to complete their assignments. The training does not include discussion or airing of complaints.

A series of role-playing experiences teaches parents how to use social reward (reinforcement), mild social punishment, ignoring, and time-out procedures. For each of these child management techniques there are specific behaviors to encourage them; for example, when praising their children, the parents should smile and lean toward their children, commending them in a warm tone of voice immediately after

Table 7-2
OUTLINE OF CURRICULUM

I. Purposes and rationale
  A. Ground rules and deposit
  B. Readings and assignments
  C. Our consulting contingent on home-recorded data

II. The causes of behavior and how behavior can be changed

III. The social learning model

IV. What is a behavior?
  A. Observation and specification
  B. Normal versus abnormal (disturbing) behavior
  C. Assigning parents to begin thinking about one behavior to work on

V. What is learning?
  A. The ABCs of behaviors (antecedents, behavior, consequences)
  B. Reinforcement and motivation: increasing rates of desirable behavior
    1. Types (social, nonsocial) of reinforcers
    2. Advantages of social reinforcers
    3. Behavioral components of effective social reinforcement (role playing)
  C. Modeling
  D. Shaping techniques, the importance of reinforcing approximations to one's expectations

VI. Ways of decreasing undesirable behavior
  A. What is punishment?
    1. Punishment not defined by type of pain inflicted
    2. Functionally, punishment defined by its suppressing effect on behavior
    3. Pain and aggression unnecessary, thus reducing parental guilt and anxiety
  B. The forms of punishment
    1. Ignoring
    2. Mild social punishment
    3. Time out from reinforcement
  C. When and where to use each type
  D. Behavioral components of effective punishment (role playing)
  E. Special problems in the use of punishment

VII. Combining reinforcement and punishment to change behavior
  A. Special motivational systems
    1. Tokens, points, stars
    2. Contingency contracting

VIII. Forecasting behavioral problems as a parent and learning how to handle future relationship between parents and child the appropriate behavior has occurred. Parents practice each of these techniques as they would be used in a typical setting. Group leaders model appropriate interactions and give feedback to each parent on the nonverbal and verbal behavioral components of their performance. Behavioral rehearsal with modeling can be effectively augmented by using a "bug-in-the-ear" device so that instructions and feedback (Weathers and Liberman 1973) can be given to the parents while they are trying to manage the behavior of their child or that of the person in the workshop taking the role of the child. Parents usually learn quickly with this prompting and reinforcing device. If the direct approach to training is used in the home, the therapist and the parent usually continue to alternate roles in managing the child's behavior until the parent becomes proficient.

This form of behavioral family therapy—training parents to serve as therapeutic mediators for their children—is based on the following principles and strategies.

Behavioral Analysis

The behavioral approach to family therapy is still often equated with specific behavioral change techniques, such as contingency contracting or operant conditioning procedures. Behavior therapy, although based largely on the principles of social learning theory, is somewhat set apart in its willingness to experiment with a broad range of intervention methods, if they can be empirically shown to be effective. This emphasis on measuring the effectiveness, at any particular treatment modality, on a person, group, or family system is more basic to the approach than is its adherence to a specific intervention or package of interventions. The uniqueness of every individual and his or her interpersonal environment is emphasized.

During the assessment phase, behavior therapists may see the family together or conduct interviews with individual family members. These initial interviews seek to:

1. Gather detailed information about each informant's observations of and thoughts and feelings about the presenting problem.
2. Gather information about each informant's interaction within the family system; his or her attitudes, feelings, and behavior toward the other family members; and his or her motivation and ability to change the presenting problem.

3. Gather information about each informant's function outside the family system and his or her assets and deficits.
4. Build rapport with the informants.

The presenting problem is used as a starting point for analyzing the family system. Each part of the system is examined in order to discover the dysfunctional system that underlies the problem. Once each household member has been interviewed, a picture of the problem behavior is formed, and the problem can be better defined. In addition, there may be a number of testable hypotheses concerning the meaning or function of the problem situation within the family system. It is assumed that the problem is the result of the family's best effort at coping with their current life situation. The family comes for therapy because they are unable to sustain their coping efforts, are suffering from the wear and tear of their coping efforts, or anticipate a breakdown in their coping performance. This is not to say that the problem is *caused* by defective coping but that with more effective coping the distress associated with the problem would not have led to professional consultation.

In addition to the exhaustive behavioral analysis of the family members, the behavioral therapist examines the interaction among the family members. Whereas traditional family therapists examine the interaction of family members in a therapy group setting, behavioral therapists will make naturalistic observations. This approach was pioneered by Dr. Gerald Patterson in Oregon, where he coded in detail the behavior of families at home (Patterson et al. 1967). Although much more information may be acquired from a single home visit, alternative ways of observing the family pattern of interaction have been developed. Perhaps the most widely used method is to observe, in the clinic, the family's attempting to solve a family problem. This method has been used for assessing communication and problem-solving deficits in marital (Weiss et al. 1973, Liberman et al. 1976) and family therapy (Falloon et al. 1982). Some of these communication problems include poor eye contact, interruptions, speaking for the other person, digressing from the subject, and inappropriate nonverbal expression. Problem-solving defects may include lack of problem definition, lack of discussion of potential solutions, lack of knowledge of alternative suggestions, and lack of evaluation of the consequences of a proposed solution.

Assessments of family interaction may be recorded for detailed analysis later and may be repeated at intervals during and after treatment to assess progress. In addition to examining general communication and problem solving, specific behavior may be observed. Patterns of interaction, excessive use of criticism or coercion, sequences leading to aggressive behavior, or intrusive comments may be analyzed when a particular hypothesis is being considered.

Each problem is discussed, including whether or not its correction will lead to positive change, which in turn forms the basis for further observation. The principal problem usually is revealed here, even though it may not be able to be treated effectively. For example, it was hypothesized that the parents of Liza, a 20-year-old girl with a fear of sharp objects, scapegoated her with incessant criticism and gave her minimal encouragement to develop her independence, which contributed to her feelings of insecurity and incapacitating fears. While attempting to have her parents identify and express positive feelings toward Liza, it became clear to the family therapist that the major family problem was not her fears but the father's lack of confidence, which was manifested in a serious drinking problem. Liza's anxiety appeared linked to father's alcoholic binges and his unpredictable behavior toward both her and mother at those times. Liza feared leaving her mother alone with her father for fear that he might seriously harm her. She had noted that her fears were related to both threatening gestures that her father had made and sharp objects, particularly when her father held them. She was afraid that the sharp objects might fly out of control and damage her eyes or genitals.

The initial therapeutic emphasis on communicating positive feelings proved surprisingly difficult for the family in the realization that a more serious problem existed. After three sessions the family secret was revealed, and a new approach was adopted that required an analysis of the impact of the father's drinking behavior on the family system. It was ascertained that father began drinking after mother nagged him about his unsuccessful career, and so the intervention plan was modified to deal with this.

Functional Analysis: A Behavioral System

The behavioral approach postulates that patterns of family interaction are learned over repeated episodes and many trial-and-error experiences. In time the most frequently occurring behavior is that which proves the most rewarding for each member of that family system, given the system's constraints on him or her. In an optimal family setting, each member's potential is enhanced by the reciprocal exchange of reinforcement with the other members. In a dysfunctional system, the converse is true, and so each person's potential is thwarted or only his or her weaknesses are reinforced. The pleasing behavior is ignored or taken for granted, whereas the unpleasant behavior is accorded considerable attention. Even deficits and negative interaction patterns may be considered coping mechanisms, however, and may represent the family's best efforts to deal with their mutual problems. This mutual reinforcement paradigm is similar to the systems theory concepts used in other models of family therapy.

Thus, a functional analysis defines how individuals, their family members, and social network respond to the problem behavior, either to reduce its threat or to incorporate it into their accepted pattern of interaction (i.e., to cope with it). Coping may range from passive acceptance of the problem, to attempts to eliminate the problem, to active support of the problem. It is assumed that the problem behavior provides positive as well as negative functions within the family system. Liza's behavior in supporting her mother from her unpredictable alcoholic father helped her parents' marriage, but prevented her from becoming independent. Thus, in the functional analysis the family therapist tried to answer the following questions:

1. How does this problem handicap this person (and his or her family) in everyday life?
2. What would happen if this problem were ignored?
3. What would happen if this problem occurred less frequently?
4. What would this person (and his or her family) gain if the problem were removed?
5. Who reinforces the problem with attention, sympathy, or support?
6. Under what circumstances is the problem reduced in intensity? Where? When? With whom?
7. Under what circumstances is the problem increased in intensity?

An example of this functional analysis process can be found in a further assessment of Liza. Liza's major complaint was a fear of sharp objects, especially those associated with her father. The problem handicapped her in her family life, making her afraid to be at home with her father. When she visited women friends, however, she was much less fearful, though men friends who appeared attracted to her increased her phobic anxiety, and so she avoided anything more than superficial contacts with men. She had had several clerical jobs, but none had lasted. Invariably, casual contact with a man at work had upset her and led to her leaving the job. Her fear of sharp objects was greatest in the presence of her father, particularly if he had been drinking. It was least when she attended a women's exercise group at a community college. The neuroleptic medication that several psychiatrists had prescribed (based on a diagnosis of schizophrenia!) did not reduce her fears but slowed her thinking, made her feel tense inside, and caused her to pace excessively.

Had Liza's problem been less intense, she believed that she could lead a nearly normal life. She wanted to leave home and share an apartment with a friend, get a job, and begin dating men. She thought the stress that this problem caused at home would be relieved, her mother would be happy again, and her father would stop drinking. Her mother agreed that there would probably be less tension in the household but did not believe that this would change her father's drinking. Liza's mother said she would miss Liza's company and "wouldn't know what to do with her time." Her father blamed Liza and insisted that his drinking would be controlled if only his daughter were "cured."

Liza and her parents claimed that sometimes they had ignored the problem, which had resulted in brief improvement, after which Liza's fears had become worse. The mother and father used much of their shared time discussing Liza, and their conversations with Liza centered on "how her fears were," and "did she feel well enough to do such and such?" Her mother accompanied Liza almost everywhere, never went to bed before her, and carefully planned family interaction to minimize her fears; for example, she prepared Liza special meals that she ate alone in her room so that she would not have to interact with her father while he was eating with a knife and fork.

It is clear that this family accorded special status to Liza's fear of sharp objects, which not only kept her mother and father from discussing their own problems but also was considered to be the major contributing factor in the problems of the other family members. Avoiding her father and leaving the house were two coping methods described. But as described earlier, Liza feared the consequences of leaving her mother alone with her alcoholic father. Liza's commitment to her mother was strong, and although she appeared to gain much from leaving home, she was unwilling to move out until her father had over-come his alcohol dependence. She daydreamed of a wonderful man rescuing her but believed she could not leave home without help from a person that her mother would listen to, probably a doctor. She would not consider making any decision that her mother would not fully endorse.

As a result of this functional analysis, the following treatment plan was devised:

Goal: To enable Liza to live an unrestricted life, regardless of her fears.

Steps: 1. Liza to spend one hour four days a week visiting friends on her own without consulting mother for approval.
2. Family to eat evening meal together three nights a week with conversation about everyday events, avoiding any mention of Liza's fears.
3. Mother and father to discuss their personal difficulties twice a week for 20 minutes without mentioning Liza's problem.
4. Father to attend alcohol rehabilitation program.
5. Liza to attend therapy to learn behavioral techniques for coping effectively with her fear of sharp objects.
6. Family therapy sessions to be held to assist in the implementation and monitoring of progress of the plans.

Patterns of Family Reinforcement

Patterns of human behavior are seldom random, although at times they may appear confused and disorganized. If we take the time to observe a family in their everyday lives, we will see sequences of behavior being repeated. Such patterns have been learned by the family members to have the most reinforcing consequences for the family system. In other words, families do the things that bring them the greatest rewards and do not do the things that result in few rewards. Although the sum of the rewards is usually positive, this is not always the case. At times, finding the least undesirable solution may be the best possibility. Not every family member may find the solution rewarding for himself or herself and may be the scapegoat from time to time. Nevertheless, no matter how unpleasant or destructive the pattern of behavior may appear to the extrafamilial observer, if it is the most frequent response to a specific situation, then it is probably the best alternative the family has in its current repertoire. This does not imply that it is the *only* alternative the family uses or that the family cannot be taught to adopt more effective and more rewarding sequences.

How can we determine which patterns of interaction are the most frequently used? There are several methods. The first is the clinical interview. We ask each family member what happens in response to any specific situation. This method is straightforward but has the disadvantage of being subject to the family members' perceptual distortions, as they each may observe different aspects of the response or remember only those sequences that involve them the most dramatically. Few families consistently agree on these behavioral patterns. The therapist's observation of spontaneous interaction among family members is seldom practical in the clinic, but it does provide more objective data. A compromise is to have the family observe their own responses to a specific situation and keep a diary or chart themselves. These diaries may reveal patterns of which the family members are quite oblivious and may constitute an effective therapeutic intervention.

The behavioral method does not accept potentially biased, indirect reports of family interaction but seeks to validate these reports through observation. An examination of the subjects' responses frequently reveals a considerable adaptive repertoire of family coping skills, including desirable alternatives. The therapeutic problem then is to cause the desired alternatives to occur more frequently than the unwanted responses. This is much easier than having to train an entirely new response.

The Reinforcement Survey

A helpful strategy in analyzing family interaction is a reinforcement survey. Family members are invited to describe their main activities and the people, places, and objects on which they spend most of their time, as it is assumed that these represent their most reinforcing situations. The family members are then asked on which activities, people, places, and things they would like to spend more time, if possible. Any discrepancies between the current interaction and the desired interaction are noted, as they may help disclose the individual's daily goals and motivations. A comparison of family members may reveal current or potential sources of conflict that may need to be considered in the treatment plan. One mother wanted her son to spend more time with her pursuing church activities, whereas the son wanted to spend his time with his girlfriend or on a sport or social club. Such a conflict of short-term goals did not seem to have an easy compromise, and restructuring the mother's expectations of her son was an essential part of the treatment.

As well as examining current and desired positive reinforcers, we also note situations that are avoided. These aversive stimuli may vary widely and, in addition to common phobias, may include a variety of family situations such as arguments, discussions about finances or sexual concerns, family meals, or family outings.

The reinforcement survey provides a fascinating picture of the family members' everyday activities and their intertwining sources of mutual reinforcement. Some families may show a clear pattern of

Table 7-3
REINFORCEMENT SURVEY

PEOPLE	Current Behavior: With whom does the subject spend most time (e.g., family members, friends, co-workers)?
	Desired Behavior: With whom would the subject like to spend more time?
PLACES	Current Behavior: Where does the subject spend most time (e.g., work, bedroom, kitchen, living room, yard, car, stores, church)?
	Desired Behavior: Where would the subject like to spend more time?
ACTIVITIES	Current Behavior: What activities does the subject spend most time doing (e.g., work, hobbies, social pursuits, doing nothing)?
	Desired Behavior: What activities would the subject like to spend more time doing?
OBJECTS	Current Behavior: What things does the subject spend most time with (e.g., books, hobbies, foods, drink, clothes, TV, stereo)?
	Desired Behavior: What things would the subject like to spend more time with (buy, possess)?
NEGATIVE REINFORCERS	What situations are aversive stimuli for subjects? What situations are avoided (e.g., people, activities, fears, social isolation)?

avoidance of intimacy, whereas others may show an overinvolved, interdependent pattern. Such reported behavior is used merely as a guideline for further exploration and is not in itself a valid representation of actual interactions. As we have already seen, reports of interaction behavior are subject to considerable distortion. In addition to the reinforcement survey, we often have family members keep diaries of their daily activities.

The reinforcement survey may reveal current or potential sources of reinforcement that could be valuable resources in the treatment program. These people, activities, or objects that are current reinforcers offer a positive basis on which to mediate change. For example, a meal that an adolescent son finds enjoyable may be used to reward him for helping with the household chores, or an activity that he would like to engage in more often, such as playing baseball with his father, could be the basis for more positive interaction between them. A knowledge of such reinforcers greatly enhances the therapist's ability to facilitate positive changes in the family system.

INTEGRATING THE FAMILY SYSTEM: PROVISIONAL TREATMENT PLANS

We have discussed several assessment procedures used in the behavioral approach to family problems. We should note that a considerable amount of time is required for a comprehensive behavioral assessment. The interviewer, like a skillful detective, tries to amass enough evidence to prove the relevance of the unwanted behavior to the family system. Like a detective, the approach must be flexible, including interviews as well as onsite inspection and observation of interaction. There should be little inference. Until the therapist is sure what part the dysfunctional behavior plays in the family, he or she should refrain from making a definitive treatment plan. Moreover, after a treatment strategy has been defined, the therapist should constantly monitor the changes so that the plan can be further modified to provide more efficient progress toward the specific goals. Sessions with family members may use various combinations of intervention strategies with various formats. No one format is considered useful for every case. The success of the approach depends more on the adequacy of the assessment phase than on the treatment techniques used subsequently. An incomplete assessment results in a situation akin to driving in a foreign city with an incomplete street map—a considerable amount of time may be spent trying to reach an unseen goal. The few extra hours spent completing the "map" may uncover surprisingly few steps to the destination.

Types of Behavioral Interventions

The interventions used by behavioral family therapists tend to be specific and directed toward helping the family resolve the problem. Once the initial behavioral assessment phase has been completed, the therapist reviews his or her findings with the family, and together they decide on one or more specific goals for their therapy. Such goals must be clearly defined before beginning any specific intervention and are structured so that they can be achieved readily within an agreed-upon time. Whenever possible the goals are chosen by the family, not imposed by the therapist. Throughout the therapy the therapist continues to serve as a teacher and facilitator of learning and change, though there may be occasions when he or she may need to take greater control over the family situation. In such situations, usually a major crisis, the therapist may take responsibility for solving the problem. At other times the therapist may teach the family, through modeling and then reinforcing the family's attempts, a new communication or problem-solving skill.

The choice of therapeutic strategy and the method by which it will be applied is determined in accordance with the behavioral goal to be achieved and the contingencies that have been elucidated through the behavioral analysis. It may be helpful to consider each family intervention as an experiment in behavior change. The therapist and the family collaborate to develop novel solutions to their problems by using their particular assets. Small, well-defined goals should be chosen initially so that this collaboration will be successful. This leads to increased confidence in the family's ability to change successfully, to an increased willingness to take responsibility for change, and to more data that can be used for subsequent interventions.

Although the techniques used in behavioral family therapy are not rigidly ordained, several strategic interventions that have been empirically derived from learning theory principles should be noted. These include contingency contracting; operant reinforcement strategies, including shaping and token reinforcement; rule setting; time out; behavior rehearsal, modeling, and communication skill training; and problem solving.

Contingency Contracting

The contingency contract is an interaction between two or more individuals that is governed by a set of rules that balances the rewards and costs. Stuart (1969), Patterson and Reid (1970), and Liberman (1970) applied these reciprocity concepts to family interaction in which conflicts had resulted from the excessive use of aversive control to solicit rewards, cooperation, and compliance from another family member. Such nagging, demanding coercive behavior was frequently reciprocated by the recipient with unpleasant responses. Thus, the goal of the contingency contract was to reverse this exchange by means of a mutual exchange of pleasant interaction behaviors. A written agreement between the warring factions was negotiated on the basis that each person was expected to give more than he or she received from the contract. The written contract was then signed by both parties, and compliance with the agreement was reviewed at subsequent sessions. A written contract may often be unnecessary, but it does have the advantage of spelling out the agreed responses and representing a firm commitment to behavior change. The contract frequently may have to be amended, and the therapist and the family should negotiate a specific exchange of pleasing behavior. Wherever possible, common everyday behaviors are preferred to occasional behavior.

> Example: Mr. and Mrs. V. expected their 15-year-old son, James, to spend most of his leisure time with them and his 9-year-old sister. But James refused to go on family visits to friends and relatives. The parents accused him of being lazy around the house, doing nothing to help, and lounging about in disgusting clothes watching rubbish on television. At times he lost his temper with both parents, swearing and calling them names.
>
> James felt his parents were always picking on him, showed no interest in him or his friends, and when they did talk with his friends, his mother embarrassed him by ridiculing him in front of them. He avoided family outings because his mother always told stories about how bad he was at home. He had pestered his father to help him with his math homework, but father always said he was too busy.

In the course of five meetings with the family, several contracts were negotiated, as listed below.

RESPONSIBILITIES	PRIVILEGES
JAMES	
Complete one major household chore to mother's satisfaction, e.g., clearing kitchen, taking out trash, vacuuming living room, watering plants.	Payment of 50 cents upon completion of chore.
Wear clean jeans every day when watching TV.	Watch 30 minutes of TV of own choosing.
Go on one family outing each week.	An ice-cream treat of own choosing.
MR. V.	
Help James with math for two hours in the evening.	A cup of tea in bed in morning.
Watch James play football.	Car washed.
MRS. V.	
Make two positive statements about James to his friends or relatives.	Tell mother one thing I like about her.

These contracted behaviors are highly specific, and a specific reward is contingent on completion of a clearly agreed-upon behavior. Another form of contract, known as the "quid pro quo" strategy, has been criticized in some circles. This variant makes the positive behavior of one person contingent on the positive behavior of the other. For example, Mr. V. would help James with his homework only when James carried out a household chore. If James did not first achieve his desired behavior, his father would not carry out his part of the contract.

The contracts negotiated by James and his parents were carried out reasonably well by all three. James had great difficulty expressing positive feelings toward his mother as a reward for her praising him to other people. He rehearsed this in the sessions on several occasions, and although it was evident that he had considerable affection for his mother, he would not verbally express these positive feelings. He was able to hug his mother without difficulty, although he expressed some embarrassment that a 15-year-old boy should be doing this.

Operant Reinforcement Strategies

The principles of operant reinforcement are central to all behavior therapy interventions. These interventions are successful when the therapist is able to guide the family members into changing their ways of dealing with one another. In behavioral therapy we can translate these ways of dealing with one another into consequences of behavior, or *contingencies of reinforcement*. Instead of rewarding maladaptive behavior with attention and concern, the family members learn to acknowledge and approve the desired behavior. It is clear that in daily interaction, relatively few of the actions performed in the family system engender either a positive or a negative reaction. Most of our daily activity passes without remark. But observations of distressed families reveal more and more angry attention to displeasing behaviors, which does not help solve the problems. This anger may be focused on one member, the scapegoat, or shared among a number of family members. The punishment that is apparently aimed at discouraging the undesired behavior has the paradoxical effect of perpetuating the deviant behavior, as a result of the attention and recognition that behavior receives. This is particularly so when less attention is gained for pleasing behavior. The mother who says, "Why should I praise Jimmy for all the good things he does when he wets the bed every night?" illustrates this dilemma.

Anything that tends to increase the future occurrence of the behavior that immediately preceded it is termed a *positive reinforcement*. In other words, people do the things that produce the rewards they want. Verbal and nonverbal means of giving attention and recognition are termed *social reinforcers*, in contrast with food or sex, which are termed *primary reinforcers*. Social reinforcement is one of the most powerful motivators of human behavior, and as such its skillful use can have powerful therapeutic effects.

Punishment is considered to occur when an agent tends to reduce the likelihood that the behavior that immediately preceded it will recur. In other words, people tend to stop doing things that produce unpleasant results. Some forms of aversive response (e.g., electric shock, pain, vomiting) have been used therapeutically (e.g., induced vomiting by disulfiram may reduce alcohol consumption). But the withdrawal of recognition, attention, and support, that is, the lack of social reinforcement, may also help extinguish behavior, for example, cooking, cleaning, paying the bills, being reliable, playing quietly, sexual behavior. Taking things for granted may thus have as profound an effect on a relationship as does the more overtly destructive negative behavior discussed above.

We have already discussed the contingency contracting methods that attempt to enhance levels of positive reinforcement. But there are other reinforcement strategies of encouraging behavior change.

Shaping (or Successive Approximation).   The process of encouraging a person to approximate his or her behavior according to a clearly defined goal is known as *shaping.* A parent's encouraging a baby to walk demonstrates this skill. With each attempted step the parent praises the child's efforts, and the baby shows slowly increasing competence. Negative features are ignored.

Token Economy.   One of the earliest behavioral strategies to enhance positive interaction on long-stay mental hospital units is known as the *token economy.* As the term suggests, an entire social structure is devised around the receipt of tokens for a specific desired behavior. These tokens are exchanged for tangible reinforcers, for example, food, entertainment, and privileges (Ayllon and Azrin 1968). Although it is difficult to apply this approach in its original form to an entire family system, variations have proved useful. This approach is particularly valuable if there is little motivation to change.

Extinction.   The absence of any reinforcement for a specific behavior leads to a reduction in its performance, according to social learning therapy. This rationale forms the basis of a strategy known as *extinction.* Simply stated, family members are instructed to ignore any undesirable behavior that they wish to extinguish in other family members. This strategy has several shortcomings that limit its applicability, however, the most obvious disadvantage is that the behavior to be extinguished must be ignored by *all members* in the target person's environment. This may extend beyond the immediate household to any persons who may acknowledge, attend to, or sympathize with the selected behavior. But when used in combination with the selective reinforcement of desired behaviors, extinction may be useful.

Time Out. *Time out* is a more structured form of extinction and is usually used when the social reinforcement of undesirable behavior is almost unavoidable. The family member exhibiting the unpleasant behavior is removed from contact with others for a brief period of time out. This strategy has proved useful in modifying severe behavioral disturbances in children whose parents have been trained to deal with temper tantrums or violent behavior by sending the child to a nonrewarding room for several minutes (duration clearly specified) with minimal fuss. The goal is to change the child's environment from one that reinforces the problem behavior to one that contains minimal reinforcement for that behavior.

The application of time-out procedures to adolescent and adult family members is somewhat difficult but has been successfully used as a means of reducing excessive family tension. Schizophrenics have been trained to monitor their tension levels and to excuse themselves from stressful discussions and take a walk or relax in their rooms. Parents have been similarly taught to cut short a discussion that appears to be getting out of hand and leading to ineffective, potentially violent problem solving.

Rule Setting

Defining the rules of family behavior is an important therapeutic intervention. When family members clearly violate the rights and expectations of the family as a whole, setting specific limits may help define the structure of family interaction. Covert rules exist in most families. Clearly specifying such rules may in itself help control inappropriate behavior. In other cases, rule setting will enable a consistent approach to modifying behavior considered undesirable by the consensus of the family group.

Behavior Rehearsal

Communication among family members includes both expressive and receptive behavior, by means of both nonverbal and verbal expression. Nonverbal communication is frequently the main expression of emotions such as affection or anger. Married couples often complain about the spouse's nonverbal behavior, such as "he doesn't look at me anymore," "she doesn't cuddle me as she used to," "he comes in drunk and beats me," "I can't get an erection," "she says she loves me, but she doesn't do anything to show it."

The behavioral approach to improving emotional communication uses the technique of *behavior rehearsal*. The situations in which communication is considered unsatisfactory are repeatedly rehearsed in therapy. The therapist and family members provide coaching and constructive suggestions for improvement. Particular attention is paid to nonverbal communication skills, such as eye gaze, facial expression, and feedback.

Communication training may include restructuring the expression of feelings through repeated rehearsal. The goal is to help the family members explore various behavioral responses in a nonthreatening setting, not to program individuals in stereotyped communication skills. The therapist may also suggest more effective communication behavior and may demonstrate these skills by taking the part of a family member in a role play with another therapist or other family members.

The communication skills most frequently introduced in family therapy are giving praise or compliments; making positive requests of family members in a nondemanding way; expressing negative feelings toward another family member; and active, empathic listening skills.

The use of behavior rehearsal as a means of changing interaction patterns is also a way of inducing accompanying attitude change. The behavioral approach maintains that attitude change is most efficiently achieved through inducing behavior change. At times, these induced behavior changes may not feel comfortable to the family member in his or her initial rehearsals and practice outside the sessions. Family members are warned that this is normal and that they will become accustomed to this new response.

Homework Tasks

Behavioral family therapy sessions are seen as training workshops in which family members can try out different response patterns. We should emphasize that performance between sessions in the everyday setting is necessary for ensuring durable and generalizable improvement. Specific homework assignments are always prescribed to help transfer the skills acquired during the sessions into the family's repertoire. These homework tasks usually are carrying out the skills rehearsed in the sessions, completing contingency contracts, and following problem-solving plans. The therapy's success is measured according to the changes in the real-life environment, and the therapist tries to ensure that these changes occur and are sustained.

Problem-solving Training

Rather than try to remediate separately each of many specific and different family problems, a more efficient approach is to teach family members general problem-solving skills. Training families to use a structured problem-solving strategy when faced with stressful situations is a technique that we have developed over the past few years. Family members are taught a six-step problem-solving method: (1) discussing and coming to an agreement on the exact nature of the problem, (2) generating a list of five or more alternative solutions without judging their relative merits, (3) discussing the pros and cons of each proposed alternative, (4) choosing the best solution or combination of solutions, (5) formulating a plan to implement the solution, and (6) reviewing the implementation and praising people's efforts. Almost any problem may be addressed in this manner, and so problem solving can be used as a basic therapeutic structure on which specific interventions are planned. In addition, once a family has mastered this approach, they may use it in the absence of the therapist.

Families are encouraged to take notes on a form that outlines the above six steps. This maximizes group participation and focuses attention on the task. The approach seeks to diffuse the burden of coping with a problem to all members of the family system and to draw on the resourcefulness of the entire family. Moreover, the structured nature of problem solving tends to reduce the level of family tension and negative feelings when discussing emotionally charged issues.

PROGRAM OUTCOME

The outcomes of the Parent Workshop Program have been measured by evaluating the conceptual and behavioral skills of the parents, the behavioral changes produced in the children of the workshop participants, and the training effects as determined 12 and 24 months after the termination of each workshop. Since the workshop curriculum focuses on the intellectual and cognitive education of the parents through lectures, reading assignments, demonstrations, and verbal discussion of the effects of parental interventions guided by the workshop leaders, the program's outcome can be partially determined by changes in pretests and posttests of conceptual knowledge about child management procedures. Conceptual knowledge was assessed using a 50-item true-false test of basic social learning principles and behavioral intervention procedures. Over the past four years of administering tests, parents have shown a 61 percent mean increase in correct answers on the posttest taken at the end of the workshop.

Because of the expense and inconvenience of sending observers into the homes to assess directly the change in children's behaviors, the self-reports of parents and their data graphs have served as indirect measures of change in the children. These graphs contained the parents' recorded observations of the behaviors targeted for change in their children during baseline and treatment periods. A parental intervention or treatment was considered successful if it changed the specific behavior by 30 percent or more in the desired direction from the average frequency recorded during the baseline period. Sixty-two percent of the targeted problem behaviors responded to treatment by either desirable increases or decreases in frequency. To substantiate parental

Table 7-4

TREATMENT INTERVENTIONS REPORTED BY PARENTS
TO BE SUCCESSFUL IN MODIFYING PROBLEM
BEHAVIOR IN THEIR CHILDREN

INTERVENTION	PERCENTAGE OF ALL SUCCESSFUL INTERVENTIONS
Social reinforcement	20
Token reinforcement	19
Activity reinforcer	13
Time out from reinforcement	19
Extinction	14
Enuresis alarm	8
Mild social punishment	5
Other interventions	2

reports, observers have been sent directly into homes on five occasions and have verified the data brought in by the parents. Less than 2 percent of the parents did not complete at least one child management intervention. In almost every case, these individuals were attending the workshop by court order and avoided active participation in the parent training program.

The most meaningful measure of outcome in the parent training efforts should be in the performance or behavior of the parents themselves as they attempt to carry out the child management procedures that they have learned. A series of 12 brief, role-played scenes of parent-child interactions has been devised to evaluate parenting skills before and after participation in the Parent Workshop Program. For example, a parent is told, "Jamie and Todd are fighting with each other again. Despite your repeated requests that they stop, the brothers continue to fight and argue. What would you do in this situation?" This introduction is followed by a role-played scene in which two of the staff from the workshop program portray children fighting with each other. The parent is instructed to behave as he or she might in trying to handle this type of sibling conflict. A third workshop staff person assesses the adequacy of the parent's intervention, using a predetermined set of evaluative criteria.

For each of the role-played scenes, one or two child management strategies are chosen as the most appropriate; for the fighting example above, mild social punishment or time out is the most effective. If in a role-played scene a parent began delivering mild social punishment to the fighting children, he or she would be given "correct" checkmarks for each of the following behavioral components:

1. looks at children
2. moves to within 3 feet of children (physical proximity)
3. exhibits "disapproving" facial expression
4. gives brief verbalization (less than three sentences)
5. verbalizes with low volume and slow, fluent pace
6. makes a nonverbal gesture consistent with disapproval
7. early delivery of punishment (within five seconds of start of fight)
8. tracks children's behavior to reinforce positively the first sign of desirable change

A similar series of evaluative criteria is used for each of the parenting strategies required by the role-played scenes. Results using the role-playing format for evaluating the workshop program indicate that the pretests and posttests are sensitive to changes in the parents' child management skills and to different types of workshop curricula. Twenty-eight parents were assigned to two groups receiving a standard workshop curriculum limited to didactic presentations and to two groups receiving the standard approach plus 30 minutes of behavioral rehearsal with modeling and feedback on intervention strategies such as social reinforcement, time out, ignoring, and mild social punishment.

Using the 12 scenes in the pretests and the posttests, comparisons between the standard didactic approach and the role-playing training indicate that the role-playing group members showed significantly greater improvements in their parenting responses after training ($t = 4.51$, df $= 15$, $p < .01$).

As more has been learned about the process of behavior change and the dynamics of family systems, methods for modifying maladaptive family behavior have been developed that are transferable to the nonprofessional, including the parent. The directness and simplicity of the behavioral approach allows parents, who are responsible for setting values, standards, and goals for their children, to serve as therapists for their own children. Our evaluation of a family treatment model—incorporating systems and social learning perspectives—has provided a large body of evidence attesting to the effectiveness of training parents to successfully, and cost-effectively, modify their children's undesirable behavior (Weathers and Liberman 1978).

REFERENCES

Ayllon, T., and Azrin, N. H. (1968). *The Token Economy.* New York: Appleton-Century-Crofts.

Azrin, N. H., Naster, B. J., and Jones, R. (1973). Reciprocity counseling: a rapid learning-based procedure for marital counseling. *Behavioral Research and Therapy* 11:365–382.

Boyd, J. L., McGill, C. W., and Falloon, I. R. H. (1981). Family participation in the community rehabilitation of schizophrenia. *Hospital and Community Psychiatry* 32:629–632.

Eimers, R., and Aitchison, R. A. (1977). *Effective Parents/ Responsible Children.* New York: McGraw-Hill.

Falloon, I. R. H., Boyd, J. L., and McGill, C. W. (1982). Behavioral family therapy for schizophrenia. In *Social Competence and Psychiatric Disorder Theory and Practice,* ed. J. Curran and P. Monti, pp. 117–158. New York: Guilford Press.

———, Liberman, R. P., Lillie, F. J., and Vaughn, C. (1981). Family therapy with relapsing schizophrenics and their families: a pilot study. *Family Process* 15:94–107.

Jacobson, N. S., and Margolin, G. (1979). *Marital Therapy: Strategies Based on Social Learning and Behavioral Exchange Principles.* New York: Brunner/Mazel.

Liberman, R. (1970). Behavioral approaches to family and couple therapy. *American Journal of Orthopsychiatry* 40:106–118.

———, King, L. W., De Risi, W. J., and McCann, M. (1975). *Personal Effectiveness: Guiding People to Assert Themselves and Improve their Social Skills.* Champaign, Ill.: Research Press.

———, Levine, J., Wheeler, E., Sanders, N., and Wallace, C. J. (1976). Marital therapy in groups: a comparative evaluation of behavioral and interactional formats. *Acta Psychiatrica Scandinavica* Supplementum 266.

———, Wheeler, E., DeVisser, L., Kuehnel, T., and Kuehnel, J. (1981). *Handbook of Marital Therapy: A Positive Approach to Treating Troubled Relationships.* New York: Plenum.

Patterson, G. R., McNeal, S., Hawkins, N., and Phelps, R. (1967). Reprogramming the social environment. *Journal of Child Psychology and Psychiatry* 8:181–195.

———, and Reid, J. B. (1970). Reciprocity and coercion: two facets of social systems. In *Behavior Modification in Clinical Psychology,* ed. C. Neuringer and J. Michael. New York: Appleton-Century-Crofts.

Stuart, R. B. (1969). Operant-interpersonal treatment for marital discord. *Journal of Consulting and Clinical Psychology* 33:675–682.

Vaughn, C. E., and Leff, J. P. (1976). The influence of family and social factors on the course of psychiatric illness: a comparison of schizophrenic and depressed neurotic patients. *British Journal of Psychiatry* 129:125–137.

Weathers, L., and Liberman, R. P. (1973). The porta-prompter— a new electronic prompting and feedback device. *Behavior Therapy* 4:703–705.

———, and Liberman, R. P. (1975). The family contracting exercise. *Journal of Behavior Therapy and Experimental Psychiatry* 6:208–214.

———, and Liberman, R. P. (1978). Modification of family behavior. In *Child Behavior Therapy*, ed. D. Marholin, pp. 150–186. New York: Gardner Press.

Weiss, R. L., Hope, M., and Patterson, G. R. (1973). A framework for conceptualizing marital conflict, a technology for altering it, some data for evaluating it. In *Behavioral Change: Methodology, Concepts and Practice*, ed. L. A. Hamerlynck, L. C. Handy, and E. J. Mash, pp. 309–342. Champaign, Ill.: Research Press.

❧ 8 ❧

Incest

Nicholas C. Avery, M.D.

The current interest in protecting women and children who are the victims of sexual abuse, including incest, has caused a sweeping review of the various treatment modalities offered to such patients.

The literature on the subject of overt incest can be roughly divided into three attitudinal or conceptual phases. In the first, an epidemiological-descriptive phase with some anthropological material (Bender and Blau 1937, Bender and Grugett 1952, Lewis and Sarrel 1969, Lindzey 1967, Schwartzman 1974, Sloane and Karpinski 1942), investigators stressed how underreported the phenomenon was, understandably, and tended to present the child as a victim of the parental sexual deviate. It was also frequently debated whether the child growing up was (Lewis and Sarrel 1969) or was not (Yorukoglu and Kemph 1966) psychologically harmed by the experience. In the second, a psychological-investigative phase (Gordon 1955, Kaufman et al. 1954, Rascovsky and Rascovsky 1950, Tompkins 1940, Wahl 1960, Weiner

1962), the family members were studied in more detail as to their individual dynamics in the etiology of overt incest. Here, incest was seen as a collusive act, with the child active, and even seductive, and the parents driven by specific instinctual motivations to repeat certain childhood experiences or conflicts with a new generation.

As family psychiatry emerged, the concept of incest entered the third, or family process, phase (Eist and Mandel 1968, Hersko et al. 1961, Lustig et al. 1966, Machotka et al. 1967, Raphling et al. 1967) in which overt incest represented family conflicts and disequilibria put into action. As with so much of psychiatric symptomatology, the pathological entity was less the problem than an attempted solution (though crude and overdetermined) to stresses and dangers confronting the family as a whole.

Psychoanalytic and psychodynamic family theory initially selected unresolved oedipal conflicts as a root cause (Rascovsky and Rascovsky 1950, Tompkins 1940); today almost all family theorists emphasize primitive character deformation and pregenital causal factors (Gutheil and Avery 1977, Krieger et al. 1980, Spencer 1978). The configurations of father-daughter incest families are, with small modifications, typical of other types as well. Such configurations demonstrate a loss in the pregenital period, including emotional indifference, emotional abuse, frank desertion, or absence due to other factors.

In the instances of father-daughter incest reported in the literature, there is a fairly consistent family pattern, although as Lustig and colleagues properly point out, it is not specific to incest itself. The mothers in such families are typically described as feeling unloved by their own mothers (Kaufman et al. 1954, Lustig et al. 1966, Machotka et al. 1967) and, as a consequence, shun the maternal role. Instead, they unconsciously demand to be mothered by their daughters (Kaufman et al. 1954, Rascovsky and Rascovsky 1950, Weiner 1962). The strong oral fixation to their own mothers results in a confused sexual identity and sometimes in the overt repudiation of their feminine sexual rôle (Kaufman et al. 1954, Lustig et al. 1966). Feeling rejected by their mothers, they resent the marital claims of their often dependent husbands and, in an identification-with-the-aggressor fashion, spurn the dependency wishes coming from husband and children. The incest relationship between husband and daughter thus gives the mother relief from her own confused sexual identity and allows a vicarious gratification of her incestuous longings (Lustig et al. 1966, Rascovsky and Rascovsky 1950).

An added incentive to promote the father-daughter liaison is the distance it provides the married couple. Such distance affords scope for mother's counterdependent defense and allays her fears of merger (Eist and Mandel 1968). For these reasons, all the case reports agree that although incest represents a total family involvement, the mother is pivotal in establishing the father-daughter incestuous bond. This is so to the degree that mother either grossly denies evidence of the incest or takes no consequent action if she does acknowledge it (Hersko et al. 1961, Lustig et al. 1966).

The seductiveness observed in these daughters led early theorists to stress their collusion with the incestuous father (Rascovsky and Rascovsky 1950). More recently the concern with child abuse swung the perspective over to a victim-perpetrator model in which the child was seen as a passive victim. As Rosenfeld (1979) argued, such a sharp dichotomy is inadequate in light of recent data from the treatment of abused children. It is true that these children are often actively and tenaciously seductive (Bender and Blau 1937, Weiss et al. 1955); however, "the child has learned that sexual behavior is a way to gain attention from grown-ups. . . . If the sexually arousing behavior is not responded to by adults, the depression it seems to be defending against emerges" (Rosenfeld 1979, p. 408).

Marital Impasse and the Threat of Loss

Gutheil and Avery (1977) observed competitive clashes between deprived, immature parents as to who would get more "supplies" from the sexual encounter. The couple's immaturity, low frustration tolerance, and competitiveness cause them to avoid sexual contact rather than be "exploited" through such means. Although the wife is often seen as initiating the sexual rejection of her husband, my own experience is that such couples take sadomasochistic turns playing hard-to-get rejector to the other's spurned petitioner. Whether the loss is one of sexual rejection or enforced abstinence from death, divorce, or abandonment, loss is the most common precipitant to the incestuous behavior (Gutheil and Avery 1977, Browning and Boatman 1977). The rejected figure turns to the child as a substitute and is reluctantly accepted because these exploitative terms are the best the child can command. The sexually rejecting spouse colludes with the incest, because however dependent he seems to an external judge, she fears her husband may leave her for another woman. Other factors promoting the collusion include binding, through guilt, the daughter, especially a soon-to-be adolescent, in an effort to forestall her separation from the family. When the adolescent attempts to date, the incestuous parent displays envy and anger (Gutheil and Avery 1977). If there are younger children, they are commonly turned to sequentially in an attempt to bind them as well (Gutheil and Avery 1977). The previously "preferred" or "special" child generally feels repudiated and unprepared to make a suitable heterosexual peer choice outside her family. Hurt, frustrated, and in turmoil, she may at this point alert outsiders to her plight and defy the family injunction not to reveal its "secret."

TREATMENT

My own experience with incestuous families concurs with the dichotomy described by Weinberg (1955). In his *promiscuous* type, grossly chaotic, impulse-ridden, and antisocial features prevail, and the incest is just one of the rampant, polymorphous expressions of primitivity. Whenever these families in turmoil allow a clinician to study them, the clinician discovers enormous losses in the families' past and formidable defenses against further loss. The more "mature" incestuous family Weinberg calls *endogamic*. Here the family appears unremarkable to outsiders with its superficial conformity to social norms. Alcoholism, fragmentation, and regressed behavior are much less common, as is criminality.

The promiscuous family type predominates over the endogamic in the clinic population I see. Here the cases are referred by a court, and legal proceedings have been initiated to separate the abusive parent and/or the exploited child from the home. Ten or more years ago professionals felt that they had belatedly come to recognize the high prevalence rate of incest and the emphasis was on the victim-perpetrator model (Rosenfeld 1979). The common illusion was that we were helping the victims of incest by vigorously punishing the offender.

In America, the variability among the states in the length of incarceration for the crime of incest is between 6 months and 50 years (Giaretto 1976). Analyzing the results of the past decade, we can now see that professionals have unwittingly contributed to the destruction of entire families in their effort to salvage the abused child. In many instances enormous pressures were brought to bear on the child to describe, often in open court, the graphic details of her parent's sexual violation. Although it is obvious that these children emphatically wished to be protected from further molestation, they were nevertheless crushed by the burden of being the instrument that banished the father from the home, put the family on welfare, and deprived the members of whatever scraps of warmth and cohesiveness the father could provide. In some cases a skilled defense lawyer was able to place the girl's sexual "complicity" in a particularly damaging light, and she often felt further punished if the court remanded her to a foster home.

As unsatisfactory as these Draconian legal steps against the "perpetrator" are, equally short sighted is the exclusive adherence to a medical model of illness. Experience shows that alliance formation with these frightened, distrustful, loss-sensitive families is impossible to obtain if psychiatric treatment is merely recommended. Indeed, the rate of compliance with treatment recommendations varies with the skill and energy of the probation officer (Giaretto 1976).

Many clinicians are uncomfortable with the double agent role they play, both as upholders of law and social convention and as advocates of their patient's rights to a mostly private relationship (Hastings Center Report 1978). Many others, however, understand that it is possible to resolve this role conflict when the entire family appears relieved that its drifting chaos promises to be stablized. Given the enormous losses that the parents have suffered at the hands of their own indifferent or inadequate parents, the family therapist, with the court behind him or her, is seen initially as a frighteningly authoritarian figure and gradually as a mostly trustworthy, and sometimes highly idealized, authoritative person.

From the central position of the loss themes in my understanding of the genesis of incest, it follows that I emphasize such ideas in my explanations to the family. This crucial loss theme allows me to address much of the sexual impasse (when the parents, but not the children, are scheduled) as a failure of trust and a fear of loss. Similarly, the fear of family fragmentation is advanced to account for turning to the child for warmth and the collusion of the nonabusing parent and the other children. Often, all the other family members are quite angry with the abused child. But when these rationalizations are stripped away, this rage is based on the assumption that in choosing the abused child, the father "gave" her something valuable that he denied the others. Here the therapist can highlight the abused daughter's sense of isolation and often can achieve a tearful and empathic reappraisal of the assumed privilege. Once I feel that the family has accepted the loss motif as underlining its behavior, I am in a good position (with the additional legal weight of the court) to insist on their commitment to try to find more adaptive solutions to the threat of loss.

In my work I emphasize the importance of the marital (sexual) impasse in structuring the therapy. That is, initially I prefer to work mostly with the couple in an attempt to correlate their rejection of each other with the residual rage over the multitudinous losses they suffered as children. The parents usually respond by vigorously denying such losses and defensively idealizing their parents. But gradually they acknowledge them, and then anger and grief emerge as the painful memories are mobilized. These painful feelings from the old hurts are then connected to the contemporary traumata when each spouse was unable to support and nurture the other. The repetitive and blindly acted out search for warmth, indeed the demand for such in the marriage, can then be understood in the light of the childhood rejections. Once the marital rupture has begun to heal, the children are immediately aware of it and hope, as a shared family experience, is stimulated. The therapist encourages the parents to share anecdotes of their painful past with their children, whose usual response is that they knew the broad outlines of such rejections but rarely the details. The family draws closer in its grief which expresses the mutual understanding that the sexual exploitation in the current generation tragically recapitulates commensurate exploitation in the parents' childhood.

To the extent that families (especially the parents) can bear their sadness, hurt, and anger, the prognosis is favorable. For many, however, a defensively idealized parent is seemingly better than no parent at all. These couples prefer to displace their rage from their parents to each other in a way that spares archaic ties at the expense of contemporary ones. In this way some parents steadfastly deny their grief and rage, and although they may not resume their incestuous behavior as long as the judicial threat hangs over them, they do not move beyond the emotional plight of a defeated enemy. While they no longer act out, their sense of coherence and meaning remains shattered. Here the question of physically separating the abusive parent from the child seems moot. True, some increased security is won, but it is largely offset, in my view, by the profound sense of guilt and disastrous disintegration. The children from these families often make impulsive marriages to inadequate mates, and a new cycle for the repetition of exploitative behaviors seems likely.

Even when the parents can grow in therapy, the clinician needs to be alert to incongruent lags in the children's growth. A daughter who for much of her life has been valued largely as a means to an end is not necessarily going to heal at the same rate as her parents' marriage may. She and her siblings may very well need concomitant and extensive individual therapy in order to deal with ego maturational deficits. The more primitive the family is, the more likely the child was abusively exploited. Such children universally need individual therapy. Conversely, with healthier, endogamic incestuous families that show some mixture of support and exploitation, more of the corrective burden can fall on family therapy.

RESULTS

Treatment-result figures are almost as difficult to ascertain as are the incest-incidence rates. A rough estimate is that one-fourth to one-third of the promiscuous incest families can be helped and about half the endogamic types can. In a particularly vigorous program with a very alert court probation officer backup, these percentages can be significantly improved.

One such program in Santa Clara, California, which enjoys very good rapport with legal authorities, provides its patients with a wide array of psychiatric, social, vocational, and financial planning services. Among the interventions they offer is a mix of individual, couple, family, peer, and group therapy (Giaretto 1976). The results of their treatment of 400 cases of father-daughter incest indicate that although their population is largely middle class, the success rate is extraordinary.

For example, they are able to retain in treatment 75 percent of their cases, return 90 percent of their abused children to their homes within a month, salvage an equal percentage of the marriages, treat the offending parent during his incarceration, and claim no recidivism in the successfully terminated cases (Giaretto 1976).

Quite obviously, this program is atypical, if not unique, in its staffing, funding, and liaison to legal-judicial services. It may appear utopian to some to expect to replicate the results of this project. But when one considers that incest negatively affects all members of a family and that, if untreated, it tends to be perpetuated seemingly indefinitely, zealously funded programs may, in the long run, be the least expensive alternative.

REFERENCES

Bender, L., and Blau, A. (1937). The reaction of children to sexual relations with adults. *American Journal of Orthopsychiatry* 7:500–518.

———, and Grugett, A. (1952). A follow-up report on children who had atypical sexual experience. *American Journal of Orthopsychiatry* 22:825–837.

Browning, D., and Boatman, B. (1977). Incest: children at risk. *American Journal of Psychiatry* 134:69–72.

Eist, H., and Mandel, A. (1968). Family treatment of ongoing incest behavior. *Family Process* 7:216–232.

Giaretto, H. (1976). The treatment of father-daughter incest: a psycho-social approach. *Children Today* 5:2–6.

Gordon, L. (1955). Incest as revenge against the pre-oedipal mother. *Psychoanalytic Review* 42:284–292.

Gutheil, T., and Avery, N. (1977). Multiple overt incest as family defense against loss. *Family Process* 16:105–116.

Hastings Center Report (1978). *In the Service of the State: The Psychiatrist as Double Agent*. Hastings-on-Hudson, N.Y.: Hastings Center.

Hersko, M., Halleck, S., Rosenberg, M., and Pacht, A. (1961). Incest: a three-way process. *Journal of Social Therapy* 7:22–31.

Kaufman, I., Peck, A. L., and Tagiuri, C. K. (1954). The family constellation and overt incestuous relations between father and daughter. *American Journal of Orthopsychiatry* 24:266–279.

Krieger, M., Rosenfeld, A. A., Gordon, A., and Bennett, M. (1980). Problems in the psychotherapy of children with histories of incest. *American Journal of Psychotherapy* 34:81–88.

Lewis, M., and Sarrel, P. (1969). Some psychological aspects of seduction, incest and rape in childhood. *Journal of the American Academy of Child Psychiatry* 8:606–619.

Lindzey, G. (1967). Some remarks concerning incest, the incest taboo and psychoanalytic theory. *American Psychology* 22:1051–1059.

Lustig, N., Dresser, J. W., Spellman, S. W., and Murray, T. B. (1966). Incest: a family group survival pattern. *Archives of General Psychiatry* 14:31–40.

Machotka, P., Pittman, F. S., and Flomenhaft, K. (1967). Incest as a family affair. *Family Process* 6:98–116.

Raphling, D., Carpenter, B. L., and Davis, A. (1967). Incest: a genealogical study. *Archives of General Psychiatry* 16:505–511.

Rascovsky, M., and Rascovsky, A. (1950). On consummated incest. *International Journal of Psychoanalysis* 31:42–47.

Rosenfeld, A. (1979). Endogamic incest and the victim-perpetrator model. *American Journal of Diseases of Children* 33:406–410.

Schwartzman, J. (1974). The individual, incest and exogamy. *Psychiatry* 37:171–180.

Sloane, P., and Karpinski, E. (1942). Effects of incest on the participants. *American Journal of Orthopsychiatry* 12:666–673.

Spencer, J. (1978). Father-daughter incest: a clinical view from the corrections field. *Child Welfare* 57:581–590.

Tompkins, J. (1940). Penis envy and incest: a case report. *Psychoanalytic Review* 27:319–325.

Wahl, C. (1960). The psychodynamics of consummated maternal incest. *Archives of General Psychiatry* 3:188–193.

Weinberg, S. (1955). *Incest Behavior.* Secaucus, N.J.: Citadel Press.

Weiner, I. (1962). Father-daughter incest: a clinical report. *Psychiatric Quarterly* 36:607–632.

Weiss, J., Rogers, E., Darwin, M. R., and Dutton, C. E. (1955). A study of girl sex victims. *Psychiatric Quarterly* 29:1–27.

Yorukoglu, A., and Kemph, J. (1966). Children not severely damaged by incest with a parent. *Journal of the American Academy of Child Psychiatry* 5:111–124.

❧ 9 ❧

School Problems

Martin R. Textor, Dipl.-Paed.

The life of any child or adolescent is intensely influenced by three social units: the family, the school, and the peer group. For young children, the family is the most crucial group, largely determining their development, socialization, and personality growth. Behaviors, communication skills, emotional expression, values, and attitudes are learned in interaction with their parents, siblings, and relatives. But as the children grow older, the influence of the family decreases. Many of the family's tasks and functions are taken over by preschools, kindergartens, and schools. These institutions teach basic skills, pass on the fundamental knowledge of the respective culture, offer social training, and prepare the child for adult life. Children and adolescents spend more than one-quarter of their waking hours in schools which, therefore, have great impact on their cognitive, emotional, and social growth. These institutions must build on what the family has achieved— in their thinking, communication skills, achievement motivation, and

159

attitude toward authority, though the family continues to influence the children's fate at school. The amount of cognitive stimulation offered, the specific interests supported, the type of life goals encouraged, and the impact on their emotional well-being are of great importance in this respect.

The more that children are permitted to explore their surroundings on their own, the more influential their peers become, and during puberty they become the most influential group. Children acquire social and leadership skills, develop many different interests, and experiment with heterosexual relationships within their peer group. But they will have positive experiences only if they learned the necessary interpersonal skills in their family, and they can become autonomous and independent from their parents only if they are supported by their peers. The school will either promote or hinder the development of long-lasting, informal peer groups, according to the kind of environment it provides (e.g., course or class system, the size of its classes, yard, or playground). And it can create formal peer groups, such as school bands, clubs, or sports teams. The school can also help determine who will have high status in the peer group (e.g., good or bad students). On the other hand, peers largely influence classroom atmosphere, attitudes toward learning, and relationships with teachers.

Thus, family, school, and peer group are three systems that operate in relation to and interact with one another. Each unit influences children and adolescents in positive, neutral, or negative ways, and these influences can be additive (exponential increase) or mutually neutralizing in their effects. If therapists treat children being referred for school problems, they should assess the impact of all three systems, for then they can treat the most destructive group, the unit that is the easiest to change, or all three systems. Professionals trained in family therapy are well qualified to intervene in families, schools, and peer groups, as they have learned how to deal with systems. We shall now discuss the etiology and treatment of learning disorders, school behavior problems, and school phobia.

LEARNING DISORDERS

Learning disorders such as underachievement, reading problems, or communicative disorders (not including learning disabilities that are caused by physical factors) can affect perceptive, integrative, or expressive processes. Children suffering from learning disorders usually have low self-esteem and a negative self-concept, as they constantly experience failures and punitive consequences from their surroundings. They react to failures by becoming depressed or angry, acting out, lowering their achievement motivation, or avoiding learning situations. This usually leads to even more problems and negative experiences (positive feedback cycle).

In some cases, these children did not adapt to school life, are not accepted by their peers, or compete with more capable (younger) siblings, thus losing their parents' affection and approval, as they are not as successful (cf. Foster and Culp 1973). Adolescents might underachieve in order to reach independence by challenging parental or societal values or by rejecting inappropriate or unrealistic goals. But they may also be afraid of growing up and may fail classes in order to remain dependent on their parents.

Interpersonal causes for learning disorders may also lie in the parents' achievement expectations (Friedman 1973b, Friedman and Meltzer 1973, Philage et al. 1975). Excessive pressure for high marks results in anxiety or rebellion and is detrimental to academic success, whereas indifferent or laissez-faire attitudes toward learning do not motivate children to achieve. Expectations of failure often become self-fulfilling prophecies, and disagreement between parents concerning school work leads to inconsistent rewards which do not motivate these children to give their best. Parents may also present their achievement expectations in an ambiguous or confusing way so that their children do not know what their parents want.

Much research evidence suggests that these parents were unsuccessful at school or suffer from low self-regard (Friedman 1973b, Friedman and Meltzer 1973, Foster and Culp 1973, Pannor 1973, Peck 1971). They may see their children as competing with them and fear that the latter may surpass them. Thus, they often covertly discourage learning, for example, by provoking negativistic behaviors, undermining their children's performance, or using double-bind messages ("I want you to succeed, but then I will become depressed"). These parents, moreover, are bad models, as they do not stress academic achievement, have negativistic attitudes toward schools and universities, or do not offer any cognitive stimulation. Similar problems occur if the other-sex parent stresses learning and the same-sex parent is a bad learner. Then the child may associate academic success with sex-linked traits that he or she should not acquire.

Friedman and Meltzer (1973) described two patterns in the behavior of fathers with children suffering from learning disorders. In the first, the father had been unsuccessful at school, functioned at an occupational level below his potential, regarded himself as a failure, and often felt helpless. In the second pattern, father is a more successful and aggressive person and is the acknowledged authority figure in the family. "Unfortunately, success and assertiveness only cover over a deep sense of inferiority and frustration stemming from early failures in life" (Friedman and Meltzer 1973, p. 49, cf. Peck 1971). In any case, these fathers may project their weaknesses onto their children, be unable to express satisfaction with their achievement, or refrain from supporting them. Their sons are frequently caught in oedipal conflicts, perceive success as competition with their fathers, exhibit castration anxiety, or identify with their underlying passivity. If the fathers are cold and rejecting, their children may retaliate by not learning.

In regard to mothers of children with learning disorders, Friedman and Meltzer wrote in their review: "Some mothers have extremely close bonds with and an intense fear of losing the special intimate relationship with a particular child. So long as this child does not learn, he will not lose his mother, will remain dependent on her, and be free from the anxieties of growing up" (1973, p. 46). These mothers may overprotect or infantilize their children, induce fears of separation, divert them from their homework, or imprint myths onto them ("My child is disabled"). If the mothers have low self-esteem or feel intellectually stupid, they may feel ambivalent toward their children's academic performance and refrain from encouraging success (cf. Friedman 1973b, Peck 1971).

Families of children with learning disorders are often characterized by power struggles, open fights, or suppressed conflicts. The spouses are angry and hostile, depressed and tired, or fearful and anxious. They may try to keep the system intact by carrying out numerous irrelevant interactions, avoiding sexual and emotional intimacy, or preventing any changes (cf. Peck 1971). Their children may become preoccupied with family problems and, therefore, cannot individuate or concentrate on learning. They may also fail at school in order to distract their parents from their fighting by allowing them to focus on the school problems (and not on their marital conflicts), to voice their frustrations, and to vent their suppressed tensions. Thus, the children become scapegoats and stabilize the family, while at the same time call for community help. The parents criticize and punish these children but also reward them, either covertly or overtly, for their sacrifice.

Learning disorders may also result from sociocultural factors. For example, the surroundings of many children living in urban Western societies do not allow for much exploration (e.g., small apartments), offer little stimulation (incomprehensible technology, uncreative toys), restrict social relations (isolated nuclear families, anonymity in apartment blocks), offer few opportunities for imitation (washing and preparation of meals done by machines), and rarely make it possible for them to observe and help adults at work. Problems may also be caused by the family's frequent moves, which make it difficult for children to establish stable relationships with peers or to adjust to their teachers. Or these problems may result from social change, as more and more adults are uncertain about what is required from them as spouses and parents or feel insecure in these roles. Many parents may also have problems at work, with institutions, or in their social life, which distract them from supporting their children.

Socioeconomic factors are also important. Children from slums or lower-class areas often come from disorganized or one-parent families or arrive at school malnourished, sleepy, or in poor health. They may be afraid of their teachers, lack achievement motivation, have a limited vocabulary, or use different communicative codes and modes of thinking. Their parents often do not appreciate education or are resentful of the school system. Thus, these children may underachieve or develop learning disorders. Similar problems are encountered by children of minorities, immigrants, exiles, or foreign workers. The educational system may show little respect for their languages, traditions, values, and mores. And so these children feel discriminated against, are suspicious of their teachers, and cannot give their best.

School Behavior Disorders

School behavior disorders like disruptiveness, aggression, stealing, lying, truancy, or withdrawal may also be caused by family problems. Conflicts in marital, parent-child, or sibling relationships, live-in grandparents, drug abuse, or family crises (death, illness, loss of employment, and so on) result in family stress which might be acted out by children at school. Parents suffering from marital conflict often use their children as scapegoats, go-betweens, allies, or ersatz partners which may lead to inappropriate behaviors at school. If the spouses are separated or divorced, their children frequently act out their parents' bewilderment, sadness, or anger, suffer from separation anxiety, or are burdened by guilt feelings. The divorced parent may neglect or parentify the children or use them as a means of retaliation. Thus, these children may express their troubles by misbehavior at school.

Behavior disorders may also result from problems with authority. If the parents are harsh, punitive, or rejecting, the children may express their hostility toward them by challenging the teacher's authority or by becoming fearful and withdrawn. If the children come from an overly strict home environment, they may try to find behavior release at school. If the parents are overpermissive, the children may not internalize norms or develop inner controls and so are unable to follow the teacher's rules. According to Friedman's (1973a) review, children may also act out a parent's repressed wish to defy authority (and provide him or her with vicarious satisfaction) or to follow a family value of nonconformity. In these cases, the parents often encourage (also by ambiguous messages) or condone the misbehavior. They will also tolerate it if they identify with their children's resentful feelings toward school. Children may also develop behavior disorders if they identify with a misbehaving older sibling or if they fail in competition with more gifted siblings.

Quite often, the relationship between family and school is disturbed. If parents are frequently called to school because of chronic problems with their children, they may see themselves as failures (especially if they see their children as extensions of themselves) and become defensive (cf. Boyd 1974, Moynihan 1978). The communications between teachers and parents may also be disrupted if the parents were unsuccessful in school and, therefore, hold negative attitudes toward it, if they use their children as the only message bearers, or if both sides resort to mutual blaming instead of helping these children.

Certainly, behavior disorders can also be caused by the school system itself. Schools are often too big and anonymous, lack warmth and personal relations, or place unattainable demands on some students. Teachers are frequently unable to care for their pupils if they have too many or too large classes, are overburdened by bureaucratic tasks, or concentrate only on teaching (believing that they are not responsible for their students' interpersonal and intrapsychic fate). Many teachers are not trained to deal with the children's problems, do not understand them, and may even aggravate them by the techniques they use (e.g., reinforce them positively). Moreover, many teachers often do not discuss their problems in handling certain students with their colleagues or school psychologists, as they are afraid of being labeled as pedagogical failures. Consequently, they do not learn better methods of teaching and child management by means of supervision. Many teachers are also afraid of using educational situations, modifying the informal class organization, representing values, or speaking privately with their students. Thus, school learning degenerates to purely cognitive learning—and the children's emotional, social, and personality growth is left open to chance. School behavior disorders may also be caused by peers who admire students who are aggressive or challenge the teacher's authority.

School Phobia

School phobic children exhibit panic attacks, extreme fears, and psychosomatic complaints such as nausea, vomiting, or stomach pains. In rare cases, these symptoms are reinforced by physicians prescribing medication and become chronic, while the family, school, and community adjust to this pathological situation. But most cases are acute, usually occurring after holidays or family crises (hospitalization, death, and the like) but also when children have to attend school for the first time. According to Skynner (1974), school phobic children frequently overvalue themselves, have a very positive self-image, and have unrealistic achievement goals. Therefore, they may avoid school and peers because these threaten their self-esteem and feelings of omnipotence. Their fantasies and goals, however, are not challenged at home, where these children have a strong and magical position, dominate or exploit their parents, and are not restrained in any way. In rare cases, school phobia may result from real or imagined fears of mistreatment by teachers and peers or from dislike of certain aspects of school life.

Most researchers (e.g., Davis 1977, Skynner 1974, Veltkamp 1975) believe that the mothers of school phobic children usually have very close relationships with their own mothers and transfer these to their own children, that they were unable to relinquish the exclusive relationship with their infants and now maintain it through childhood and puberty, or that they were disappointed with their spouses and developed intimate relationships with their children as ersatz partners. Quite often, they value their children more than their husbands. These mothers are overindulging, infantilizing, and overprotecting, but they may also feel slightly ambivalent or hostile toward their offspring. Their children are extremely dependent and suffer from great separation anxiety. They want to stay at home even if this requires that they develop painful symptoms. As their fathers are usually detached, passive, and insecure, cling to their wives, or spend little time at home, they cannot disrupt or weaken these symbiotic relationships and force their children to go to school. In some other cases, one parent may be depressed or sick, fear the spouse, or expect an unwanted separation. Their children may sense these anxieties, be extremely concerned with what might happen to their parents while they are at school, and thus decide to stay at home.

DEALING WITH SCHOOL PROBLEMS
IN FAMILY THERAPY

If school problems are caused by family pathology, family therapy is indicated—and this has already become obvious to many parents, teachers, and professionals. Many parents, therefore, who contact family therapists do so because of learning and school behavior disorders. Often they are referred by teachers, principals, or guidance workers. Moreover, many school counselors and school psychologists have been trained in family therapy and offer it to selected clients.

Usually only those families that refer themselves express a need for change and a willingness to collaborate in order to solve their problems. If only one parent contacts the therapist, if the family is referred by the school, or if they are invited by the school psychologist, the family members may feel threatened or forced and become resistant and defensive. The parents may then try to shift the responsibility for their child's change to the therapist or argue about who will control the sessions. Many fathers resist treatment, as they regard child rearing as their wives' responsibility. Family therapists should overcome these resistances by interpreting them and by being friendly, warm, congruent, and empathic. They should mobilize the family's desire for change, overcome some initial shyness by scheduling a home visit, and insist on always seeing the whole family, thereby taking a position of real authority. If a father really cannot come to sessions during office hours because of work-related problems, the therapist could offer therapy during the evening.

The assessment usually takes place in the therapist's office and should involve the whole family or at least the parent-child triad. Sometimes the spouses and the problem child should be interviewed separately for a while. In many cases it is necessary to invite teachers to the first session or to contact them by phone, to arrange for classroom observation, to plan a home visit, or to refer the child for a medical exam in order to rule out organic causes of the disorder. This way, the therapist obtains much information from different sources and viewpoints as well as from his or her own observation.

At the beginning of the assessment interview the focus should be on the learning or behavior disorder. The family therapist asks for a detailed description of the problems, its onset, antecedents, and consequences, discusses the ideas of each family member concerning the causes of the disorder and inquires about solutions tried before. Afterward the therapist takes a short family history, asking about the parents' school experiences and performance, the child's development and socialization, family crises, and factors related to social class, economic situation, and minority status. With that, the interview acquires a broader focus, and more detailed questions are asked. The therapist explores the child's feelings and attitudes toward school, his or her achievement motivation, school adjustment, and relationship with teachers and peers (classroom status). As well, the therapist assesses the child's maturity, self-concept, and confidence, looking for feelings of inadequacy, inferiority, or separation anxiety. The therapist may also ask about the school, the requirements, the classroom atmosphere, and the remediation services offered.

The family therapist also assesses the mother-child and father-child relationships for symbiosis, dependency, infantilization, overprotection, disengagement, scapegoating, rejection, and the like. The therapist should also inquire about achievement goals, behavior expectations, values, child-rearing techniques, and the family-school relationship. Friedman (1973b) even recommended conducting "a brief homework or tutoring lesson with the parent as supervisor or tutor for the purpose of direct observation of parent-child interaction in an authority-related, task-oriented, and possibly conflict-laden situation" (p. 90). Finally, it is important to look for power struggles and conflicts between the spouses. At the end of the assessment phase, the family therapist should also have an impression of the overall family functioning, quality of communication, role performance, and individual psychodynamics. Then he or she is able to determine the nature and extent of the connection among individual, family, and school problems. The therapist may explain these links in a nonblaming way so that all sides arrive at a common view of the problem, recognize their part in it, and become motivated to solve it together.

Afterward the family and the therapist discuss treatment goals. They should arrive at the same ones and state them in such a way that progress can be measured against them. General goals are the modification of situations that negatively affect learning and school adjustment, the resolution of marital and family conflicts, the facilitation of individual growth, and the promotion of good child-management techniques. Then the family therapist can outline the treatment program, thereby building on individual and family strengths. If deemed necessary, a treatment contract is formulated.

During the treatment phase, the family therapist helps the parents recognize that experiences with their own parents or their own unfulfilled educational goals determine their responses to their children, thereby encouraging them to treat their offspring as individuals with their own rights. If the family has undergone any traumatic events (separation, death, job loss, and the like), the therapist may use crisis intervention, help the parent(s) voice their feelings of loss and disappointment, stimulate the mourning process, and alleviate stress. As well, he or she should facilitate therapeutic interactions among family members and encourage open and honest communication about marital and family conflicts. The family therapist makes the family share their thoughts and feelings, explore one another's attitudes and life-style, and achieve a greater understanding of one another. He or she uses interpretations to help the family members gain insight into the causes of their conflicts, focuses on nonverbal communication in order to show hidden conflicts, confronts the family with rules and myths, and intercepts manipulative relationship patterns and scapegoating, thereby demonstrating and teaching effective communication.

The family therapist often has to disrupt the symbiotic relationship between mother and child as well as increase the closeness between father and child, for example, by encouraging mutual help and joint activities. The therapist reassures the parents that nothing is physically wrong with their child, emphasizes the results of diagnostic tests, and points out the child's capacities, strengths, and vulnerabilities. The parents are urged to give up unrealistic goals or behavior expectations and help their child to accept himself or herself and to stop competing with more gifted siblings. The therapist informs the parents about the bad effects of an authoritarian, permissive, or overprotective relationship on their children and teaches them better child-rearing techniques and democratic methods (e.g., contracting, family councils). He or she helps them set and enforce rules, structure the child's life at home, and develop trust by listening effectively and looking for the causes of a behavior. The therapist may model missing parental behaviors and teach them by means of shaping and role playing.

Parents should help children with learning problems gain more self-confidence by providing successful learning experiences. If the child is school phobic, the parents should make him or her relinquish omnipotent demands for total control of the mother, alleviate fears of separation, and send him or her back to school. Sometimes the family therapist must make it clear that residential placement will be arranged if a return to school is not enforced. If the problem person is an adolescent, the therapist may use contracting to force him or her to take responsibility for his or her own behavior and performance at school and to gain more autonomy from the parents. In these cases, the therapist may also invite peers to the sessions so that they can support the adolescent, offer clarification, and prevent the parents from blaming them for their child's problems.

Friedman (1973c) developed the Parent-Tutor Therapy: If a parent is an inadequate learning model, unconsciously accepts the bad performance and behavior of the child, or does not support the child's learning, he or she will be trained as a tutor. The family therapist explains or models a constructive tutoring approach and then makes the parent teach his or her child. In this way the parent remains responsible for the child's performance and eventually becomes an effective tutor and role model. The therapist works as a supportive coach, helping the parent choose suitable learning material for the child, suggesting better techniques, and modifying the parent-child interaction. Working separately with the parent or child, the therapist may comment on the tutoring or learning behavior, convey confidence, model fair expectations, or interpret feelings and experiences. Tutoring may also be given as homework after the parent has become a better learning model.

A comparable approach was developed by Patterson and colleagues (1975), who train mothers to work as remedial reading teachers for 30 minutes a day. Each mother receives a manual, data sheets, and a programmed reading text listing the sounds and words to be introduced. They are trained to use this material in one tutoring session, in which they learn reinforcement techniques and teaching methods. Afterward they are contacted by telephone weekly in order to discuss their progress and to help with any problems. Philage and associates (1975) also offer special remedial programs. These therapists work with groups of children, using a token system, discussing feelings, improving social skills, and modifying manipulative devices. The remedial work is gradually taken over by parents who learn to do it by observing, modeling, and role playing.

While these approaches seem to be effective for children with learning problems, Group Filial Therapy was developed by Ginsberg and colleagues (1978) to treat children with school behavior disorders. At first, parents read a training manual on client-centered play therapy, and then they observe the therapists treating groups of children at their school. Later on, the parents become more and more involved in playing with their children until they become the primary therapists. The group leaders meet with the parents at the end of the play session to discuss practiced skills, give feedback, and suggest changes in the home. The treatment principles are to develop a nondirective, accepting, and child-focused atmosphere, to set limits providing a secure and safe environment, to foster communication and trust between parent and child, to teach reflective listening, and to enhance the children's interpersonal skills. The parents, moreover, can learn from each other and are encouraged to generalize their new behaviors to the home situation, whereas the children are helped to accept themselves, gain more confidence, become responsible for their own behavior, and transfer their new skills to the school environment.

A comparable approach was developed by Williams (1973) who trains parents to use operant conditioning to make their preschool children change their disruptive behaviors. Williams uses videotape feedback to show cueing and bad reinforcement techniques, explains and models better child-rearing methods, and points out bad communication patterns that confuse or overwhelm the child.

Several therapists (e.g., Durell 1969, Hillman and Perry 1975, Skynner 1974) use Multiple Family Therapy (MFT) to alleviate school problems. Though they have comparable goals and use techniques similar to those that therapists use for conjoint family therapy, they believe that MFT has several advantages. For example, families can learn from one another through identification and imitation and can benefit from interventions directed at other families. Fathers can interact with fathers, mothers with mothers, and children with children, empathizing with and supporting one another as representatives of the same role. Members of other families can also be more objective and helpful, offer advice, and help resolve conflicts and problems.

Many therapists like Boyd (1974), Downing (1974), and Philage and associates (1975) use parents' groups to alleviate learning and school behavior disorders. These groups may be available in schools or agencies, and their members may be referred or take part voluntarily after having heard about them by news releases, school reports, or public addresses. They may be therapeutic or discussion groups, training groups (e.g., in behavior modification techniques), enrichment groups (e.g., Parent Effectiveness Training), or lecture groups. The discussions may focus on common problems, parent-child and marital relationships, child-rearing or remediation techniques, communication and problem-solving skills, and feelings of guilt, frustration, or protectiveness. The therapists explore specific problematic situations, increase insight into the causes of conflicts, and try to change parenting behaviors, attitudes, and values.

A few family therapists also work as consultants. They help parents identify and meet their children's developmental needs, improve marital and parent-child relationships, and develop strategies to reduce inappropriate behaviors and increase appropriate ones. In these cases, the therapists remain outsiders who see their main function as giving advice (as well as clarifying, analyzing, and interpreting) and who let the parents decide how to use this information.

All the family therapy approaches mentioned so far have in common the belief that working on the parent-child and marital relationships and resolving family conflicts will result in changing the children's behavior and performance at school.

SCHOOL INTERVENTIONS

Many schools offer remedial programs, especially for children with learning disorders. Many teachers, however, notice that their efforts are greatly enhanced by the interest, support, and cooperation of the parents—and are minimized by hostility, disinterest, and power struggles. Moreover, if the symptom has a function within the family, the children and parents will want to maintain it (at least as long as no help is provided for the whole family) and collaborate to defeat the remedial teacher (or if they cannot, the child will develop a new problem in an area out of this teacher's reach). Many remedial teachers, therefore, try to involve the parents as part of the helping team. They inform them about the school program and try to persuade them to support it, for example, by motivating their children, helping them accept responsibility for their problems, and supervising their homework. These specialists also discuss the parents' feelings of anger or worry, criticisms, and manipulative devices.

If remedial teachers cannot win the parents' cooperation, if the family suffers from great pathogenic conflicts, if long-term treatment is indicated, or if the school counselor does not feel competent to offer treatment to the family, the school may refer the problem child and his or her family to an agency or private practitioner for family therapy. This makes it necessary for the school staff to be informed about available community resources (including drug abuse centers, vocational rehabilitation offices, public health services, and the like) and also about these services' primary theoretical approaches and waiting periods. If the family is afraid or resistant, the referral can be facilitated by having the first meetings on the school premises or having the teacher or school counselor invite the family and take part in the first sessions (at the school or agency). However, the referring school staff remains responsible for the family: They should maintain contact with the agency and coordinate the efforts of the school (e.g., continued remedial work), family, and therapist.

Family therapists must also cooperate with the school staff in order to obtain relevant information, influence the child's treatment at school, and improve the parent-teacher relationship—and they often feel as though they have two clients, as the referring agent may seek help, too. Thus, family therapists should offer consultation to remedial teachers and counselors, invite them to strategic sessions and case reviews, and work on problems among them, the problem children, and the parents. This has the advantages that the therapists can help where the problems occur, that the school staff continues to be involved with the children, and that all sides accept part of the responsibility for change. On the other hand, family therapists sometimes have to avoid being identified with school personnel, as the family may perceive them as prejudiced and biased in that they represent the (hated) school system. They must emphasize that they are working for the family.

Cooperation between family therapists and the school staff can be improved if they confer frequently. For example, Moynihan (1978) meets with the problem child's teachers after having dealt with the family's and the child's reluctance, embarrassment, or anxiety and after having gained the permission of all family members and the principal. She often includes the problem children in these conferences but always shows positive regard for them before inquiring about their problems. She makes the children and teachers communicate more directly and openly with one another, encourages them to share feelings, experiences, and disappointments, helps them better understand one another, and motivates them to solve problems together. Thereby, she models a positive relationship between teachers and students. Moynihan also serves as a consultant and teaches child-management techniques. She provides the school staff with a picture of the problem child's home environment and thus helps them empathize with the family and their problems. She also mediates between parents and school, helping the parents take a more positive and cooperative stance toward the teachers, control their feelings, and communicate more effectively. The children are then no longer surrounded by combating adults and can focus on age-appropriate achievements and competition with peers.

Some family therapists go even further and require that part of the treatment take place at the school. Many of them are behavior therapists who believe that changes in the child's behavior at home will not automatically generalize to the classroom. After the parents have "earned" the additional investment of professional time by effectively applying behavior modification techniques at home, Patterson and colleagues (1975), for example, involve teachers in reducing the rate of disruptive behaviors and ameliorating learning problems. They organize conferences with the parents and teachers in order to improve their communication, create an alliance between staff and family, and explain the treatment program. Then they ask the teachers to list all the problems with the student on a card which is given to him or her. This card has to be presented at the end of each class to the teacher, who marks each problem behavior that has occurred. Then the child has to show this card to his or her parents, who assign a consequence for each positive or negative behavior according to a token program. The parents also maintain contact with the school by telephoning the teachers once a week in order to obtain an overview of the child's behavior.

In more difficult cases, Patterson and associates (1975) teach behavior modification techniques to teachers and even demonstrate them *in situ*. They may also use a work box which signals and counts good behaviors (often operated by the parents). If the problem student scores a certain number, the whole class can leave earlier for recess. This increases the positive reinforcement contingency from the peers, raises the child's status, and improves his or her academic skills. Later on, the work box is discarded and is replaced by the token system. The therapists may also arrange for consequences if a crisis should occur (e.g., the parents have to fetch their child at once and make him or her work at home if he or she attacks another child). Philage and colleagues (1975) also involve teachers in a token program, ask them to report any progress, seek their recommendations, and discuss problems with them.

Foster and Culp (1973) organize Home-School Conferences. As parents and teachers see children from different vantage points, experience them in different situations, and have different concerns and goals, they should share their views in these meetings. Thus, they will become more objective about one another and the child, better understand one another's feelings, attitudes, and problems, and recognize the impact of ethnic or cultural values and of class or language barriers. The therapists prevent mutual blaming, establish meaningful communication, and explore the consistency of the parents' and the teachers' approaches, as well as their similarities and differences (e.g., those concerning philosophy of discipline, child-management techniques, or guidelines). They also offer a more realistic view of the child and his or her problems and needs. Including the students in the conferences alleviates their fears about secret machinations and allows them to explain misunderstandings, express their feelings, and develop motivation for change. Later, parents, teachers, and children can establish more realistic behavior expectations and achievement goals, devise a mutually acceptable approach to the child's management, and draw up a problem-solving plan. The therapists teach them better techniques, such as reward systems, behavior extinction, shaping, and other reinforcement methods.

Another group of family therapists (e.g., Andolfi et al. 1977, Aponte 1976, Freund and Cardwell 1977) intervenes in schools, using a systems approach. They conceptualize family, school, and peer group as different systems embedded in even larger systems (neighborhood, community, school bureaucracy, government, economy, culture, and so on). Each system is separated from the others by nearly impermeable boundaries and has some impact on the others. Each system consists of horizontal (family: spouse and sibling subsystems; school: subsystems of administrators, of guidance workers, counselors, psychologists, and social workers, of teachers, and of students; peer group: leader and member subsystems) and vertical subsystems (family: grandparent-parent and parent-child subsystems; school: administrator-teacher, administrator-counselor, administrator-student, counselor-teacher, counselor-student, and teacher-student subsystems; peer group: leader-member subsystems). These subsystems usually have more permeable boundaries and interact more frequently with one another. Each subsystem contains several individuals (who are also conceptualized as systems made up of subsystems like body and psyche) whose behavior is related to and dependent on the behavior of any other member of the subsystem. Here we find the most permeable boundaries and the highest frequency of interaction. An individual can be a member of several subsystems and will behave differently in each one.

Each system or subsystem has a different internal structure and operates according to different rules and transactional patterns. It always tries to maintain its equilibrium even if this can be achieved only by pathological processes (e.g., scapegoating, repression of conflicts) or by extruding members (e.g., sending them to hospitals or agencies). Systems therapists believe that they can help an individual only by modifying the subsystems that have a pathogenic impact on him or her. But then changes in one subsystem will "cause" changes in all other subsystems and the total system because of their interrelatedness. These therapists, then, tend to work with those subsystems that can be most easily entered and modified. But interventions in one system (e.g., family) have only little impact on other systems (e.g., school or peer group), as they do not interact frequently with one another. This explains why a child's learning or behavior disorder may disappear at home after family therapy but still be evident at school: It fulfills a certain function for the school system or is caused and maintained by pathogenic processes within it. Therefore, these therapists intervene in all important systems and subsystems to which the problem person belongs.

These family therapists should be familiar with systems theory and the characteristics of family, peer-group, and school systems, maintain contact with key school personnel, bureaucracies, parent associations, and community agencies, and have techniques for systems intervention. They either work with all systems themselves (often being assisted by cotherapists), or they use a specialist at their agency who intervenes only in schools. They always consider the impact of any intervention on all subsystems and systems.

Systems-oriented family therapists can proceed in three different, but not mutually exclusive, ways.

1. They may work with individuals or horizontal subsystems, like spouses' and teachers' groups. For example, they help children understand themselves and their behaviors, discuss feelings and personal concerns, gain some control over their lives, and solve their own problems. Working in a group may help these students share similar experiences, support one another, and acquire social skills. Or the

therapists help teachers better understand problem children, learn new techniques in behavior management and instruction, discuss their concerns, and learn from one another. Sometimes it is helpful to organize classroom visits.

2. Systems therapists may also work with vertical subsystems like teacher-student groups or with total systems like families and peer groups. They facilitate interaction within these systems, increase their flexibility and adaptability, solve conflicts, and change structures, boundaries, functions, and rules. For example, they have a group of teachers, administrators, and counselors openly discuss their problems, break away from hierarchical decision making, develop a plan for handling the problems, and support one another in carrying it out.

3. The therapists may also combine different systems or some of their subsystems in order to alleviate mutual blaming or defensiveness, solve conflicts, intervene in intersystemic failures, and encourage collaboration. For example, they may organize a conference with family members and the involved school personnel, get them acquainted in a friendly and confidential atmosphere, and urge them to communicate openly about the problem child (e.g., how he or she behaves in different systems, how they feel about him or her, which goals and expectations they have), their own difficulties (e.g., family crises, problems with the whole class or exorbitant requirements), and how they perceive one another. Each individual develops empathy for the others, recognizes and accepts different viewpoints, learns more about the presented problem, and understands other systems, their significance, and their impact on the problem child. The therapists describe the different systems, their boundaries, distribution of power, psychological and sociological linkages, and vectors of interaction (e.g., by drawing a model). Then all members of the conference together can draw up a mutual problem-solving plan, review it step by step to prevent complications of interpretation, collaborate in carrying it out, and evaluate it. The therapists leave if the plan is successful but offer their help in case any unexpected crisis should occur.

Family therapists tend to neglect to modify the social, cultural, and economic context in which these systems are embedded. They should contact newspapers, TV stations, politicians, and bureaucrats in order to point out problems and negative developments in the school system (unattainable demands, school stress; lack of warmth, no help for personal problems, little consideration of social, emotional, and personality growth; negative side effects of school reforms; and the like). They should also describe the problems of minority and lower-class children, recommend solutions, and improve the situation by organizing self-help groups or community activities. Family therapists should also offer lectures and discussion groups in which they can point out dangers for the healthy development of children (e.g., TV, lack of social contacts), advise people on how to provide a better environment for them (one that is more stimulating and offers more opportunities for observation, exploration, imitation, and help), and improve the cooperation between community and school. They should also help establish marriage and family preparatory classes at schools, colleges, universities, adult education centers, agencies, or churches in order to prepare people for the most difficult jobs of their lives—being a spouse and a parent.

REFERENCES

Adamson, W. C. (1972). Helping parents of children with learning disabilities. *Journal of Learning Disabilities* 5:326–330.

Andolfi, M., Stein, D. D., and Skinner, J. (1977). A systems approach to the child, school, family, and community in an urban area. *American Journal of Community Psychology* 5:33–43.

Andrey, B., Burille, P., Martinez, J. P., and Rey, Y. (1978). Traitement d'un cas d'inadaption scolaire par une thérapie breve de la famille. *Enfance* 31:143–164.

Aponte, H. J. (1976). The family-school interview: an eco-structural approach. *Family Process* 15:303–311.

Bernstein, M. E. (1976). Psychotherapy in the schools: promise and perplexity. *Journal of School Psychology* 14:314–321.

Boszormenyi-Nagy, I., and Spark, G. M. (1973). *Invisible Loyalties. Reciprocity in Intergenerational Family Therapy.* New York: Harper and Row.

Boyd, R. E. (1974). Working with parents and community resources. In *Student Personnel Work in General Education: A Humanistic Approach*, ed. H. A. Moses, pp. 297–329. Springfield, Ill.: Chas C Thomas.

Davis, J. (1977). School phobia in adolescence. *Nursing Mirror and Midwives Journal* 144:61.

Downing, C. J. (1974). Worry workshop for parents. *Elementary School Guidance and Counseling* 9:124–131.

Durell, V. G. (1969). Adolescents in multiple family group therapy in a school setting. *International Journal of Group Psychotherapy* 19:44–52.

Foster, A. H., and Culp, W. W. (1973). School guidance with parents. In *Family Roots of School Learning and Behavior Disorders*, ed. R. Friedman, pp. 284–320. Springfield, Ill.: Chas C Thomas.

Freund, J. C., and Cardwell, G. F. (1977). A multi-faceted response to an adolescent's school failure. *Journal of Marriage and Family Counseling* 3:49–57.

Friedman, R. (1973a). School behavior disorders and the family. In *Family Roots of School Learning and Behavior Disorders*, ed. R. Friedman, pp. 65–81. Springfield, Ill.: Chas C Thomas.

—— (1973b). Structured family interviewing in the assessment of school disorders. In *Family Roots of School Learning and Behavior Disorders*, ed. R. Friedman, pp. 85–107. Springfield, Ill.: Chas C Thomas.

—— (1973c). Structured family-oriented psychotherapy for school behavior and learning disorders. In *Family Roots of School Learning and Behavior Disorders*, ed. R. Friedman, pp. 133–162. Springfield, Ill.: Chas C Thomas.

——, and Meltzer, D. (1973). Family factors in learning disability. In *Family Roots of School Learning and Behavior Disorders*, ed. R. Friedman, pp. 45–64. Springfield, Ill.: Chas C Thomas.

Friedrichsen, G. (1981). Kinder können auch "hinausgefördert" werden. *Frankfurter Allgemeine Zeitung*, September 16, pp. 9–10.

Friesen, J. (1976). Family counseling—a new frontier for school counsellors. *Canadian Counsellor* 10:180–184.

Ginsberg, B. G., Stutman, S. S., and Hummel, J. (1978). Group filial therapy. *Social Work* 23:154–156.

Hillman, B. W., and Perry, T. (1975). The parent-teacher education center: evaluation of a program for improving family relations. *International Journal of Family Counseling* 3:11–16.

Kaslow, F. W., and Cooper, B. (1978). Family therapy with the learning disabled child and his/her family. *Journal of Marriage and Family Counseling* 4:41–49.

Moynihan, S. K. (1978). Utilizing the school setting to facilitate family treatment. *Social Casework* 59:287–294.

Neraal, T. (1982). Familien- und Sozialtherapie. In *Theorie und*

Praxis der Familientherapie ed. M. R. Textor. Forthcoming.

Pannor, H. (1973). The family approach to school problems in an agency setting. In *Family Roots of School Learning and Behavior Disorders*, ed. R. Friedman, pp. 177–194. Springfield, Ill.: Chas C Thomas.

Patterson, G. R., Reid, J. B., Jones, R. R., and Conger, R. E. (1975). *A Social Learning Approach to Family Intervention*, Vol. 1. Eugene, Ore.: Castalia.

Peck, B. B. (1971). Reading disorders: have we overlooked something? *Journal of School Psychology* 9:182–190.

Philage, M. L., Kuna, D. J., and Becerril, G. (1975). A new family approach to therapy for the learning disabled child. *Journal of Learning Disabilities* 8:490–499.

Sampson, N. (1972). Family therapy for the child with a communicative disorder. *Journal of Communication Disorders* 5:205–211.

Seidmon, B. L. (1978). The marriage, family and child counselor and public education. *Marriage and Family Counselors' Quarterly* 12:47–49.

Skynner, A. C. R. (1974). School phobia: a reappraisal. *British Journal of Medical Psychology* 47:1–15.

Tucker, B. Z., and Dyson, E. (1976). The family and the school: utilizing human resources to promote learning. *Family Process* 15:125–141.

Veltkamp, L. J. (1975). School phobia. *International Journal of Family Counseling* 3:47–51.

Waldron, S., Jr., Shrier, D. K., Stone, B., and Tobin, F. (1975). School phobia and other childhood neuroses: a systematic study of the children and their families. *American Journal of Psychiatry* 132:802–808.

Williams, F. S. (1973). The family approach to psychoeducational treatment in the preschool setting. In *Family Roots of School Learning and Behavior Disorders*, ed. R. Friedman, pp. 163–176. Springfield, Ill.: Chas C Thomas.

✖ 10 ✖

Sexual Complaints and Dysfunctions

Martin R. Textor, Dipl.-Paed.

Sex is one of the most important spheres of human life, influencing people from their first until their last day. It can be a source of great satisfaction and pleasure, deep frustration and disappointment, or isolation and shame. Sex is the arena in which the most intimate feelings or the most severe conflicts may be expressed. It may lead to high self-esteem or to a negative self-image, to social approval and support, or to rejection and derogation.

Family therapists cannot avoid dealing with sex. They must assess sexual relationships in order to enhance relatively positive ones and to alleviate sexual complaints. Sometimes they must also treat sexual dysfunctions, sexual variations such as homosexuality and gender identity disorders, or sexual deviance.

Nearly all family therapy cases include sexual complaints. One or both spouses may complain about no sex, too little sex, or too much sex. Some partners are less interested in sex and see their spouses as oversexed and too demanding. In long-standing relationships both partners may experience a loss of mutual physical attraction. Other spouses complain about unsatisfactory sex characterized by a lack of stimulation and caressing, insensitive or inadequate techniques, or constricted and mechanical sexual expression. These partners feel frustrated, deprived, or cheated and often become depressed or hostile.

Sexual complaints can frequently be traced back to intrapsychic causes. Some spouses experience problems with their bodies; for example, they feel unattractive, are uncomfortable with nudity, or suffer from real or imagined deformations. They often have defenses against erotic pleasure—and especially men may be out of touch with tender or loving feelings—which can lead to a lack of sensitivity. Sexual problems can also be caused by shame, denial of sexual wishes, or unconscious guilt or anxiety. Individuals with little ego strength may be afraid of letting go, feel threatened by intimacy, and experience discomfort with giving or receiving.

Some sexual problems originate in early or late childhood. Many adults grew up in a constrictive environment in which physical closeness and caressing were forbidden. The parents punished pleasure-seeking or erotic behaviors like masturbation and induced guilt feelings, shame, and inhibitions by their negative attitudes toward sex. Psycho-analysts trace sexual problems to unresolved oedipal conflicts which cause castration fears and transference distortions. Traumatic sexual experiences during childhood can also have long-term negative consequences.

Sexual complaints may also result from dyadic causes. Sometimes both partners are inexperienced, uncomfortable with each other's body, or ignorant of ways to please each other. This is often aggravated by a lack of open communication and reciprocal feedback about sexual likes and dislikes, feelings, and reactions. An unsatisfactory sexual relationship is frequently caused by one or both partners' being exclusively orgasm oriented, thus neglecting erotic stimulation and caressing. Some people approach sex as work or associate it solely with reproduction and, thereby, eliminate all fun and spontaneity.

Very often sexual difficulties are caused by marital problems. They frequently reinforce each other in a circular and increasingly destructive way. The marital relationship is usually disturbed in one of the following ways: (1) Both spouses see their marriage as shaky or feel insecure in it. They are afraid of being abandoned, rejected, or hurt. (2) Both partners are disappointed with each other, become alienated, and lose (sexual) interest in each other. (3) Both spouses are excessively dependent on each other and may regress to a nongenital relationship, taking turns in parenting each other. (4) In most cases, however, the marital relationship is characterized by discord and conflict, overt or covert hostility, and ambivalence, which may lead to mutual humiliation and sexual sabotage or result in a continuous power struggle in which sex is seen as conquest and submission.

Sociocultural influences may also contribute to sexual problems. For example, each society defines norms of sexual attractiveness and thus determines feelings of personal regard and self-acceptance. Some societies constrict the expression of sexual feelings by religious or social norms. Many Christian groups, for example, equate sex and sin, thus inducing inhibitions, shame, and a fear of eternal punishment. Other societies and social groups are overpermissive and exaggerate the importance of sexuality. In addition, the media in Western societies spread destructive myths like those of macho behavior and mutual orgasm. They portray sex as something to be taken (and to be given) and as something ending with intercourse. Noncoital forms of physical closeness are rarely described in books or shown in American movies.

Social change, especially if it involves the sex roles, may lead to confusion and disturbed sexual relationships. For example, many spouses misunderstood the goals of feminism and ended up with a never-ending struggle between the sexes, thus wreaking havoc on their marital relationship. For women, especially those with children, the stress caused by strenuous or full-time work often results in physical exhaustion and loss of sexual interest. Problems can also be caused by an antierotic environment like that found in small, overcrowded, or unpleasant dwellings.

Family therapists must deal not only with sexual complaints but also with sexual dysfunctions such as impotence, premature ejaculation, and retarded ejaculation in the male and frigidity, orgastic dysfunction, and vaginismus in the female. These problems are caused by factors similar to those described above and are usually aggravated by fear of failure, performance anxiety (need to excel or compete), spectatoring, early conditioning (early sexual failures), fear of the partner's sexuality, or the spouse's demand for performance. In some cases sexual dysfunctions are also caused by physical factors (pathology of the genitals), illness, drugs, and medication. For further information, see Masters and Johnson (1970), Hartman and Fithian (1972), or Kaplan (1974, 1979).

Sex therapists usually use individual diagnostic categories and distinguish between symptomatic and asymptomatic partners. They thus sometimes neglect the total relationship, which allows the asymptomatic partner to assign blame and to limit his or her participation in therapy (e.g., by striving to become a "cotherapist"), causing the symptomatic spouse to feel like a victim or culprit and to become defensive. Family therapists usually avoid these pitfalls by focusing on the total (marital, sexual, parental) relationship and by making both partners responsible for change. Their approach is supported by an empirical research project carried out by Cole and associates (1979). They divided 130 individuals taking part in sex therapy into symptomatic and asymptomatic partners and compared them with respect to parental attitudes toward sex, the age at which heterosexual dating began, early sexual experiences, sexual knowledge, current sexual practices and attitudes, sexual communication, wishes, and the like. They found nearly no significant differences and concluded, "One could argue, therefore, that classifying individuals into symptomatic and asymptomatic categories did not serve as a useful analytic dichotomy for comparing predisposing factors leading to sexual dysfunction or predicting outcomes for treatment" (p. 85). Thus, family therapists should always consider intrapsychic, interpersonal, and sociocultural causes of sexual complaints and dysfunctions—and couples usually state their sexual problems in terms of dissatisfaction with their total relationship.

Another difficulty should be mentioned in this context. Some couples try to keep the treatment focus on the sexual complaint or dysfunction in order to prevent an overall assessment and treatment of their total relationship. They resist talking about more fundamental problems and do not want to change their marital relationship. Using the sexual complaint as a myth they try to sabotage the treatment and tend to attack and humiliate each other. Family therapists have to consider this possibility and deal with it in the same way as they do other resistances.

TREATMENT OF SEXUAL COMPLAINTS

Family therapists should be able to treat sexual complaints effectively. They need to be acquainted with the physiology and psychology of the sexual response, common sexual problems, and specific treatment techniques. They should also be comfortable with talking about sex, provide a permissive atmosphere, facilitate discussion, and model sexual communication by maintaining an information-seeking, nonjudgmental stance.

Inquiries about the spouses' sexual adjustment are nearly always necessary. In the presence of all family members, family therapists may discuss intimacy, affection, body contact, sex-role behavior, or attitudes related to sex. Children can often contribute much to the assessment of the nongenital aspects of their parents' (sexual) relationship, and the discussion may give them valuable learning experiences, lead to more open and honest communication, and increase the closeness among family members. If the therapist deems it necessary to explore the physical aspects of the spouses' sexual relationship or if the partners want to talk about unsatisfactory sex (techniques) or dysfunctions, the children should be excluded from the sessions.

Family therapists can approach sexual issues by mentioning that sexual behavior is important to the spouses' relationship and that it, therefore, has to be evaluated in the context of the total relationship. If the partners do not accept the definition of their sexual complaint as a relationship problem, the therapist should help them explore the interactional components of their complaint and recognize the impact of (and its impact on) marital problems. But if the definition is accepted, the family therapist can proceed to inquire about the onset of the sexual problem (takes a history), problems occurring at the same time (developmental crises), and the sexual problem's causes. The therapist should also assess relationship needs, modes of communication and problem solving, role flexibility, affectional responses, attitudes, values, and so on before deciding whether the sexual problem must be treated separately (either by the therapist or a specialist) or together with other problems, or whether it will disappear by itself after more fundamental conflicts have been resolved.

Intrapsychic causes of sexual complaints can be treated by using cognitive insight methods such as interpretation and confrontation, experientially oriented (Gestalt) methods, and/or behavioral techniques. Family therapists can assist individuals to work through negative thoughts and feelings concerning their bodies and genital organs, help them overcome shame and embarrassment, and encourage them to explore their own bodies (some women know very little about their genitals). They can also relieve guilt feelings, work on inhibitions and childhood strictures against erotic pleasure, and give permission to enjoy sex, have fun, and indulge in sexual play and fantasy.

Treating interpersonal causes of sexual complaints usually involves teaching the spouses to communicate openly about sexual likes and dislikes and reactions and preferences. Family therapists alleviate the anxiety about talking about sex, clarify the sexual interaction, and help the partners share their feelings and verbalize appropriate expectations. They have the couple discuss how to please each other and encourage them to explore each other's body. They also help the spouses confront avoided problems, teach conflict-resolution, deal with power struggles, and alleviate fears of being rejected or hurt. It is often necessary to remove rewards from sexual symptoms or to rekindle sexual interest in the partner.

Another important function of family therapists is to educate and inform about the physiology and psychology of sexual behavior. They eliminate misconceptions and clear up confusions, talk about alternative ways of giving erotic pleasure, teach more sensitive or adequate techniques, and encourage the partners to experiment. Quite often the therapists have to change negative attitudes or destructive myths (e.g., of mutual orgasms). Meisel (1977) wrote, "Men often need help in allowing themselves to be given to sexually, to take a more passive role and enjoy being receptive. Women often operate with the myth that sex is something a man does to a woman, and need help in feeling comfortable being more assertive about giving and getting" (p. 206).

Sex Therapy

Family therapists are usually not trained to treat sexual dysfunctions and, therefore, sometimes need the help of sex therapists. The latter see their primary goal as relieving sexual dysfunctions and improving the overall sexual functioning. Accordingly, they use a symptom-focused form of therapy which is usually rapid and task oriented. Because of this limited focus, family therapists should refer clients for sex therapy only if the marital relationship is relatively healthy and if the partners are motivated and do not suffer from any severe psychopathology. Otherwise, the family and marital conflicts or the disturbed partner(s) should be treated first before referring them for sex therapy. If the sexual dysfunction, however, is central and impedes any progress in family therapy, concurrent sex therapy is indicated, or the spouses are referred to sex therapists and later returned by the latter. Less severe cases of sexual dysfunction (e.g., secondary impotence) can be treated by family therapists if they incorporate techniques from sex therapy (thereby recognizing the limitations of their experience and knowledge) or use sex therapists as consultants. It is important to maintain good professional relationships with sex therapists and to confer with them as often as necessary.

A sex therapist usually works with a heterosexual cotherapist. Together they sort out the physical causes of the sexual dysfunction by means of a (joint) medical exam. Then they assess intrapsychic and interpersonal causes and treat them in a way similar to those described earlier. In addition, they usually start the treatment by prescribing the "sensate focus" exercise (see Kaplan 1974, Masters and Johnson 1970). They help the partners relax by removing the pressure for intercourse (forbidding it) and encouraging physical closeness and caressing instead. Thereby, the couple experiences new erotic pleasures and develops trust. The demand for performance is replaced, and the therapists receive new information about the sexual behavior and the causes of the dysfunction by exploring the partners' reaction to these exercises.

Later, the sex therapists use various systematically structured erotic tasks and prescriptions in order to treat the specific dysfunction or cause. They may use systematic desensitization or flooding to alleviate fears, teach techniques to stop distracting thoughts or spectatoring (like concentrating on sexual fantasies), prescribe muscular exercises to make the partners relax, and undo early conditioning with the help of reinforcement techniques. They describe nondemand coitus, give responsibility to each spouse for his or her own erotic fulfillment, and teach the principle of taking turns in order to dispel the fear of failure or performance anxiety. Women suffering from sexual dysfunctions are encouraged to experiment with masturbation and vibrators or are taught how to heighten vaginal and clitoral arousal, while at the same time their partners learn better ways of genital stimulation. These tasks are usually performed at home and are of great effectiveness in relieving sexual symptoms. They are described in detail by Masters and Johnson (1970), Hartman and Fithian (1972), Kaplan (1974, 1979), Meyer (1976), and Lo Piccolo and Lo Piccolo (1978).

The chances are great that the spouses will return for family therapy with their sexual dysfunctions having disappeared. This usually has a beneficial effect on their overall marital and family functioning. The partners have more positive and warm feelings for each other and are more optimistic and confident. They have found that they can cooperate effectively and solve problems—now they might even tackle other conflicts on their own. Besides, their attitudes toward therapy are more positive, and they are more willing to change.

Sometimes, however, sex therapists are not successful, as the main problems lie in the marital or family relationships. In some cases, improvement in the sexual sphere leads to the exacerbation of other family problems as the family tries to maintain its homeostasis (e.g., by developing new symptoms or by the children's acting out). Sex therapists then can provide new data on the relationship and the problem that will help the family therapist be more successful.

PSYCHOSEXUAL IDENTITY DISORDERS AND SEXUAL VARIATIONS

Sex-role and sexual behaviors are not inborn but are learned during childhood and adolescence. Children experiment with different ways of expressing their own gender, thereby growing into their sex roles and developing a sexual identity. But it is also common for them to imitate the opposite sex in play and fantasy or participate in activities that society reserves for the other gender. This is normal as long as it does not occur too often or in combination with adjustment problems. If parents are upset by these behaviors, they need only some reassurance. The same is true if they worry about their child being a homosexual if he or she plays only with peers of the same sex: This is normal for children during the latency period. The awakening of the heterosexual drive in puberty may lead to confusion, as the adolescents have not yet learned how to express it appropriately. Accordingly, they may experiment with heterosexual, homosexual, or masturbatory behaviors. Parents should be reassured that this is common and that no therapy is indicated as long as the children do not show symptoms of any psychopathology.

But there are also cases in which children indulge in the activities, habits, and behaviors of the other sex. For example, boys might wear dresses, jewelry, or makeup (openly or in secret), consistently move and talk with feminine mannerisms, prefer girls' games and toys, avoid the company of males, and converse only about topics that women are interested in. They frequently pretend to be girls in play and fantasy or even express the desire to be a woman or to change their sex organs. These behaviors are often very distressing to their parents and usually lead to rejection by relatives, teachers, and peers, often causing these boys to feel isolated, lonely, and unhappy. If girls behave like boys, it is usually accepted by their environment, as a greater variety of sex-role behaviors is permitted for girls.

Parents of children with psychosexual identity disorders usually have unhappy marriages without affection and real communication and with much conflict and frustration in the marital and sexual relationship. Higham (1976) noticed that "gender transposition in the child paralleled the direction of parental dissatisfaction: When the father disparaged his wife, the daughter rejected femininity; when the mother disparaged her husband, the son rejected masculinity" (p. 55). This is often aggravated by disturbed sex roles and negative or confusing gender attitudes which prevent these children from accepting their sex and developing a secure sexual identity.

The relationship between the parents and their child is often disturbed. For example, fathers of feminine boys are often absent from their families, tend to be cold and distant, or are only a little emotionally involved with their children. They thus are not available as models for masculine behaviors. Moreover, they may be indifferent and unconcerned or avoid, reject, and punish their sons instead of helping them alter their feminine behaviors. The mothers of these boys often feel incomplete, depressed, and empty, use their children to find sense in their lives, and cling to them in a symbiotic way. They try to make them into "female" companions by encouraging every feminine trait, regarding their effeminate behavior as graceful and sensible, and shielding them from a critical environment. In this family situation the boys do not pass through the oedipal phase, as they cannot develop incestuous feelings and do not experience their fathers as rivals inducing castration anxiety.

As feminine boys (masculine girls less so) usually suffer from rejection and ridicule, feel isolated and unhappy, and nearly always want to become like their same-sex peers, family therapy is indicated. The probability of treatment success is very high, as reported by Bates and colleagues (1975), Newman (1976), and Metcalf and Williams (1977), as long as the children are between 5 and 12 years old. Treatment programs usually consist of play therapy with the child conducted by a same-sex therapist. He or she acts as a role model, encourages identification, reinforces activities typical for the respective gender, teaches lacking sex-role behaviors, and tells stories to develop normal interests. Bates and colleagues (1975) also use group therapy to encourage peer interaction and social skills. They use a behavior modification (token) program which is also taught to the parents in order to increase masculine behaviors. Metcalf and Williams (1977) train parents and teachers to use an operant conditioning program.

But family therapists also have to treat the relationship between parents and child. They should explore the parents' feelings about the child's behavior; make the distant parent give up shaming, rejecting, and punishing the child; increase his or her involvement with the child (e.g., by motivating joint activities typical for the respective gender); and help the symbiotic parent give the child some autonomy. Both parents need to be educated about masculinity and femininity and should define their gender roles sharply for a while so that the child can more easily develop a sexual identity. Metcalf and Williams (1977) recommend that the child should take part only in those activities and domestic duties that are typical of members of his or her gender and that are also performed by the same-sex parent. Family therapists also should improve the marital relationship so that the spouses no longer need to derogate the opposite sex.

If psychosexual-identity disorders, cross-dressing, or experimentation with homosexual relationships are maintained through adolescence, they usually become irreversible, as these young adults usually have accepted that they are homosexuals or lesbians, transsexuals, or transvestites. They want to be accepted as such and rarely are motivated to change their sexual orientation. Therefore, if family therapists are contacted by the parents, they should aim at rehabilitation and not at therapy—especially as there is no legal (and little social) pressure to treat these young adults against their will (which, anyway, is not possible). They can help them sort out their feelings, become more knowledgeable (e.g., about the homosexual life-style or sex changes), and enhance the quality of their sex life. These young adults often need help in accepting themselves, handling social disapproval, and achieving independence. Family therapists also should show the parents that rejecting their child will only add one more burden to his or her difficulties. Then they can encourage them to accept their child's sexual identity and his or her right to make decisions about his or her sexual behavior. The parents should support their child, keep the channels open for meaningful communication, and show empathy and understanding.

Family therapists rarely have to treat families in which both partners are homosexuals or in which one spouse is a transvestite. They should treat them in the same way as other clients and promote their growth and happiness, whether or not they come with problems related to their sexual behavior. Most family therapists have to make a special effort to understand a different life-style and to work through prejudices and negative countertransferences (DiBella 1979). There is the danger of their focusing too much on sexuality and, thereby, losing sight of the total person and other interpersonal aspects.

Sexual Variations and the Law

The sex drive is very malleable and diffuse and can be aroused and satisfied in many different ways. Anthropologists describe a great variety of allowed or forbidden sexual behaviors in primitive and developed societies, and historians note that the range of permitted sexual behaviors changes in the course of time within one society. For example, homosexuality was considered to be a disease and legal offense in the United States some 20 years ago. But today it is better tolerated. Society determines which are the best and right ways of sexual expression, which ways are criticized but permitted, and which are forbidden and punished. The family and the peer group are the most prominent social institutions which transmit the society's norms, values, and attitudes regarding sex to its younger members, whereas other institutions (churches, courts, councils, and so on) control the adults' sexual behavior.

Western societies permit a wide range of sexual behaviors. In many countries even sexual variations such as homosexuality, transsexualism, transvestism, and fetishism are tolerated officially. Individuals expressing their sexual feelings in these ways may still be criticized or stigmatized by some social groups, but they can find subcultures of people who desire similar sexual experiences. They are permitted to gather in bars, form clubs, publish journals, and voice their interests in national organizations. Other forms of sexual behavior, however, are considered to be deviant. All Western societies prosecute and punish pedophilia, incest, childhood prostitution, rape, and exhibitionism.

Sex offenders are usually incarcerated, though the treatment facilities in the prison system are usually inadequate, and few therapists are interested in working with these individuals. Family therapists are generally not trained to deal with sex offenders and rarely see them as patients. As well, few families will travel to the prison in order to take part in weekly family therapy sessions, though in at least some cases the wife can be involved in the treatment.

REFERENCES

Apperson, L. B., and McAdoo, W. G., Jr. (1968). Parental factors in the childhood of homosexuals. *Journal of Abnormal Psychology* 73:201–206.
Bates, J. E., Skilbeck, W. M., Smith, K. V. R., and Bentler, P. M. (1975). Intervention with families of gender-disturbed boys. *American Journal of Orthopsychiatry* 45:150–157.

Cole, C. M., Blakeney, P. E., Chan, F. A., Chesney, A. P., and Creson, D. L. (1979). The myth of symptomatic versus asymptomatic partners in the conjoint treatment of sexual dysfunction. *Journal of Sex and Marital Therapy* 5:79–89.

DiBella, G. A. W. (1979). Family psychotherapy with the homosexual family: a community psychiatry approach to homosexuality. *Community Mental Health Journal* 15:41–46.

Hartman, E. W., and Fithian, M. (1972). *The Treatment of Sexual Dysfunctions*. Long Beach, Calif.: Center for Marital and Sexual Studies.

Higham, E. (1976). Case management of the gender incongruity syndrome in childhood and adolescence. *Journal of Homosexuality* 2:49–57.

Kaplan, H. S. (1974). *The New Sex Therapy*. New York: Brunner/Mazel.

—— (1979). *Disorders of Sexual Desire*. New York: Brunner/Mazel.

Lo Piccolo, J., and Lo Piccolo, L., eds. (1978). *Handbook of Sex Therapy*. New York: Plenum.

Masters, W. H., and Johnson, V. E. (1970). *Human Sexual Inadequacy*. Boston: Little, Brown.

Meisel, S. S. (1977). The treatment of sexual problems in marital and family therapy. *Clinical Social Work Journal* 5:200–209.

Metcalf, S., and Williams, W. (1977). A case of male childhood transsexualism and its management. *Australian and New Zealand Journal of Psychiatry* 11:53–59.

Meyer, J., ed. (1976). *Clinical Management of Sexual Disorders*. Baltimore: Williams and Wilkins.

Newman, L. E. (1976). Treatment for the parents of feminine boys. *American Journal of Psychiatry* 133:683–687.

Resnik, H. L. P., and Wolfgang, M. E. (1972). New directions in the treatment of sex deviance. In *Sexual Behaviors: Social, Clinical, and Legal Aspects*, ed. H. L. P. Resnik and M. E. Wolfgang, pp. 397–428. Boston: Little, Brown.

Sederer, L. I., and Sederer, N. (1979). A family myth: sex therapy gone awry. *Family Process* 18:315–321.

Sherman, S. N. (1976). The therapist and changing sex roles. *Social Casework* 57:93–96.

Witkin, M. H. (1977). Sex therapy as an aid to marital and family therapy. *Journal of Sex and Marital Therapy* 3:19–30.

❧ 11 ❧

Separation and Divorce

Janice Goldman, Psy.D., and
James Coane, Psy.D.

Families, we now know, continue to exist well after the divorce is over. Divorce doesn't "end it all" but, rather, alters the family, creating two subsections. In this view, divorce is not so much an event as a process and a way of life. The family therapist and the family must appreciate that once there are children, the spouses can not be done with each other. Further, the child is often an agent who actively tries to encourage the parents to stay together, by acting out and other maneuvers. The child's desire to maintain the family is related to his or her perception of developmental survival. A family therapy approach to the whole family through the process of separation and divorce attempts to work with these factors and to facilitate for all of its members interaction and developmental progression in the next phase of the family's life. The primary goal is this preservation of the parental coalition. The purpose of this approach is to enable the parents to maintain a coparenting alliance while separating from the marital bond. Therapy helps establish new roles in the postdivorce period, especially in regard to fair play, allocating family resources, and freeing the children from the parental fight. The therapist is defined as the children's advocate, a referee, and a facilitator who enables the family to move from one transitional stage to another.

Families in the process of separation and divorce live with two important existential paradoxes. The first is that "We are and we are not still a family." The resolution of this paradox and the therapeutic directive following from it lie in promoting the view that we are a family, but in an altered form, and that the children need to be able to continue to call on the resources of both parents through their developmental years. The second paradox is that the divorce of the marital pair represents a failure of the system that they have developed, and the work with the family after divorce seeks a new modus vivendi that must adhere to the terms of this untenable system. Put another way, the therapist must understand the system that the spouses have developed and use it to make modifications for the postdivorce period. Anger must be isolated. When old issues surface, the therapist must point out that "that is why you don't want to be married to each other" and concentrate on the present need to cooperate for the children's sake. It is important to stress that each parent needs a relationship with the child for his or her own growth and development, not for the other's sake. In this manner, individuated relational ties can replace the group cathexis of the family as a whole.

A second, and more ambitious, goal of divorce therapy is to foster the couple's emotional divorce while maintaining ties to the children and the parental coalition. This is difficult because people avoid being in the "nothing" state and are afraid of ultimate losses. Hate is as warming an emotion as love is, and many cling to it for this reason. Specific therapeutic techniques to foster an emotional divorce may include encouraging individual responsibility for problems, supporting the spouse's growth as a trade-off for his or her support of one's own growth, mobilizing hate as a way to transform it into love, and refocusing conflicts with the spouse backward to each spouse's parental generation.

In recent years, there has been a rapid increase of interest in and awareness of the therapeutic problems associated with a divorce. The focus is frequently on the child who often carries the invitation for treatment in the guise of various symptoms. Reder and Eve (1981), Derdeyn (1977), and Fine (1980) all describe the perspective of the child in this situation. Wallerstein and Kelly (1974, 1975, 1976, 1977) link the child's reaction to divorce with developmental stages.

It is clear that creative interventions in this process are imperative. Kressel and Deutsch (1977) investigated many therapists' views and concluded that the basic strategies in divorce treatment were the resolution of the couple's psychic divorce and the primary welfare of the minor children. Suarez, Weston, and Hartstein (1978) and Elkin (1977) described the special treatment considerations of divorce.

Family therapy is a particularly appropriate way of approaching these problems. Beal (1979) described the divorce process in family system terms. Kaplan (1977) suggested structural family therapy. Baideme and associates (1978) offered conjoint techniques following divorce. Goldman and Coane (1977) delineated a four-stage model that describes the phases necessary for final disengagement of the marriage and maintenance of the coparenting function. Bohannan (1970) outlined the six stages of divorce. Rosenthal and Hansen (1980) discussed single-parent family treatment. Weisfeld and Laser (1977) suggested therapeutic approaches with children in residential settings. Ritchie and Serrano (1974) considered a treatment of postdivorce families with adolescents called *multiple-impact therapy*. And Ransom and colleagues (1979) expressed the need to facilitate the stepparenting process.

This involvement by the therapist in the area of divorce necessitates discussions of the meaning of divorce (Hancock 1980) and the relationship between the therapist and the legal system (Steinberg 1980). Whitaker and Miller (1969) eloquently described the particular dilemmas for the therapist involved with divorce.

Working with families on the issues of separation and divorce may be viewed as a process of stages with specific tasks and therapeutic directives corresponding to each. The stages are (1) deciding to divorce or separate, (2) negotiating the separation, (3) the short-term and long-term effects after the separation and/or divorce, and (4) rebonding to a new partner. We shall consider each of these stages, with the appropriate techniques for that stage and then case illustrations.

DECISION TO SEPARATE

The point at which a couple decides to get divorced is preceded by an intricate history. The tensions, fears, resentment, and emotional pain are usually intense and awesome. When a family enters therapy in crisis, the therapist needs to make a provisional assessment of the status of its members' intentions. Families can be roughly categorized as the decided and undecided.

The decided family has either consciously or unconsciously decided to end the marriage. Their quest in therapy is to separate as a marital unit and to minimize the pain to themselves and their children. The goal of retaining some later coparenting alliance in the service of the children is often far from their immediate plans.

The undecided family is considering options in its desire for emotional health, of which divorce is one option. This choice often is suggested by one of the spouses as a means of expressing enormous dissatisfaction and forcing the marriage into crisis. The therapist in this instance must recognize the desire for divorce as a symptom and not a solution. From this perspective, conjoint marital therapy may be the best approach.

If the family is undecided, several assessments need to be made. One possible intervention is to view the stated causes for difficulty and possible divorce as stylistic labels. The labels often are the ones most commonly encountered by therapists: money, children, sex, family of origin, and they are strategic maps of communication patterns, family alliance, and overt and covert power struggles. The nature of the surface conflicts can also be used to assess the individuals' ego structure and strengths.

To clarify and amplify family dynamics it is helpful to have diagnostic family interviews even if conjoint marital therapy is ultimately the approach chosen. The children in these situations often freely express fears of divorce and report revealing data and observations.

If the therapist and couple are undecided about divorce, it is then the therapist's responsibility to facilitate the decision-making process. Briefly, the goal at this stage is to humanize the marriage and its individuals to the point that each member has at least a sense of the existential and intrapsychic issues that have led to their decision.

Each spouse should explore his or her fantasies about what is to be gained or lost by divorce. The therapist aids in constructing an experimental separation. The husband and wife, even though there is no physical separation, may indulge in a full fantasy experience. Sometimes an actual separation may be necessary. This is useful, first, because the individuals get a chance to "get the wish" or "have the fear come true." This expression tends to reveal both beneficial and catastrophic expectations. Also, each spouse gets to know the other's hopes and fears and then may view that person more sympathetically.

When marriages are in crisis and divorce is being considered, there is a complementary process of holding on and letting go. This holding-on/letting-go ratio is sometimes fixed and sometimes variable. Often a couple arrives for treatment with one wanting to leave and the other wanting that person to stay. The person that is afraid of letting go is encouraged and supported to let that happen. This move tentatively increases the anxiety of the holding-on person. But as the holding-on person's anxiety is desensitized, the letting-go person's anxiety rises. This path ultimately leads to an investigation of the couples' symbiotic need for each other, their fears of aloneness and isolation, their sense of failure, and their feelings of guilt. When the couple can recognize these experiences, they can foster an alliance that allows them to make a decision. The therapist's support for a responsible decision permits the couple to respond according to the other's welfare as well as his or her own. The therapist and couple decide either to remain married, in which case further marital therapy follows, or to consider the marriage as untenable. It is when both people see this untenability that the therapist can help achieve an active, conscious, and caring separation and divorce. The second stage of actually separating can be complicated by a return to indecision or a resistance to therapeutic help by assuming strong positions, both relationally and legally.

> The F. family consisted of a very compulsive mother, a very
> impulsive father, and two daughters aged 12 and 8. The
> parents' marriage had always been a struggle for control.
> Their marriage of 14 years had produced little understanding,
> and they frequently had bouts of judgmental, blaming
> arguments. The father's individual psychotherapy shifted the
> balance of the relationship. He became more willing to stop

blaming and recognize how his wife represented his need for self-control. Instead of trying to persuade her to reject him, he now was considering leaving. This provided a panic in Mrs. F., as she preferred this sadomasochistic style to isolation.

In conjoint therapy, Mr. and Mrs. F. recognized the power of their unresolved dependency issues and explored their fears of independence. They agreed that a trial separation would be useful in discovering their own capabilities. They came to their decision by fantasizing worst-case scenarios and allowing candid thoughts to be expressed. They disclosed many secrets and came to see that they had little in common. The children were divided in their loyalty, the 12-year-old strongly identifying with her mother and the 8-year-old allying herself with her father. The children were seen as symbolizing the dramatic lack of family and marital interaction. After using fantasy techniques and dynamic explorations, Mr. and Mrs. F. decided to separate.

SEPARATION PROCESS

Once a couple has decided to separate, they have strong contradictory feelings of relief, coupled with anxiety. The relief comes from the notion that this painful period will soon be over. The anxiety stems from anticipatory fantasies of being alone and dealing with new financial, social, and parental responsibilities. Some of this anxiety can be transformed into the excitement of the unknown. The therapist can help ease tension, not only by acknowledging the difficulty of the situation, but also by actively teaching and encouraging the transformation of stress into excitement. The therapist's own style is a model of identification and a source of positive energy, and he or she should be impartial and able to ally with both parties, which Boszormenyi-Nagy and Krasner (1980) call *multidirectional partiality*. The underlying commitment is to the growth and welfare of all individuals.

Early in treatment the therapist creates a monitoring, reality-testing ego. The family system is described in such a way as to sensitize the individuals to the fact that they should be on guard for breakdowns in problem solving during divorce, similar to those they have had during marriage. This leads to the establishment of an ego alliance which sets realistic expectations for the difficulties ahead.

The process of separation and divorce can be described as an abandoning of old agreements and a recontracting for new agreements that enhance separate functioning. These renegotiations most commonly become mired in the complexities of parenting and custody. All other issues (property, family of origin ties, social consequences) seem resolvable. The children, however, are a link in the union that cannot be removed. Out of desire for the children's welfare, long-term agreements are necessary and are the essential therapeutic challenge: how to get two adults who cannot make workable agreements to make a workable agreement.

Often the clients place the therapist into the position of a Solomon. Because of the pain and anxiety in the separation process, the children's welfare is not only neglected but is also negatively affected by scapegoating and parentification. It can be helpful strategically to take on the role of Solomon as a means of getting each parent to appreciate the complexity of the process. The Solomon technique is to offer a superficially fair settlement that is patently destructive to the child, and this often mobilizes the best parental instincts.

The parents should know that the separation is marital and must not be confused with parenting responsibilities. They should be aware that the children are not the only ones to gain from a constructive divorce. It is helpful to encourage them to discuss their fears of exploitation and manipulation by each other. The therapist also can describe the advantages of mutual support during this termination process.

Although the couple has acknowledged their inability to cooperate, they need not believe that this must be overcome totally in order to reach a workable solution. A helpful technique here is to persuade the couple to accept a level of destructiveness that each can tolerate. By pointing out the level of pathology in the relationship, both people can recognize the irony of the task and accordingly adjust their expectations. Humor is useful in that it can reduce anxiety and anger, solidify a task-oriented alliance, and describe paradoxical dynamics.

The therapist then can appeal to the most mature aspects of the person's ego. Often the system distorts in pathological ways the destructive and unhealthy parts of people's functioning. By acknowledging the system as destructive, each person is given a chance to feel dignity and to begin the task of creating new meaning as a person. By stressing the agreement responsibilities and not demanding that these be pleasant, each person is more willing to accept a temporary burden that will be beneficial in the long run. The marital partners may become more cooperative and effective parents by recognizing that they both are in the same position.

Typically, married men and women separate as a prelude to divorce. This serves two purposes. First, it removes the dissatisfied parties from frequent contact and reduces tension and discord, and, second, the separation is an experiment in this new life-style. Therapy sessions during this time are extremely helpful, as the therapist can help create new modes of living, especially an acceptable arrangement for the children.

The therapist can avoid failure by describing the inevitable breakdowns of agreement that will take place and predicting regression to pathological relational styles. By anticipating this problem, there will be fewer complications, and they will be viewed as acceptable deviances.

In addition, adequate time should be assigned to the mourning process. Sometimes couples are resistant to this aspect because of the pain involved. But with the proper preparation, the death of the marriage can be worked through. When the children are informed of the impending separation and divorce, they can be included in family therapy sessions. The therapist can function as a transitional object of nurturance for the children as the family mourns the loss of one organization and creates another.

We should point out that there is a serious difficulty in divorce therapy once the decision to divorce is made. The legal system encourages the adversary nature of divorce and often discourages healthy, therapeutic, and cooperative modes. Questions of responsibility for divorce, who is right and who is wrong, financial arrangements, and custody decisions become enormous obstacles to continuing cooperation. The legal system can promote the most pathological aspects of family functioning, and it is at this point that there can be a wavering in commitment to family treatment. Legal advice often counsels secrecy, self-protectiveness, and false statements. This can be somewhat neutralized by narrowing the treatment's focus and holding occasional individual sessions. But, this plan is somewhat risky, as the therapist may be inadvertently drawn into the adversary process. The therapist must insist on a goal of cooperative, mutually beneficial separation. At times the legal process is so contrary in its direction that therapy has to be suspended until some of the legal issues are settled. The therapist's position can remain relatively neutral if he or she can maintain the child advocate role.

> Mr. and Mrs. M. were separated and had decided to get divorced. They had three sons, aged 12, 9, and 7, and were greatly disturbed by the negative effect on both the children and their own lives. They came into therapy desiring help in separating and divorcing. At no time did they reconsider their decision to divorce.
>
> Therapeutically it was necessary to define the difficulty of the problem. It was agreed that what they had in common was a desire to leave each other and give the children what they needed. But this acknowledgment did little to offset their arguing and bickering. The therapist at one point became the problem solver by suggesting that the children be sent to a relative's or foster home, as they were too complex a problem for two "inadequate" people to resolve. Such suggestions became a splash of cold water on this couple when they heatedly contested each other.
>
> Gradually, their relational script became obvious to the point that it could be discussed humorously. They often made fun of themselves by exaggerating their styles. They also demonstrated more control of their hurt and fear. The parents and the therapist became a team to work out coparenting issues. The therapist modeled techniques of care and supported the more mature sides of the couple's personalities. Mr. and Mrs. M. discovered that they had much to gain by separating their roles as parents from their roles as spouses.
>
> At this point a mutual depression set in. Therapy proceeded through a mourning phase that resulted in a more profound acceptance of each other, despite their incompatibility. The divorce process followed a smoother route with significantly less scapegoating of the children.

AFTER THE SEPARATION AND DIVORCE

The stage of separation and divorce may be divided into two substages. Time is the crucial variable here, and therapists need to be

alert to the short-term versus long-term effects of the separation/
divorce. Short-term effects are signaled first by the eruption of symptoms, particularly in a previously healthy and stable child. When this
occurs, if such symptoms are not transient adjustment reactions, it is a
sign of a poor resolution of one of the foregoing stages. Such symptoms
may also be the expression of serious psychopathology in one of the
parents whom the breakdown of the marriage now leaves exposed.
The first reaction may be to recreate the marriage in order to regain the
stabilizing ego function, attempting to use one of the children as a
partner or to invoke care-taking activity by the former spouse because
of pathological neediness.

> Mrs. R. used to minister to a borderline husband in a manner
> that allowed his pathological defenses to continue to organize
> the family's functioning. For example, though quite trim
> physically, Mr. R. had extreme fears of oral incorporation
> and used to run 10 miles or so before eating a normal
> Sunday breakfast of pancakes. Mrs. R. cooperated in
> disciplining herself and her two young children to wait until
> this ritual had been completed. Finally, she entered
> individual treatment with the express goal of working toward
> a separation from this pathological marital system. When this
> goal was achieved and she had moved out, the couple's
> oldest child, a daughter of 8, took on the role of stabilizing
> her father's functioning. Within several months the child
> became symptomatic with severe tension headaches, for
> which no physical cause could be found. A brief therapy
> intervention, with the mother, father, and daughter
> interviewed separately, was successful in clarifying the issue
> of the daughter's attempted monitoring of her father's depression.
> The father was made aware of the pressure his daughter was
> experiencing and was encouraged to seek individual
> treatment for himself. He did, although he ultimately
> suffered a breakdown and had to be hospitalized. The
> daughter's wish to fix things for her father was explored
> and its impossibility declared, at which point her tension
> headaches stopped.

Long-term effects of the poor resolution of divorce-related issues
are more subtle and more difficult to uncover, since they typically
occur years later enmeshed in a matrix of other presenting problems.
Therapists need to be sensitive to the ways in which divorce-related

issues interact with development and provide a framework for seemingly unrelated issues. These issues then should be addressed by allowing the deficiency to be identified and worked through.

The O. family presented with problems of delinquent acting out in the youngest daughter, a girl just 16, who had been discovered to be drunk following a near-fatal car accident. The accoutrements of drug use were at the same time discovered in her room. Her school grades had been going down, and over time her friendships had become more secretive and more objectionable to her parents. The O. family had had a history of three marriages and two fathers. The four children all were now adolescents and young adults. The current father, the mother's third husband, had been a bachelor until his marriage to the mother some five years previously, and he had had no experience in parenting before his entrance into this family. He doubted his legitimacy and entitlement to aid the mother in setting limits for the adolescent daughters and needed therapeutic sanction for expression of his fatherly role. Acting-out behavior in adolescence in all four children was tied in part to the poor resolution of issues surrounding the loss of the two fathers. The children's contact with one biological father was quite sporadic, almost nonexistent for three of the offspring. Contact with the second father, the biological father of one and the psychological father of two, was allowed only to the biological child and was limited to Christmas and summer vacations. Both men had remarried and established new families far away. There was much fantasy about each father and ambivalent longing for reunion. Early premature heterosexual behavior of the three daughters was begun in an attempt both to replace the father and to have a male figure to aid in the adolescent task of separating from the mother. These issues had to be introduced and a period of mourning allowed. The technique used in this case involved the precipitation of feelings concerning mourning and loss. The effect of the mourning process, in which three daughters and the mother participated (a son was far removed geographically), was enough to abort the beginning delinquent behavior of the youngest daughter and to allow a closer bonding among all family members. Mr. O.'s role during the mourning process was peripheral, but his presence was important in sanctioning the work and bringing the whole family, as now constituted, into a common present.

THE PERIOD OF ADULT REBONDING

Adult rebonding is the period when the family system enlarges to include the new partner or partners of the former marital pair. It is most useful to conceptualize the family as having subsystems, with the child or children belonging to both or several of them. The salient psychological work is to help the relevant adults accept this fact of life. In practice this may mean helping the child with reentry problems as he or she moves between households with different rules and different styles of living. Excesses must be prevented through cooperation and communication between the subsystems. These are boundary issues, and it has been documented that such blended households have to have more permeable boundaries than do ordinary nuclear families.

Another major area of concern in this phase is working through the loyalty issues. It is essential that the stepparent tolerate without undue jealousy the child's cathexis of the natural parent. When this becomes difficult, the therapist must determine how the child's love for the parent reminds the parent of his or her former spouse.

Issues in the marriage can also be precipitated by the arrival of an unplanned child. For example, in one case, the arrival of a child after the death of the custodial parent precipitated marital stress, since having children was not part of the original marital agreement. When such is the case, the family is more willing to enter therapy as a family and to work on issues of how to be a family. Discussing the historical development of each person's family in the presence of the other family members can be especially helpful. With children, this technique can include the use of play materials as aids in illustration. One child, for example, chose a set of dominoes and used them as abstract building blocks, cars, and people to illustrate his memories of life from early childhood up to his present age of 10, while his father and stepmother watched from the sidelines.

In summary, we considered the most helpful therapeutic techniques for each stage of the separation and divorce process. Our choice includes working with two existential paradoxes as the baseline of our approach: the first being that the family is and is not still a family, and the second that an unworkable system can be used to develop a new workable system. The family crisis of separation and divorce can be a "dangerous opportunity." If this moment in the family's history can be used constructively, the postdivorce period can be improved for all of the family members.

REFERENCES

Baideme, S., Hill, H., and Seritella, D. (1978). Conjoint family therapy following divorce: an alternative strategy. *American Journal of Family Therapy* 6:55–59.

Beal, E. (1979). Children of divorce: a family systems perspective. *Journal of Social Issues* 35:140–154.

Bohannan, P. (1970). The six stations of divorce. In *Divorce and After*, ed. P. Bohannan, pp. 33–63. New York: Doubleday.

Boszormenyi-Nagy, I., and Krasner, B. (1980). Trust-based therapy: a contextual approach. *American Journal of Psychiatry* 137:767–775.

Derdeyn, A. (1977). Children in divorce: intervention in the phase of separation. *Pediatrics* 60:20–27.

Elkin, M. (1977). Postdivorce counseling in a conciliation court. *Journal of Divorce* 1:55–56.

Fine, S. (1980). Children in divorce, custody and access situations: the contribution of the mental health professional. *Journal of Child Psychology and Psychiatry and Allied Disciplines* 21:353–361.

Goldman, J., and Coane, J. (1977). Family therapy after the divorce: developing a strategy. *Family Process* 16:357–362.

Hancock, E. (1980). The dimensions of meaning and belonging in the process of divorce. *American Journal of Orthopsychiatry* 50:18–27.

Kaplan, S. (1977). Structural family therapy for children of divorce: case reports. *Family Process* 16:75–83.

Kressel, K., and Deutsch, M. (1977). Divorce therapy: an in-depth survey of therapists' views. *Family Process* 16:413–433.

Ransom, J., Schlesinger, S., and Derdeyn, A. (1979). A stepfamily in formation. *American Journal of Orthopsychiatry* 49:36–43.

Reder, P., and Eve, B. (1981). Some considerations on the clinic treatment of children of divorce. *British Journal of Medical Psychology* 54:167–173.

Ritchie, A., and Serrano, C. (1974). Family therapy in the

treatment of adolescents with divorced parents. In *Therapeutic Needs of the Family: Problems, Descriptions and Therapeutic Approaches*, ed. R. E. Hardy and J. G. Cull, p. 240. Springfield, Ill.: Chas C Thomas.

Rosenthal, D., and Hansen, J. (1980). Working with single-parent families. *Family Therapy* 7:73–82.

Steinberg, J. (1980). Towards an interdisciplinary commitment: a divorce lawyer proposes attorney-therapist marriages or, at least, an affair. *Journal of Marital and Family Therapy* 6:259–268.

Suarez, J., Weston, N., and Hartstein, N. (1978). Mental health interventions in divorce proceedings. *American Journal of Orthopsychiatry* 48:273–283.

Wallerstein, J., and Kelly, J. (1974). The effects of parental divorce: the adolescent experience. In *The Child and His Family*, ed. E. Anthony and C. Koupernik, pp. 479–505. New York: John Wiley.

———— (1975). The effects of parental divorce: experiences of the preschool child. *Journal of the American Academy of Child Psychiatry* 14:600–616.

———— (1976). The effects of parental divorce: experiences of the child in later latency. *American Journal of Orthopsychiatry* 26:256–269.

———— (1977). Divorce counseling: a community service for families in the midst of divorce. *American Journal of Orthopsychiatry* 47:4–22.

Weisfeld, D., and Laser, M. (1977). Divorced parents in family therapy in a residential treatment setting. *Family Process* 16:229–236.

Whitaker, C., and Miller, M. (1969). A reevaluation of "psychiatric help" when divorce impends. *American Journal of Psychiatry* 126:611–618.

❧ 12 ❧

Therapy with the Remarried Family System

*Clifford J. Sager, M.D., Elizabeth Walker, M.S.W.,
Hollis Steer Brown, R.N., Helen M. Crohn, M.S.S.,
and Evelyn Rodstein, M.S.W.*

In 1976 we began to be aware that the customary family and child therapy methods of our agency were not adequately meeting the needs of the growing population of remarried (Rem, blended, second, reconstituted, or step) families seen in our clinics. The family systems were different from and more complex than those of the usual intact family, or even the so-called single-parent family. Old models were no longer applicable. A special service with its own staff, the Remarried Consultation Service, was established to study the remarried (Rem) family in its many polymorphous states. Our objective was to develop a better understanding of the structure and dynamics of Rem and to devise improved and preventive measures.

We define the Rem family as one that is created by the marriage (or living together in one domicile) of two partners, one or both of whom have been married previously and then divorced or widowed, with or without children who visit or reside with them. The couple and the children (custodial or visiting) comprise the Rem family system. The *metafamily* system is composed of the Rem family plus former spouses, grandparents, stepgrandparents, aunts, uncles, and others who may have significant input into the Rem system. The children are part of each of their bioparents' household systems. Because of the high divorce rate, both the Rem system and the metafamily system have now become permanent common family variations.

Visher and Visher (1979) were the first to publish a professional volume on stepfamilies, in which they emphasized a meaningful prophylactic approach. Walker and colleagues (1979) prepared an annotated bibliography of the literature on Rem and in another article, Sager and associates (1980) reviewed our knowledge of Rem and stepfamilies.

In this article we shall discuss how the Rem family structure differs from the intact family, some principles of therapeutic intervention, and the problems of clinicians working with Rem.

Structural Differences

In a nuclear family, the membership is well defined, and the family boundaries clearly distinguish external from internal. There is input from significant others, but this input does not usually endanger the system's functioning. Family expectations, rules, roles, tasks, and purposes are also clear and conform with the generational boundaries and sexual taboos defined by society.

In contrast, membership in the Rem system is open to interpretation: some members may belong in two systems, or they may feel they do not

belong in either parental household. The system has permeable boundaries (Messinger 1976) and significant input from others in the metafamily. Not only former spouses, grandparents, and children, but also
institutions can have a marked impact on the Rem family's viability
and functioning.

Generational and sexual boundaries are often vague and can be
more easily trespassed. Expectations, rules, roles, and tasks in the Rem
system have remained ill defined by society. Each Rem system has to
generate itself with no pattern on which to model itself. Rem marriages
start with at least one spouse's having suffered the ending of a primary
relationship with all its attendant pain and with continuing responsibilities and ties to children and possibly ties to a former spouse. Often
these spouses are financially encumbered and their children have suffered serious life disruption and losses, all of which affect and condition
future attitudes and relationships.

The structure of Rem always takes into account the metafamily
system. Thus, we disagree with Ransom and colleagues (1979), who
examine only the type of Rem family in which a child is raised primarily
in one family unit. They seem to deny the existence of the metafamily
and advocate "the actual reconstitution of the family" as the objective
of the new marriage. That is, the stepfather plays the role of father to
the child, and the role of husband to the wife, reconstituting a facsimile
of the intact nuclear family.

We believe this reconstituted family model denies the existence of
the metafamily system. We have observed several possible Rem structures and are as impressed as are Baideme and associates (1978) with
how often both bioparents desire to participate in child rearing and
will share responsibility.

When a divorced or separated couple has children, there is first a
two single-parent phase. Single-parent family is an erroneous apella-
tion except when one parent has disappeared and abdicated all responsibility, contact, and support. When one parent remarries, there is then
a Rem household system and a single-parent household system. Children are part of both of these systems, each of which is part of the
metafamily system. Not to comprehend or to ignore this dual family
structure makes incomprehensible much that otherwise may be readily
understood on a structural, dynamic, and behavioral basis.

We do agree with Ransom and colleagues that the Rem family must be consolidated—but not as a replacement for the nuclear family. It will always be different. To gloss over this difference makes for a common source of trouble for the Rem family and for the work of the therapist. A guiding principle for our work flows from our recognition of the necessity to involve both bioparents and any stepparents in the treatment process when any of these have input into the system that affects the others. Using the potential of the metafamily system does make the task for families and therapist more difficult but, ultimately, more rewarding for all.

ENTRY TO TREATMENT

Treating the clinical population of Rem families can be an effective and exciting process for family and therapist, but also a time-consuming one because of the complexity of the family systems involved. Instead of having been a system that functioned well at one time and then began to malfunction, Rem families often have not been able to consolidate themselves into a viable functioning unit except perhaps for a brief "honeymoon" period. Characteristically, these families call for help when in crisis and desperate, seeing the specter of another failure hanging over the adults' heads. It is not uncommon for a family to arrive at the point of having expelled a member or at the point of doing so before asking for help. The pressure on the therapist to try immediately to rectify the situation is tremendous and must be resisted.

Evaluation: Initial Phases

Therapy starts with the first telephone call. When an emergency exists (that which is beyond crisis) we attend first to the emergency while simultaneously beginning to evaluate the metafamily system. Regardless of what else may be transacted in these early sessions, the mere seeking and ordering of information brings knowledge, intelligence, and structure to the family members, as it does to the therapist, when it is a shared process.

As when treating nuclear families, the therapist has the greatest leverage in the initial phases to involve everyone who is part of, or who affects, the system. Once therapy has begun, it is often more difficult to include a former spouse, because the therapist is likely to be viewed with hostility and identified as being on the Rem system's side. We do not refuse to see those members who ask for help if we cannot enlist the others at the start, but neither do we accept a simple no as an answer—it spurs us to use our ingenuity. In the process that ensues, the metafamily learns how interrelated they are and when and how to disengage appropriately.

Whoever calls for help, whether it be the biological parent, step-parent, or child, we make every effort to include from the outset both bioparents and stepparents. Frequently clients will articulate anxiety about including their former mate, or the stepparent may be anxious or jealous about being present with the former spouse, because of ex-spouse hostilities or hidden collusive affection. The therapist will recognize the concern and point out that since the child lives in both families, it is in the best interests of the child for the adults to work together; it is the parenting and stepparenting issues, not the exmarital hurts or financial issues, that will be addressed. The therapist sets clear limits in sessions that include exspouses and stepparents. Only when all adults agree, should one include in the therapeutic contract attempts to resolve residual pain and anger or to put residual affection and love into appropriate perspective.

Work with the metafamily requires therapeutic flexibility. It may be necessary to see each bioparent separately in order to establish a connection and promote comfort with the therapist before setting up joint meetings. If the therapist is already identified with one partner of the system, it may be necessary initially to enlist another therapist to make the connection to the other partner, who may have been excluded. Sometimes we use an adaptation of MacGregor's and colleagues' (1964) multiple-impact family therapy by assigning a different therapist to each subsystem of the metafamily. But this is a costly luxury that cannot be continued for a long period of time.

Use of the Genogram

The genogram is an effective tool which we use initially with the family to map out the metafamily and to understand fairly quickly the complicated structure of this particular Rem family. We find that the multiple changes that have occurred, and most likely the multiple losses also, are dramatically highlighted and may facilitate a delayed mourning reaction in some family members. We inquire about the children's bioparents, even if one of them is not present, to soften any loyalty conflict a child may have between his or her parents and/or stepparents and to support the needed connection to both. The therapist's implicit and explicit recognition of the other important persons in the child's life does more than any statement could. Information specific to the Rem situation can be asked for directly as well as deduced from observation and interaction, including data on:

The present Rem unit: living in, living out, and visiting children; when they visit, how often, holiday schedules, who makes school visits on parent's day, and other sensitive living arrangements in the household.

How the present Rem unit was formed: the background of the couple's meeting and courtship; how and if the children were prepared for the remarriage; if the former partner(s) knew, were informed, and by whom; changes in residence, financial arrangements, and other cathected parameters.

The two single-parent household structures: the quality and quantity of time spent with each child by each parent; the role of grandparents and the relation between the separated spouses during this period.

The original nuclear family system: when, why, and how this was dissolved; what each adult's and child's understanding of that dissolution was in the past and currently; dates of the actual physical separation and the legal divorce.

The families of origin of all the adults: both Rem spouses and former spouses, assessment of input by each significant person both current and past.

It is important to observe overt and covert alliances, power structures, levels of intimacy and bonds between members, and patterns of inclusion and exclusion in the system. But one need not be compulsive about history taking: basic facts first, then the rest as therapy continues.

Two other areas in Rem should be learned as rapidly as possible: mate choice and life cycles.

1. *Mate choice*: the unconscious as well as conscious factors determining mate choice for the second as well as the first marriage. Did those who have been married more than once learn from past experi-

ences; is their choice appropriate; does it reflect a positive change in their level of maturity; are there reasonable expectations and goals? Are marriage contracts of the couple concordant, complementary, or in conflict? (Sager 1976, p. 164)

2. *Life cycles*: life, marital, and family cycle needs of Rem couples. Are the life cycle needs of each marital partner consistent with the other partner's and with the needs of their Rem family? To illustrate the marital cycle problem:

> An older man with adolescent children remarries a younger woman who has no children. She accepts in good faith his condition that they will not have children together. After a while her desire to have children with him becomes a pressing need. He persists in his position and wants to hold her to their "contract."

To illustrate the family cycle problem:

> A woman with elementary school-age children who live with her remarries a man who knows that she expects him to be a caring stepfather. He agrees, denying his own needs to have a childlike relationship with his wife. He increasingly refuses to accept any responsibility for parenting.

Treatment Goals

Goals are not a simple matter; they reflect the multiple levels of a behavior's determinants. It is necessary for the therapist to be alert to the desires beyond awareness that hinder the attainment of expressed goals. Masochistic or self-defeating needs can be revealed during anamnestic data collection by noting self-defeating patterns and in behavior and interactions observed in the family sessions. Often such patterns can be bypassed in therapy. As change begins to occur, the therapist should expect to see resistance initiated by the obstructor, often with the unconscious collusion of other system members. If negative goals cannot be bypassed, they must be brought into the open and dealt with more directly. This is one of the many complexities of human system behavior that defeats attempts at cookbook therapy and requires a broad spectrum of skills and knowledge.

There are immediate, intermediate, and long-range treatment goals. Individuals and the family as a system are helped to define achievable goals. For example, when a child says, "I want to feel like I felt when my parents were married," he or she usually means, "I want my parents reunited," an unreachable goal. One then tries to help the child achieve a more reasonable goal: to accept the loss and the irretrievability of the original nuclear family, experiencing the anger and sadness that leads to accpetance.

The therapist, too, may have goals that must be shared with the family. These goals must be agreed to by all involved. Goals and contracts are under constant evaluation and review as the treatment progresses, and this work forms the essence of the therapeutic process.

Common treatment goals with Rem families include many that are based on the acceptance and enhancement of the effectiveness of the metafamily system. For example, an early goal may be to stop scapegoating a child. This may be approached by helping former spouses and their own biofamilies (grandparents, etc.) to eschew fixing blame for the termination of the former marriage. Then, adult anger can be worked through or more readily bypassed for the children's needs, and guilt or retribution for past acts need not be utilized as a motivation for current action, thus allowing bioparents and stepparents to share some responsibility for child rearing.

Some other goals frequently encountered are (1) to consolidate the Rem couple as a unit and establish their authority in the system; (2) to consolidate the parental authority in the system among bioparents and stepparents with the formation of a collaborative coparenting team; (3) as a corollary to item 2, to help children deal with and minimize the continuance and exacerbation of loyalty binds; (4) to facilitate mourning of the nuclear family, former partner, old neighborhoods, friends, and way of life; (5) to make certain there is a secure place for the child's development through optimal utilization of the entire metafamily system; and (6) to help family members accept and tolerate their differences from some idealized intact family model. These include differences such as lack of complete control of money and children; differences in feelings for and of the bioparent and stepparent; differences in rules and expectations in the two households; and different levels of bonding in Rem household, as opposed to those of the nuclear household.

Therapy is structured to achieve goals in as orderly a progression as possible, accented by a dash of the serendipitous. Rarely have we had a treatment plan, however, that did not have to be revised (Sager 1957). For example:

The presenting complaint was of a child's recent poor functioning in school. Evaluation indicates that the child is living in a chaotic metafamily system in which none of the adults takes responsibility for setting limits with him and that this situation began after his mother's remarriage. In the Rem family there is role confusion between the mother and her spouse—each is expecting the other to parent the child. The biological father has abdicated his parental position, not only communicating hastily and uneasily with his former wife about the child, but also focusing only on entertaining the child and giving him anything that he wants when they are together. Both of the Rem adults are frustrated because the child's needs seem to interfere constantly with the fulfillment of their love needs for each other.

The immediate goal is to help all the adults: biological mother and father and stepfather form a collaborative parenting team and begin to clarify their parenting expectations, both with each other and the child. Once this is accomplished, the chaos diminishes and the child's functioning in school is restored. The Rem couple then requests further help in consolidating their relationship with each other, which becomes a new treatment goal. The biological father seeks help in working through his feelings about the loss of his former wife and family, which have been stirred anew by the remarriage and which he can now see have been interfering with his capacity to function optimally as a single parent.

The goals of the two bioparental systems may be mutually exclusive, as may be those of any subsystem or individual vis-à-vis another. These goal differences must be clearly delineated to determine if they are real or only apparent; if real, can they be reconciled or negotiated in some fashion? Some are so pervasive and mutually exclusive that family members and therapist may have to accept that the system is not viable.

TREATMENT

To achieve the immediate and long-range goals, we have available to us three general theoretical systems of psychological treatment: insight methods such as the various psychoanalytic systems, Gestalt, and transactional analysis; methods based on general systems theory such as Minuchin's structured therapy or Bowen's detriangulation therapy; and those approaches derived from learning theory such as behavior modification methods. Although many of our techniques are based on treating the family and metafamily systems, we also use our knowledge of individual intrapsychic dynamics and couple dynamics to determine some of our interventions, as well as tasks and positive reinforcement techniques. The individual should not become lost in the system; neither should the therapist lose sight of the power of the family system to shape and alter behavior.

Common Treatment Issues with Rem

We have referred previously to some Rem couples' inability to consolidate into a viable marital unit, meeting the love needs of the adults and yet allowing them to carry on with parenting and other appropriate family needs. Often there are bonds and priorities as powerful, or more powerful elsewhere, that can produce crisis, confusion, and jealousy in the current couple relationship. Such factors may lead to a concomitant failure to resolve pivotal marital issues of intimacy, power, and the exclusion or inclusion of others and to negotiate and resolve their individual and joint marital contracts (Sager 1976, Sager and Hunt 1979).

These failures may have come about through a variety of circumstances. Parents often experience guilt or confusion between loyalty to their children of a former spouse and to a current spouse. The parent, not the child or new spouse, must take prime responsibility for confronting and resolving this resolvable dilemma. One partner may have failed to mourn, appropriately work through, and accept the loss of his or her former spouse. Other couples may be involved in a bond of either pseudomutuality or pseudohostility (Wynne et al. 1958). This bond inevitably intrudes destructively into the relationship. Conversely, the former spouse may have refused to accept termination of the marital relationship and may constantly intrude himself or herself into the current pairing, at times using the children for this purpose. The remarried partner may covertly condone this intrusion out of his or her own guilt over the end of the marriage.

Some parents develop an overly close bond to a child during the two single-parent household phase. Later, neither the parent nor the child is able to alter the quality and intensity of this bond in order to make room for the entry or inclusion of the new marital partner into the system. It is a process that usually takes time and patience. The new marital partner may have been unable or unwilling to help his or her mate separate from the child and move into a closer couple pairing without arousing defensiveness and hostility. The difficulty in keeping the adult-pairing love separate from parent-child love reappears as a common problem of Rem families.

To the child, remarriage represents finality and the loss of the dream of reinstating the "old" family. Acceptance of reality may be postponed, and the child instead can enter into disruptive denial or undoing maneuvers.

Treatment Modalities

Starting with a knowledge of family systems theory and a conviction of the correctness of the concept of multiple genetic and environmental inputs to all individuals and family systems, we begin working with the Rem family, keeping in mind the family structure and individual function, values, and adaptations. Some issues are specific to Rem families, and some emotional and interactional family system dynamics are more generalized. Our point of view, for both evaluation and treatment, is to conceptualize the problems in terms of the metafamily system, while remembering the needs of the individual members and the two bioparent systems as well as the specific Rem unit. Our primary therapeutic process is to refocus and redefine the problem with the family in terms of the whole system and its subsequent needs and responsibilities. In Rem, the therapist helps the family understand the expanded system: its differences from a nuclear family, the appropriate significance and role, if any, of the metafamily nonhousehold members, and how they all may affect one another. This process helps stop the scapegoating of the children, who often are blamed for the Rem family's troubles. Insight methods are used if and when the therapist views them as applicable. When tasks are used, we are concerned with any resistance to carry them out and the feelings evoked by them, as well as the actual effects on individuals and the system of having completed the task. The reasons and feelings brought out by an incompleted task are often of great therapeutic importance. The therapist should choose tasks that are designed to produce a specifically predicted behavioral and/or attitudinal change.

Key treatment questions include whom to include, when to include them and for what purposes, and which treatment modalities to use, when, and for what ends. There are no hard and fast rules, and sensitive timing is of the essence. Familiarity and ease in working with a variety of modalities are helpful. It is easier to begin immediately with everyone involved in the problem and then work down, breaking into subunits, than it is to begin with the microsystem (for instance, the child) and try to include others later. If the Rem couple relationship is the presenting problem and the children are not involved, but there is clearly unfinished business with a prior partner, then a few couple sessions with the divorced pair, or individual sessions with that Rem partner, may be held to further completion of the divorce, while at the same time beginning to work with the current partners. We do not necessarily include all metafamily or Rem members in every session, but we do try to keep in mind the different subsystems and how the present parts fit into the whole dynamic mosaic. The therapist's capacity for both flexibility and activity is crucial; successful treatment depends on the therapist's comfort with moving in and out of the different parts of the system and with treatment in different modalities, including family, couple, individual, and child, as indicated. Since emotions in Rem families often run high, the therapist must be active and able to take charge of the sessions. These abilities are particularly necessary when (1) the session includes the former spouse; (2) there is a psychotic individual; (3) members are manipulative or form an alliance to defeat the therapist; or (4) the family's underlying feelings of hopelessness and despair are rampant.

Multiple Impact Therapy with Families

At times we use a modified multiple-impact therapy model (MacGregor et al. 1964) with our metafamily systems. A different therapist is assigned to work with, support, and model separate subsystems, such as children, an exspouse, or grandparents. In a large, joint meeting the therapist may then act as supporter, interpreter, advocate, negotiator, and spokesperson, as well as therapist for that part of the system. This modality is particularly helpful with extremely chaotic, polarized, or conflicted systems or when there are individuals who would be unable to enter treatment which he or she may consider as hostile territory, without the added support of his or her therapist. It is also recommended for large systems; for instance, if both of the bioparents are remarried and have several children with needs different from those of the original and the new family. It may be necessary to use this modality only initially for a crisis and for a brief period until some resolution takes place and clear goals are agreed upon. Ongoing treatment may then proceed as usual. We try not to use cotherapists, unless absolutely necessary; for instance, when there is strong conflict between two subunits. Cotherapy is also sometimes prohibitively expensive. A single therapist can achieve similar results through separate appointments with different subsystems of the metafamily, for instance, with the Rem system and with the single-parent system, prior to meeting with the entire system. Another way is to split a session, seeing one subsystem for part of the session, the second subsystem for another part of the session, and then all together.

The Use of Groups

Couples' groups often are the treatment of choice for many Rem couples. Our experience demonstrates that this modality best addresses several important problem sources in the Rem system, notably the lack of consolidation of the couple, ill-defined mourning of the lost relationship and spouse, and guilt and conflict regarding the children. The group can provide a structure for the couples, separate from their children and stepchildren. It provides time and privacy to work on their mutual contracts with each other, with support from others in the same situation and struggling with similar issues. At the same time, they have the opportunity to be "reparented" in a corrective emotional experience with the therapist and one another. Family meetings separate from the group can be held periodically, both to help the couple integrate their changes into the system and to facilitate the children's integration into the Rem family.

We have tried multiple family therapy groups (Lacquer 1972) of unselected Rem families but do not recommend this modality for families who are very chaotic and needy. Further, MFT makes it more difficult to include former spouses and other metafamily members, because to include these makes the group unwieldy and interrupts ongoing processes, as many metafamily members need be only transiently engaged in treatment. Adolescents, though, have found MFT to be beneficial. As a result, we currently advocate couples' groups and separate groups for children of Rem, particularly for adolescents, who often feel like "orphans" in their Rem families and isolated from their peers.

We are also experimenting with including the children in the couples' group for some sessions, after the couples have been successful at consolidating themselves and are then ready to address the parenting issues directly, within the group's supportive framework. We shall return to the use of MFT with better consolidated Rem couples, whose situations are not so chaotic as were those in our earlier experiences.

The Therapist

The therapist working with Rem family systems is constantly subjected to his or her own emotions and value systems. The first emotional assault on the therapist pertains to male/female relatedness and systems of loyalties and consanguinity. The therapist may have values markedly different from those that have allowed Rem adults to divorce and remarry, live with someone, or break up a marriage. The actions and feelings of various Rem family members may touch off emotional reactions based on experiences the therapist has had, has feared will happen, or has not dared to bring about in his or her own life because of guilt, anxiety, superego constraints, or cultural considerations. True countertransferential reactions may also occur in which the patients and/or their system involve the therapist, who reacts the way the individuals or the system unconsciously expected him or her to react.

The complexities of the Rem systems, the sense of despair, hopelessness and loss, and the chaos and crisis that are at work may spill over into the therapist's personal life. We find ourselves putting our personal relationships on "hold" and avoiding decisions about making or ending commitments to others. Depression and despair are common reactions, without clear sources, as are making moralistic judgments about clients.

These reactions can best be handled by using a trusted and support-ive group of peers; our service has provided that for the staff. Con-sultation, supervision, and the use of the group to help individual therapists resolve personal reactions have mitigated some of the anxiety and pain that seems built into the work with Rem systems. At the same time our team approach has facilitated consolidation of our clinic families, who felt cared about and "special" to the unit and less isolated once they knew that there was a specialized team of therapists sup-porting them. Within the team, we have used ourselves to identify specific areas of vulnerability for therapists working with Rem systems, and we shall outline them here.

Unrealistic Expectations. Many Rem couples marry with the hope that this marriage will right all previous relationship disappointments, including both parental and past marital "failures" and that this time their marriage contract and expectations—even if unrealistic and magical—will be fulfilled. Other family members may also expect that their unmet needs will now be gratified.

If the therapist accepts the unrealistic expectations, he or she too may be dragged down into feelings of hopelessness that so often characterize the clinic population of Rem. To accept the fantasies is to become enmeshed in disappointment and disillusionment and will lead to paralysis and despair.

Denial. If the adult partners are pseudomutual and deny their dif-ferences, conflicts, and disappointments, they are likely to focus their problems on a child or children who are scapegoated. The therapist, sensing that certain material is forbidden, may join the denial and also displace to the child, thereby encouraging the pseudomutuality and scapegoating. Therapists may also collaborate with the family in their denial of the importance of their history and the metafamily as relevant to the present problem. All too often, children are told by their re-marrying parent that the marriage is for the child's benefit or welfare, the parent denying his or her own needs to the child. This type of denial may arouse critical feelings within the therapist that, too, are often denied and come out indirectly. The key is knowledge; the more the therapist knows about Rem, the less likely he or she is to join family members in their resistance and obfuscation.

Abandonment Fears.   Loss and abandonment are prime issues for the children and adults in Rem, and may trigger the therapists' own abandonment anxieties. Thus a therapist dealing with a child who has been deserted by a parent may be drawn into becoming the good parent for the child, thus reinforcing the child's unresolved feelings toward the parent, instead of helping the child work through these feelings of loss, anger, and disappointment. Similarly, children who have been abandoned often use abandonment as a threat: "If I can't have my way, I'll leave and go live with Daddy," or "I'll leave therapy." If the therapist joins with the child, rather than challenging the threat and its meaning, then the therapist will become anxious and immobilized, which will lead to great chaos in the system and in treatment. The child is left with the feeling that no one cares enough to offer either resistance or support.

Control Issues.   The therapist may attempt to allay his or her anxiety by becoming overcontrolling, as do some harried stepparents, or by taking impulsive therapeutic action. He or she may rush too soon to try to impose order and consequently push the family away. The therapist is likely to despair when the chaos does not right itself quickly in response to interventions and may consciously or unconsciously dismiss the family. Thus, the ability to tolerate ambiguity and chaos is required, along with patience and awareness of the process that needs to take place during treatment.

As in all mental health areas, our prime concern must be prevention of distress and damage to people. What we have presented, although centered on theory and therapy, provides the underpinning for our prophylactic work. Sager and colleagues (1983) explain our therapeutic approach more comprehensively and discuss the important area of education and prevention. Working with this group of families clinically can be very rewarding. Although the complexity of Rem can create problems, it also is the basis of the richness of relationships and experiences such a family can provide to the individual, satisfying a need we all have for a variety of encounters and emotions. When we work with these families, we are attuned to both how they are alike and different from nuclear families. We attend to the metafamily as well as the Rem family, including all people who have an impact on the current situation. We look at the family's development over time and take an eclectic approach which emphasizes flexibility, understanding of behavioral and dynamic factors, and goal-directed work, as well as the play of the therapist's own reactions in his or her intervention.

REFERENCES

Baideme, S. M., Hill, H. A., and Serritella, D. A. (1978). Conjoint family therapy following divorce: an alternative strategy. *International Journal of Family Counseling* 6:55–59.

Bowen, M. (1978). *Family Therapy in Clinical Practice.* New York: Jason Aronson.

Crohn, H. M., Sager, C. J., Rodstein, E., Brown, H. S., and Walker, E. (1980). Understanding and treating the child in the remarried family. In *Children of Separation and Divorce*, ed. L. E. Abt and I. R. Stuart, pp. 292–317. New York: Van Nostrand Reinhold.

Goldstein, J., Freud, A., and Solnit, A. J. (1973). *Beyond the Best Interest of the Child.* New York: Free Press.

Guerin, P. J., and Penagast, E. G. (1976). Evaluation of family system and genogram. In *Family Therapy: Theory and Practice*, ed. P. J. Guerin, pp. 450–464. New York: Gardner Press.

Lacquer, A. P. (1972). Mechanics of change in multiple family therapy. In *Progress in Group and Family Therapy*, ed. C. J. Sager and H. S. Kaplan, pp. 400–415. New York: Brunner/Mazel.

MacGregor, R., Ritchie, A. M., Serrano, A. C., and Schuster, F. P. (1964). *Multiple Impact Therapy with Families.* New York: McGraw-Hill.

Messinger, L. (1976). Remarriage between divorced people from previous marriages: a proposal for preparation for remarriage. *Journal of Marriage and Family Counseling* 2:195–200.

Minuchin, S. (1974). *Families and Family Therapy.* Cambridge, Mass.: Harvard University Press.

Ransom, J. W., Schlesinger, S., and Derdeyn, A. P. (1979). A stepfamily in formation. *American Journal of Orthopsychiatry* 49:36–43.

Ranz, J., and Ferber A. (1973). How to succeed in family therapy. In *The Book of Family Therapy*, ed. A Ferber, M. Mendelsohn, and A. Napier, pp. 544–581. Boston: Houghton Mifflin.

Sager, C. J. (1957). The psychotherapist's continuous evaluation of his work. *Psychoanalytic Review* 44:298–312.

—— (1976). *Marriage Contracts and Couples Therapy.* New York: Brunner/Mazel.

——, Brown, H., Crohn, H., Engle, T., Rodstein, E., and Walker, E. (1983). *Treating the Remarried Family.* New York: Brunner/Mazel.

——, Brown, H. S., Crohn, H. M., Rodstein, E., and Walker, E. (1980). Remarriage revisited. *Family and Child Mental Health Journal* 6:19–25.

——, and Hunt, B. (1979). *Intimate Partners—Hidden Patterns in Love Relationships.* New York: McGraw-Hill.

Visher, E., and Visher, J. (1979). *Stepfamilies.* New York: Brunner/Mazel.

Walker, K. N., and Messinger, L. (1979). Remarriage after divorce: dissolution and reconstruction of family boundaries. *Family Process* 18:185–192.

Walker, L., Brown, H. S., Crohn, H. M., Rodstein, E., Zeisel, E., and Sager, C. J. (1979). An annotated bibliography of the remarried, the living together and their children. *Family Process* 18:193–212.

Wynne, L. C., Ryckoff, I. N., Day, J., and Hirsch, S. I. (1958). Pseudomutuality in the family relations of schizophrenics. *Psychiatry* 21:205–220.

Index